BILINGUAL
EDUCATION

OTHER RECENT VOLUMES IN THE
SAGE FOCUS EDITIONS

BILINGUAL EDUCATION
Issues and Strategies

Edited by
**Amado M. Padilla
Halford H. Fairchild
Concepción M. Valadez**

SAGE PUBLICATIONS
The International Professional Publishers
Newbury Park   London   New Delhi

For information address:

SAGE Publications, Inc.
2111 West Hillcrest Drive
Newbury Park, California 91320

SAGE Publications Ltd.
28 Banner Street
London EC1Y 8QE
England

SAGE Publications India Pvt. Ltd.
M-32 Market
Greater Kailash I
New Delhi 110 048 India

Printed in the United States of America

Library of Congress Cataloging-in-Publication Data
Main entry under title:

Bilingual education : issues and strategies / edited by Amado M.
   Padilla, Halford H. Fairchild, Concepcion M. Valadez.
       p.   cm. — (Sage focus editions ; v. 112)
   Includes bibliographic references.
   ISBN 0-8039-3638-9. — ISBN 0-8039-3639-7 (pbk.)
    1. Education, Bilingual—United States. 2. Concentrated study.
3. Language and education—United States. 4. Educational
Innovations—United States—Case studies.   I. Padilla, Amado M.
II. Fairchild, Halford H. III. Valadez, Concepcion M.
LC3731.B5515   1990
371.97'00973—dc20   89-27801
                                                                    CIP

FIRST PRINTING, 1990

Sage Production Editor: Diane S. Foster

Contents

Preface

The authors of the various chapters in this volume and in its accompanying volume were all associated in one way or another with the Center for Language Education and Research (CLEAR) at the University of California at Los Angeles at the time this project was planned. All the authors were committed to assisting in the development of a language-competent American society—that is, a society in which all residents of the United States have a realistic opportunity to develop the highest possible degree of proficiency in understanding, speaking, reading, and writing English, whether it is their mother tongue or a second language. Simultaneously, a language-competent American society includes opportunities for English-speaking individuals to develop an ability to understand, speak, read, and write a second (foreign) language while those who are not native speakers of English should have an opportunity to develop proficiency in their mother tongue.

It was our belief that the development of a language-competent society should be accorded our highest educational priority. We felt that researchers and practitioners who work within the domain of educational linguistics could play an active role in achieving a language-competent society.

Throughout the world today, there are many more bilingual individuals than there are monolingual; and there are many more children who are educated via a second language than are educated exclusively via their mother tongue. Thus, in most of the world, bilingualism and innovative approaches to education involving the utilization of more than one language constitute the status quo—a way of life, a natural experience. The phenomenon of bilingualism in most countries is not problematic, and achieving competency in more than one language is not particularly onerous or burdensome. Nor is participation in bilingual education programs or other innovative language education programs particularly novel or different.

As educators, we have much to teach others concerning the choice and sequencing of languages for purposes of initial literacy training and for basic instruction. Even more important, we have much to learn from other nations concerning the successful implementation of bilingual education in public schools.

In these days of increasing global interdependence, all American residents will benefit—personally and socially—if the largest possible number of residents can speak, read, write, and understand at least one language in addition to English. Language is an important thread that runs, albeit too often without recognition, through a variety of issues fundamental to national development and to public policy. Educational practice can be improved and social equity can be facilitated by applying knowledge gleaned from research conducted within the domain of the language sciences.

Innovative instructional programs can and should be designed to encourage the development of second-language skills for as broad a spectrum of school-age students as possible. Despite more than a decade of federal and state involvement, there continues to be much confusion and disagreement concerning the nature and goals of our programs for second-language learning.

Although the approach selected to facilitate the development of bilingual skills may vary depending upon local circumstances, it should be possible to offer an appropriate language education program for all students. We must make a societal commitment to encourage innovative language education programs, and we should make a professional commitment to offer our insights and our professional expertise to articulate appropriate educational goals for our children, to help design and implement responsive pedagogical programs, and to document and evaluate their relative efficacy. We should be able to document the course, causes, and correlates of second-language learning and to communicate the findings about the personal and societal benefits of bilingualism to others.

If members of our profession are to assume strong leadership roles, we should be able to assist in the development of a language-competent American society. It is this set of interrelated beliefs that have worked to unite our efforts to describe work conducted during the course of four years that was directed at understanding ways in which linguistic majority and linguistic minority students could achieve competence in two languages.

Amado M. Padilla
Halford H. Fairchild
Concepción M. Valadez

PART I

Issues and Perspectives

Bilingual education has undergone a number of dramatic changes during the past 20 years. Its history and concomitant political issues are reviewed in Part I.

Amado Padilla, in "Bilingual Education: Issues and Perspectives" (Chapter 1), reviews the policy, research, and programmatic debates surrounding bilingual education. Noting the strong opposition to bilingual education by former Secretary of Education William Bennett, Padilla emphasizes the need for bilingual education proponents to develop both a "paradigm" and a "mission."

Padilla reviews the research controversies concerning bilingual education, particularly with respect to the lively debate between Baker and de Kanter (1981, 1983) and Willig (1985, 1987). He also notes the importance of bilingual education in terms of demographic projections for increasing linguistic diversity in the United States into the foreseeable future. In this respect, he identifies a startling revelation: that members of the current "majority" who decry their presumed "support" of the poor are likely to be the primary "dependents" of the increasing populations of immigrant "minorities" as they get older relative to the younger and working immigrant groups.

By "paradigm," Padilla underscores the need for developing a "coherent tradition" in the development of bilingual education programs, teaching strategies, and research approaches. He notes, for example, that the majority of empirical investigations into bilingual education, because of the lack of an organizing principle or "paradigm," consist "of a loosely connected mosaic of "facts."" It is not surprising, then, that evaluations of bilingual education are inconsistent.

In terms of a "mission," Padilla calls for the joining together of people, organizations, and institutions to establish the goal of a "language-competent society." Here he prescribes the development of a commitment to bilingualism on the part of all Americans. In this respect, Padilla joins with foreign language educators who see language and bilingualism as personal and national resources (see Tucker, 1990).

Marguerite Malakoff and Kenji Hakuta, in "History of Language Minority Education in the United States" (Chapter 2), provide a comprehensive review of the public policy debates and legislative actions concerning bilingual education. Beginning with the eighteenth and nineteenth centuries, Malakoff and Hakuta identify the changing dynamics of American attitudes toward bilingual education.

For example, although bilingual education was common for a number of northern and western European groups in the eighteenth century (i.e., Spanish, French, Norwegian, Lithuanian, Dutch, and so on), in the late nineteenth century, the "new immigration" from southern and eastern Europe stimulated ethnocentric, racist, and "English-only" sentiments among the "old immigrants." "English-only" sentiments have become very dominant in the past few years. Currently, approximately two-thirds of all states have some form of English-only amendment. Crawford (1989) has documented the politics of bilingual education, including the English-only movement. Crawford's book should be mandatory reading for anyone wanting to better understand the xenophobia that has accompanied attacks on bilingual education.

Malakoff and Hakuta, however, focus their review on contemporary models of bilingual education, particularly since the 1968 passage of the Bilingual Education Act and the legislative consequences of the ruling in *Lau v. Nichols* in 1970. They identify six models of programs, including transitional, maintenance, English as a second language, submersion ("sink or swim"), and forms of bilingual immersion programs. According to their analysis, most of these programs are "subtractive" in the sense that they seek to replace individuals' native language with English, and they fail to maintain true bilingual proficiency.

In reviewing research on the effectiveness of bilingual education programs, Malakoff and Hakuta define myriad methodological difficulties in conducting effectiveness research, and call instead for research on the *process* of implementing innovative teaching strategies and curricula.

In sum, Part I provides an overview of the history of bilingual education, the changing nature of public sentiment and legislative actions, and the context for evaluating research findings and for supporting the development of new pedagogical models.

REFERENCES

Baker, K., & de Kanter, A. A. (1981). *Effectiveness of bilingual education: A review of literature*. Washington, DC: Office of Planning, Budget and Education, U.S. Department of Education.

Baker, K., & de Kanter, A. A. (Eds.). (1983). *Bilingual education: A reappraisal of federal policy*. Lexington, MA: Lexington.

Crawford, J. (1989). *Bilingual education: History, politics, theory, and practice*. Trenton, NJ: Crane.

Padilla, A. M., Fairchild, H. H., & Valadez, C. M. (1990). *Innovations in language education: Vol. 2. Immersion and foreign language education*. Newbury Park, CA: Sage.

Tucker, G. R. (1990). Second language education: Issues and perspectives. In A. M. Padilla, H. H. Fairchild, & C. M. Valadez (Eds.), *Innovations in language education: Vol. 2. Immersion and foreign language education*. Newbury Park, CA: Sage.

Willig, A. C. (1985). A meta-analysis of selected studies on the effectiveness of bilingual education. *Review of Educational Research, 55*, 269–317.

Willig, A. C. (1987). Examining bilingual education research through meta-analysis and narrative review: A response to Baker. *Review of Educational Research, 57*, 363–376.

1

Bilingual Education
Issues and Perspectives

AMADO M. PADILLA

Since the passage of the Bilingual Education Act in 1968, bilingual education has consistently been criticized as a method of instruction for linguistic minority children. Perhaps the most severe challenge was spearheaded by William Bennett during his tenure as Secretary of Education. Bennett's criticism was significant because for the first time the attack came from the highest education official in the country. The essence of Secretary Bennett's criticism of bilingual education was summed in one sentence when he stated, in a 1985 speech to the Association for a Better New York in New York City, "After seventeen years of federal involvement, and after $1.7 billion of federal funding, we have no evidence that the children whom we sought to help have benefitted" (Bennett, 1988, p. 185).

The central issue of the debate on bilingual education has been whether research supports the educational benefit of the program or whether federal monies could be better spent on other educational programs. The strongest arguments against bilingual education occurred when Baker and de Kanter (1981, 1983) concluded that bilingual education evaluation studies showed that bilingual education was not effective in meeting the educational needs of linguistic minority children (also see Chapter 2, on the history of bilingual education, by Malakoff & Hakuta, this volume).

The most critical reply to the Baker and de Kanter reports came from Willig (1985, 1987), who carried out a meta-analysis of many of the same studies reviewed in the conventional way by Baker and de Kanter. Willig's analysis led her to conclude that bilingual education programs *are* effective in raising the academic achievement (in English) of students requiring bilingual education. More recently, Willig (1987), in a rebuttal to Baker (1987), elaborated upon her earlier study and argued even more convincingly for the soundness of her original conclusion. She also identified the numerous methodological flaws inherent in the Baker and de Kanter (1981, 1983) reports that contributed to their erroneous conclusions.

⅄   Despite Willig's analyses, advocates of bilingual education are still struggling to demonstrate the educational merits of their programs to educators and policymakers who would rather eliminate them. At the same time, another challenge to bilingual education is coming from the public's perception that there is something to fear in bilingual education (Spener, 1988). Specifically, the "English-only" movement is guided by a philosophy that seeks the homogenization of linguistically diverse groups into a population of "English-only" speakers. The rationale for the "English-only" movement, as reported in Spener (1988), is that the United States owes its greatness to its ability to incorporate, through its educational system, individuals from all nations of the world into a single, amalgamated people. Deviations from the process of "Americanization," such as the emergence of ethnic and linguistic pride by Hispanics (and other ethnolinguistic groups), are viewed as a threat to the "normal order of things" and in need of reform.

Coming from another direction are other movements to reform education (e.g., National Commission on Excellence in Education, 1983). Included in these proposed reforms are recommendations that are especially significant for the educational needs of high-risk students. The impact that these reforms will have on students from non-English home backgrounds is not at all clear.

The policy questions that drove the Baker and de Kanter study are now quite moot, as Secada (1987) has so eloquently stated. The policy issues for the future should not be about "the effectiveness of bilingual education," and such things as local control for program flexibility, but about the development of effective instructional programs for limited-English-proficient students. Nor are the policy issues properly focused if the central questions concern improved language assessment instruments for the selection of students requiring bilingual education, as Baker (1987) has suggested in his rebuttal to Willig (1987).

SOME DEMOGRAPHIC FACTS

The policy-related issues requiring consideration are more profound than those suggested by Baker, other federal education policymakers, "English-only" advocates, and educational reformists. Important demographic shifts in the U.S. population must guide the direction of educational policy for linguistic minority students. For example, the Hispanic population is on a positive growth trajectory for at least the next 30 to 50 years. According to the 1980 census, Hispanics numbered about 14.6 million and represented 6.4% of the population of the United States. Five years later, Hispanics had increased to about 16.9 million, an increase of 16%, compared with a 3.3% increase for the general population (McKay, 1986). Hispanics are estimated to increase to between 23.1 and 26.9 million by the year 2000 and will constitute from 8.6% to 9.9% of the total U.S. population (Orum, 1985). With this pattern of growth projected to continue well into the next century, demographers expect that, within two generations, Hispanics may constitute over 30% of the general U.S. population (Ascher, 1987).

Without dwelling on other demographic facts relevant to Hispanics—such as the very large number of school-age children, above average levels of poverty and unemployment, higher than average teenage pregnancy rates, and a higher than average rate of school noncompletion—we need to place the Hispanic population into proper perspective as far as social policy is concerned (also see Ascher, 1987). To do this, we need to reexamine the question of who is dependent upon whom in our society. This raises the question of dependency ratios, which is the measure used by demographers to forecast the ability of a society to care for those who cannot care for themselves (i.e., dependent children and the elderly).

The dependency ratio for children under 18 has steadily declined over the past two decades and now stands at about 42 children per 100 workers. On the other hand, the dependency ratio for those 65 and over has now reached about 19 per 100 workers and is continuing to increase ("Here They Come," 1986). Using current population estimates, it is projected that, by the year 2030, American workers will be in a situation of having to care for an equal number of children and retirees. In 2030, it is expected that the dependency ratio will reach 74 per 100 workers.

Thus a disproportionate burden of caring for the children and retirees in the next century will fall upon Hispanics and other minority groups (Hayes-Bautista, Schink, & Chapa, 1988). There is nothing wrong with this except for the fact that these groups will be the least capable of shouldering the economic burden suggested by the projected dependency ratios discussed above. The social and educational implications of this dilemma are apparent and cannot be cloaked with either pseudopolicy questions (e.g., Is bilingual education effective?) or with policy debates (e.g., Is there a better instructional approach for linguistic minority students?) that are short-term, narrow, and lacking in real solutions for the pressing educational concerns that will intensify well into the twenty-first century. Viewed from this futuristic perspective, the tables are turned in terms of who needs whom in our society. Whereas it has been traditionally believed that minority groups extract a disproportionate share of the taxpayer dollars for services such as welfare, aid to dependent families and children, and so on, we are moving toward an era where minority groups will be overly taxed to maintain the standard of living of an elderly majority group population whose self-interest and lifestyle generally exclude minority groups.

In short, debates about bilingual education and equal educational opportunity cannot remain fixed on Hispanics (or other linguistic minority groups). Rather, such debates must be expanded to include economic factors, including dependency ratios, in order to understand the long-range cost of undereducating linguistic minority children.

In order to counter its critics, bilingual education needs a radical shift in focus. Researchers need to focus their attention on new research questions derived from advances in the cognitive sciences, educational technology, and foreign language instruction (also see chapters in this volume by C. Snow and Spanos & Crandall). Rather than pursuing the timeworn question of whether "bilingual education works," it is important to ask *how* new educational technologies can be used in the classroom and *how* instructional features that make use of cognitive-based theories can be made relevant to bilingual and foreign language teachers.

BILINGUAL EDUCATION: PARADIGM AND MISSION

These critical language issues remain largely unstudied because of the absence of a meaningful paradigm in bilingual research. A scientific "paradigm" orients and guides the thinking about researchable problems, theory, methods, and interpretations of data. It is important to review what is meant by a paradigm in this context. In Kuhn's (1970) terminology, a *paradigm* is an accepted and shared model where the same rules and standards are exercised and from which springs a "particular coherent tradition" of research. Kuhn (1970, p. 15) warns that, without such a paradigm,

> all of the facts that could possibly pertain to the development of a given science are likely to seem equally relevant. As a result, early fact-gathering is [far] more [a] random activity than the one that subsequent scientific development makes familiar. Furthermore, in the absence of a [sound conceptual framework] fact-gathering is usually restricted to the wealth of data that lie readily [at] hand.

When we review the literature on bilingual education, the randomness surrounding research questions and research findings becomes evident. The research consists of a loosely connected mosaic of "facts." In other words, there appears to be an absence of a paradigm in bilingual research and, consequently, a profound lack of theoretical coherence or unity. The task for the future is to reassess our thinking about bilingual education, make some decisions about the critical *knowledge* issues as they relate to instructional and educational policy, and put ourselves on track toward the development of a true knowledge base concerning bilingual education, knowledge acquisition, and bilingual proficiency. This can only be done once an agreed-upon paradigm is adopted and used as a means of taking research to a higher level. Both Willig (1987) and Secada (1987) have discussed ways to begin this process.

A practical problem that must be overcome in our quest for a paradigm is the lack of a "mission" in bilingual education. Research and development in science have historically been connected to a "mission" that is supported by a majority of the general population and by policymakers. Missions are characterized by a joining together of people, organizations, and institutions that mobilize to seek a solution to common problems. We can point to examples of "missions" in the health arena by examining the forces that were brought together to seek a solution to diseases such as polio and that are currently under way in the fight against muscular dystrophy, cancer, and AIDS.

Unfortunately, few examples in education embody the same sense of mission as in the health arena. One example might be the educational reform in science education in the early 1960s brought about by the Russian launching of Sputnik. In the area of educational programming for high-risk children, we can point to Project Headstart and even bilingual education, but these programs have not enjoyed the same fervor of a mission as have science programs or the current reformist movement in education seeking the elevation of standards and educational excellence.

Beginning with *A Nation at Risk* (National Commission on Excellence in Education, 1983), the call for excellence in education has taken on the characteristics of a mission and, as such, the call is presumably applicable to all students. Within this context, Headstart and bilingual education are perceived as "special" programs that are tied directly to a limited segment of the school-age population and, therefore, are perceived only as enactments of Congress for a limited population and for a prescribed period of time. Further, as programs without a capital "M" in their mission, it has been easy to criticize both the educational effectiveness of these programs and the political justifiability of their continuation.

Unfortunately, without a clear mission, or mandate, the necessary funds to adequately carry out research and development efforts in bilingual education are not available. As yet, there is no mandate from Congress or the Department of Education to develop a bilingual education capability that works; nor is it likely that such a mission will come to fruition. In fact, evidence such as Bennett's 1985 speech points to less, rather than more, attention to bilingual education in the future by educational policymakers. There is also little hope that this policy will be reversed under the current administration.

The mission of U.S. education continues to be the homogenization and assimilation of diverse ethnic, racial, and cultural background children despite Title VII and other educational programs for language minority children (Spener, 1988). No mandate for cultural pluralism in education exists in spite of claims to the contrary. Although there is nothing wrong with a policy that advocates English as the language of education and commerce, a policy that does not recognize the inherent value of other languages and people is shortsighted.

Bilingualism is usually recognized as the sign of an educated and cosmopolitan elite. Yet, in the United States, we have a policy that seeks to eliminate bilingualism among those who have the best possibility of becoming fluent bilinguals, that is, children who enjoy the privilege of a home language other than English. Ideally, a public education system should provide instructional support to make these children competitive in English without contributing to the loss of their home languages. These potentially "true bilinguals," then, should be viewed as a critical national resource (Campbell & Lindholm, in press). Senator Paul Simon (1980) has argued that the implicit policy of monolingualism in the United States has isolated this country with respect to the world marketplace; the consequence is that U.S. business interests are losing their economic competitiveness to countries that actively promote foreign language instruction and bilingualism in the education of their children (also see Tucker, 1990).

Another side of this monolingual policy is that educational programming in foreign languages is given only lip service. A second language cannot be learned with 30 minutes or even three hours of instruction a week. The learning of a second language is a time-intensive activity that requires the best educational technology available, dedicated teachers, and motivated learners.

⅄   It is interesting that foreign language instruction appears to be on the rise again among educational reformers and is likely to enjoy a new prominence (see Thompson, Christian, Stansfield, & Rhodes, 1990). The irony is that the renewed interest in foreign language education is occurring simultaneously with the demise of bilingual education. At every front, the need for bilingual education is giving way to English immersion for non-English-speaking children despite the growing numbers of such children in our schools. At the same time, and even within the same school district, educators are adding foreign language requirements to the list of subjects necessary for high school graduation. In addition, many universities have reinstituted their foreign language requirement for graduation.

THE POLITICS OF LANGUAGE INSTRUCTION

There is definitely a dilemma here on several counts, but the most important one involves the issue of *politics*. The political arena affects every aspect of educational policy. Bilingual education has suffered because of the lack of a paradigm and a mission. Without either, bilingual education is in a seesaw position where policymakers arrive at program or research priorities from positions of self-interest and/or limited input from experts and interested constituencies. An excellent example of this is the vetoing, by California Governor George Deukmejian, of an extension of the state's bilingual education law in 1987. As justification for his action, the governor stated that the program needed review for its cost-effectiveness prior to reauthorization despite support for the law from Bill Honig, superintendent of public instruction, as well as the California State Legislature.

With this kind of political discretion available to policymakers, it is hard to envision a change unless a mission surfaces that can capture the imagination of those that possess the power to determine language policy. It is essential for practitioners, researchers, and parents to demonstrate the relevance of what they are doing for educational excellence.

It is also important for those interested in language instruction to seek new friendships among power brokers whose attention has not yet been captured. This does not imply severing old political alliances, but it does suggest the recognition that the need for bilingual education and its companion foreign language instruction can be tied to national priorities in ways not yet completely articulated.

We must establish a paradigm that is more closely allied to educational research and development rather than to mere concerns of program evaluation. We should not ask the question: "Does bilingual education work?" Rather, "How can instruction be designed and implemented that maximizes the linguistic, cognitive, and social exchanges between students who come from different home language backgrounds?" We need to bring together the best researchers and practitioners to explore how to optimally implement bilingual programs so that all students acquire linguistic skills in English while retaining their home languages.

We need an agreed-upon mission that is politically viable; a mission that will establish the necessary dialogue among federal and state policymakers to launch a new emphasis on bilingual education. Practitioners and researchers must collaborate to get the best out of our bilingual programs. We should seek strategies for ensuring that politics is turned from "personal biases" to substantive scientific questions and ensuring that these questions can be translated into sound educational practices.

A LANGUAGE-COMPETENT SOCIETY

Our ultimate goal should be a language-competent society. What this means is a society in which all residents (citizens and immigrants) of the United States have the opportunity to develop the highest possible degree of proficiency in understanding, speaking, reading, and writing in English. At the same time, English-speaking individuals should have an opportunity to develop an ability to understand, speak, read, and write a second language.

This goal should be the force that drives the *mission* for sound language instruction, and it should be the rallying point for the *political* stance that must be taken. The goal of a language-competent society can be enhanced by research that is conceptualized according to the dictates of a *paradigm* that seeks organized facts that can build on each other to inform us about the best way to carry out language instruction practices.

Throughout the world today, there are many more bilinguals than monolinguals, and many more children who have been and who continue to be educated via a second or third language than children educated exclusively via their mother tongue. Thus, in many parts of the world, bilingualism and multilingual education constitute the status quo—a way of life, a natural experience. In most of the world, bilingualism is not an issue and it is not particularly onerous or burdensome. Nor is participation in a bilingual education or other innovative language program particularly novel or different.

In these days of increasing global interdependence, all U.S. residents, and the nation as a whole, would benefit if everyone were able to speak at least one language other than English (see Padilla, Fairchild, & Valadez, 1990, chaps. 2, 7, and 9). The language incompetence of this nation's students has been noted by several national commissions that have examined the issue of foreign language teaching in the United States. For example, the President's Commission on Foreign Language and International Studies (1979) noted that our schools graduate students who are incompetent in foreign languages and who know little about international affairs.

Therefore, not only is it important to encourage the study of other languages among English-speaking students, but it is also important to build on the existing national resource present in those who know a language other than English for the development of a language-competent society.

Recently, language educators have begun to explore a strategy called "bilingual immersion education," which couples the best of bilingual education and immersion education to foster bilingual development in linguistic minority *and* majority students (Lindholm & Dolson, 1988). Although only a handful of such programs exist around the country (Lindholm, 1987), they are proving quite promising in fostering English language proficiency on the part of linguistic minority students while at the same time encouraging the maintenance of the home language. Similarly, language majority children are acquiring competence in a non-English language while also maintaining their native English. Several of these innovative language programs are described in this volume (see Chapter 8, Lindholm & Fairchild) and in the companion volume to this, Padilla, Fairchild, and Valadez (1990, see chap. 9).

PREPARING STUDENTS TO MEET THE
DEMANDS OF THE TWENTY-FIRST CENTURY

As we enter the twenty-first century, we must develop new approaches to instruct language minority students. To do this we must combine our second-language learning strategies with advances being made in the cognitive sciences and in educational technologies. The goal should be enhancing the educational attainment and advancement of language minority students and *not* the preservation of old instructional models or antiquated ideologies. Persistence in adhering to old arguments, models, or ideologies will forecast an even bleaker and more disastrous outcome for ethnolinguistic minority students as we move into the next century.

Cole and Griffin (1987) recently discussed how new technologies can be used to improve education, especially for minorities and women in science and mathematics. At the same time, they called our attention to the fact that

> a new technology of communication is causing a new epidemic of unbalanced knowledge acquisition, instead of a rise of educational excellence across the board. Therefore, special attention has to be paid to the growing disparity between potential for reorganizing diverse people in educationally productive ways on the one hand and the consequences of the current way that new technologies are introduced into the schools on the other. (Cole & Griffin, 1987, p. 3)

Clearly we need to heed Cole and Griffin's warning. Whatever new form education for linguistic minority students takes in the future, it needs to be more attuned to the technologies that are increasingly more important in our society. Further, the introduction of these new technologies must be done in educationally sound ways that enhance learning rather than in ways that simply perpetuate *rote* learning (Cole & Griffin, 1987). We are no longer talking about simply acquiring enough English to survive in an "English-only" classroom, nor are we referring only to literacy acquisition in English; we are talking about literacy with computers and other technological innovations, irrespective of the language spoken by the student. To achieve this, teachers of language minority students should join forces with researchers involved in transferring technology to the classroom. For example, the use of interactive video in second-language instruction is still largely unexplored. It is possible with our telecommunicating systems for an exemplary science teacher in Mexico City or Santiago, Chile, for example, to simultaneously instruct students in her classroom as well as Spanish-dominant students in Los Angeles, San Antonio, or Chicago.

Further, bilingual researchers knowledgeable of advances in the cognitive sciences can collaborate with cognitive scientists in their search for "models of the mind." In the process, both sides would benefit. Bilingual researchers could then develop new strategies (and, hopefully, better pedagogy) for enhancing transfer across linguistic systems, or develop better ways for acquiring complex linguistic information. At the same time, cognitive scientists formulating "models of the *monolingual* mind" are ignoring the fact that the majority of the people in the world speak at least two languages, and that bilinguals have their languages cognitively organized in ways that cannot be accounted for by current models based on the monolingual learner (see Chapter 3 by Hakuta, this volume; and in the companion volume to this, Padilla, Fairchild, & Valadez, (1990, chap. 3).

We are also better able to attend to individual differences between learners. At the least, this implies screening and assessment instruments (and technologies) that capture differences between students and that can prescribe courses of action to remedy learner deficiencies in reasoning and problem-solving skills, factual knowledge, and language-related skills. Much of this knowledge has been generated by cognitive scientists, but it requires a specific focus on language minority students. In addition, we need information about successful learners and their intellectual processing strategies, especially when two languages are involved. In other words, we can learn more about helping high-risk students by first learning about successful students and the cognitive, linguistic, and social factors that contribute to their success.

Let us hope that, for the next 20 years, the debate about how to assist linguistic minority children is focused on some of the educational technologies described here (as well as others) and *not* just on issues concerning the effectiveness of bilingual education. The needed research is expensive to be sure, but what is at stake is even greater when viewed with the longer lens of a futurist. Today's language minority student is tomorrow's wage earner, taxpayer, and participant in the political process. With the demographic shift and dependence ratio discussed earlier, the investment in the education of language minority students is actually an investment in the future well-being of everyone.

REFERENCES

Ascher, C. (1987). Trends and issues in urban and minority education. *ERIC/CUE Trends and Issues Series*, No. 6.

Baker, K. (1987). Comment on Willig's "A meta-analysis of selected studies in the effectiveness of bilingual education." *Review of Educational Research, 57*, 351–362.

Baker, K., & de Kanter, A. A. (1981). *Effectiveness of bilingual education: A review of literature*. Washington, DC: Office of Planning, Budget and Education, U.S. Department of Education.

Baker, K., & de Kanter, A. A. (Eds.). (1983). *Bilingual education: A reappraisal of federal policy*. Lexington, MA: Lexington.

Bennett, W. J. (1988). *Our children & our country: Improving America's schools and affirming the common culture*. New York: Simon & Schuster.

Campbell, R. N., & Lindholm, K. J. (in press). Conservation of language resources. In B. Van-Patten & J. F. Lee (Eds.), *SLA:FLL: On the relationship between second language acquisition and foreign language learning*. New York: Newbury House.

Cole, M., & Griffin, P. (1987). *Contextual factors in education: Improving science and mathematics education for minorities and women.* Madison: Wisconsin Center for Education Research.

Hayes-Bautista, D. E., Schink, W. O., & Chapa, J. (1988). *The burden of support: Young Latinos in an aging society.* Stanford, CA: Stanford University Press.

Here they come, ready or not. Who's dependent on whom? (1986, May 14). *Education Week*, p. 14.

Kuhn, T. S. (1970). *The structure of scientific revolutions* (2nd ed.). Chicago: University of Chicago Press.

Lindholm, K. J. (1987). *Directory of bilingual immersion programs* (Educational Report No. 8.). Los Angeles: University of California, Center for Language Education and Research.

Lindholm, K. J., & Dolson, D. (1988). *Bilingual immersion education: Promoting language and academic excellence for language minority and majority students in the same program.* Unpublished manuscript, University of California, Los Angeles, Center for Language Education and Research.

McKay, E. G. (1986, July). *Hispanic demographics: Looking ahead.* Washington, DC: National Council of La Raza.

National Commission on Excellence in Education. (1983). *A nation at risk: The imperative for educational reform.* Washington, DC: U.S. Department of Education.

Orum, L. S. (1985). *The education of Hispanics: Selected statistics.* Washington, DC: National Council of La Raza.

Padilla, A. M., Fairchild, H. H., & Valadez, C. M. (Eds.). (1990). *Foreign language education: Issues and strategies.* Newbury Park, CA: Sage.

President's Commission on Foreign Language and International Studies. (1979). *Strength through wisdom: A critique of U.S. capability.* Washington, DC: Government Printing Office.

Secada, W. G. (1987). This is 1987, not 1980: A comment on a comment. *Review of Educational Research, 57,* 377–384.

Simon, P. (1980). *The tongue-tied American.* New York: Continuum.

Spener, D. (1988). Transitional bilingual education and the socialization of immigrants. *Harvard Educational Review, 58,* 133–153.

Thompson, L., Christian, D., Stansfield, C. W., & Rhodes, N. (1990). Foreign language instruction in the United States. In A. M. Padilla, H. H. Fairchild, & C. M. Valadez (Eds.), *Foreign language education: Issues and strategies.* Newbury Park, CA: Sage.

Tucker, G. R. (1990). Second language education: Issues and perspectives. In A. M. Padilla, H. H. Fairchild, & C. M. Valadez (Eds.), *Innovations in language education: Vol. 2. Immersion and foreign language education.* Newbury Park, CA: Sage.

Willig, A. C. (1985). A meta-analysis of selected studies on the effectiveness of bilingual education. *Review of Educational Research, 55,* 269–317.

Willig, A. C. (1987). Examining bilingual education research through meta-analysis and narrative review: A response to Baker. *Review of Educational Research, 57,* 363–376.

2

History of Language Minority Education in the United States

MARGUERITE MALAKOFF
KENJI HAKUTA

Bilingual education as an object of attitude occupies a special place in the American soul. The person on the street might support it because it offers hope for connecting individuals to their heritage language. They might support it because it symbolizes a breaking away from the image of Americans as English-centered and failing to see themselves in an international arena (Archie Bunker once said: "If God wanted me to learn another language, then why did He write the Bible in English?").

The opponent of bilingual education, on the other hand, sees it as an unnecessary coddling and spoiling of new immigrants, eroding the strength of the English language—an important symbol of American unity. Bilingual education is seen as a political lobby that caters largely to the Spanish-speaking population. Opponents frequently comment that, unlike previous immigrant groups, the current group of immigrants is failing to learn English and is demanding services in Spanish.

The degree of sentiment evoked by bilingual education is not matched by an equivalent degree of understanding about the history of language minority education in the United States or by knowledge about the state of bilingual education. For example, a national survey of attitudes toward bilingual education revealed considerable confusion about the nature of bilingual education programs (Sears & Huddy, 1987). The goal of this chapter is to briefly

27

review the history of language minority education in the United States and to discuss the role that research has played in the policy debate.

IMMIGRATION AND COMPULSORY SCHOOLING: THE LANGUAGE ISSUE IS BORN

In the United States, bilingual education was not uncommon in the eighteenth and nineteenth centuries. Linguistic pluralism and diversity were acknowledged and tolerated, if not always encouraged. In New Mexico and California, there were both English and Spanish schools; in the Midwest, German-language schools served the large number of German immigrants. In New Mexico, an 1884 law recognized public Spanish-language elementary schools, noting that the language of instruction would be left to the discretion of the director. French-language public schools served the French-speaking communities in Louisiana and northern New England (August & Garcia, 1988). In the Midwest and the East, several states allowed German-language public schools in predominantly German communities. In the mid-nineteenth century, the German-English public schools were established in Ohio (Laosa, 1984). Other languages (e.g., Norwegian, Lithuanian, Czech, Dutch) were part of the curriculum in areas with large numbers of immigrants from these countries (Anderson & Boyer, 1970).

Until the end of nineteenth century, language of instruction was not an important or prominent issue in education policy. Education policy was primarily in the hands of the towns or districts, who taxed parents the necessary tuition to support a local school. The school was supported entirely by the community, teachers were often recruited from the community, and the language of instruction was frequently the language of the community. Federal and state legislation, where it existed, generally required only that schools be established, and said little more.

In the late nineteenth century, the movement for the Common School—or public school—and compulsory education, gained momentum as large numbers of poorly educated, lower-class immigrants arrived and settled in urban centers. The influx of these "new immigrants," who were predominantly Catholic and from southern and eastern Europe, created a strong xenophobic reaction among the "old immigrants" (Easterlin, Ward, Bernard, & Rueda, 1982). City and town leaders, who largely controlled the local educational institutions, became increasingly worried about changes in their communities resulting from a swelling among the ranks of "children of foreign born."

Public policy turned to mandatory education in public schools as the means to ensure that the children of immigrants were assimilated into the "American" (read Anglo-Saxon/northern European Protestant) culture (Glenn, 1988). At the same time, the work force and humanitarians hoped to use mandatory education to keep children out of the labor market, and these groups pointed to the need to teach literacy and American values to these children. Thus public schools came to be seen as the primary institution for socializing immigrant children and producing literate individuals who were assimilated into the democratic values of American society.

This task of assimilating foreign children, along with increased regulation of education by state and county legislatures, raised the issue of a common language of instruction that would represent American society and provide a measure of assimilation. Simultaneously, the loss of the national-origin language represented the abandonment of the foreign culture of origin. State legislatures began to pass laws regulating the language of instruction in public, and then private, schools. By the end of the nineteenth century, California and New Mexico both had English-only instruction laws. In 1898, the U.S. government banned the use of Spanish in newly acquired Puerto Rico, undeterred by the fact that the entire population was Spanish speaking.

The antiforeign and, in particular, anti-German sentiment of World War I made bilingual education a moot topic. The remaining foreign language schools, most of which were German, were shut down, either by laws mandating English-only instruction or by laws reserving public funds for English-only schools. In several states, laws were passed requiring compulsory education in public schools, where the district had greater control. Numerous states attempted to ban the teaching of a foreign language in both private and public schools under laws that carried criminal penalties. By the early 1920s, 34 states had English-only requirements in their schools (McFadden, 1983).

This linguistic xenophobia was somewhat stemmed in 1923, when the Supreme Court declared, albeit rather apologetically, that a Nebraska state law prohibiting the teaching of a foreign language to elementary students was unconstitutional. *Meyer v. Nebraska* is illustrative of several cases of the time. A teacher in a parochial school was convicted for teaching reading in German to a 10-year-old child. The Nebraska Supreme Court opinion, affirming the conviction, notes:

> To allow the children of foreigners who had emigrated here, to be taught from early childhood in the language of the country of their parents ... was to ... naturally inculcate in them the ideas and sentiments foreign to the best interest of this country. (262 U.S. 390, 1923)

The Supreme Court, finding that proficiency in a foreign language was "not injurious to the health, morals, or understanding of the ordinary child," declared the Nebraska law unconstitutional under the Fourteenth Amendment. However, the Court underlined that the power of the state to "make reasonable regulations for all schools, including a requirement that they shall give instruction in English, is not questioned." The Court further noted: "The desire of the legislature to foster a homogeneous people with American ideals, prepared readily to understand current discussions of civic matters, is easy to appreciate."

Following the *Meyer v. Nebraska* decision, the strict English-only instruction laws were generally either repealed or ignored. However, Laosa (1984) noted that, in 1971, 35 states still had English-only instruction laws of some kind. Although *Meyer v. Nebraska* limited the state's power to prohibit the teaching of foreign languages in private schools, it also clearly established that the United States is an English-speaking country and indicated that schools could require the use of English (Teitelbaum & Hiller, 1977).

THE 1960s: BILINGUAL EDUCATION RETURNS

The history of bilingual education in the United States is frequently divided into two periods: pre-World War I and post-1960 (August & Garcia, 1988; Hakuta, 1986; Laosa, 1984). From the 1920s until the 1960s, little attention was given to the language needs of non-English-speaking students. Students were placed in regular classrooms, where they "sank or swam." It was not until the 1960s that the failure of English classrooms to educate non-English-speaking students began to receive national attention (McFadden, 1983).

In 1963, Dade County, Florida, initiated an experimental bilingual education program in the first three grades of the Coral Way School. The desire to meet the needs of the large number of Cuban refugees, many of whom were children, motivated the program (see Mackey & Beebe, 1977, for a detailed review). The experimental program, set up by the Ford Foundation, included children from both Cuban- and English-speaking middle-class homes; the objective was to create functional Spanish-English bilinguals. The success of the program attracted local and then national attention. The program spread to other elementary schools and junior high schools in Dade County in the following years (Hakuta, 1986). By the late 1960s, several other cities had started locally supported bilingual education programs.

In 1968, bilingual education programs in public schools were legitimized at the federal level by the Bilingual Education Act. The return of bilingual education to public schools is closely tied to the civil rights movement of the 1960s. The civil rights movement and the pressure for cultural pluralism that accompanied it produced two avenues to bilingual education: (a) Title VI of the 1964 Civil Rights Act and (b) the 1968 Bilingual Education Act. Title VI of the Civil Rights Act ultimately provided the enforcement mechanism through which the courts could order that limited-English-proficient (LEP) students be served (Title VI prohibits discrimination on the basis of "race, color, or national origin" in the operation of any federally assisted programs—45 C.R.F. Sec. 80). The Bilingual Education Act (BEA), on the other hand, established the federal role in bilingual education and allocated funds for innovative projects and support programs such as graduate fellowships and program evaluation.

In addition to the civil rights movement, national attention was concerned with reducing poverty, improving education, and supporting ethnic identity. Until the Elementary and Secondary Education Act of 1965, the federal government had left educational policy to state legislatures. However, with the general wave of enthusiasm to mobilize education as a primary means of battling poverty, there was a move for greater federal intervention, especially in the allocation of funds. The assimilationist melting pot ideology was replaced by a move toward cultural pluralism and ethnic revival. Research on bilingual programs in Canada and Europe suggested that bilingual children not only did not suffer any cognitive deficiency but outperformed monolingual children on a number of cognitive tasks (Lerea & Kohut, 1961; Lewis & Lewis, 1965; Peal & Lambert, 1962). The success of the Dade County programs had attracted national attention to the effectiveness of bilingual education. All these factors contributed to the creation of the first Bilingual Education Act (BEA) in 1968.

The Bilingual Education Act

The BEA was not an independent piece of legislation but was added as Title VII of the Elementary and Secondary Education Act. It was four and half pages long and served primarily to legitimize bilingual education programs, allocate funds for experimental programs, and foster research on bilingual education. While it legitimized bilingual education, it neither defined the programs nor mandated that bilingual programs should be created. According to a former general counsel to the Department of Education, the

Bilingual Education Act provides "funds to enlightened school districts that submitted a voluntary proposal for expenditure of those funds on special projects for a small number of limited-English proficient students" (Levin, 1983).

The Bilingual Education Act was the final product of S.428, which Senator Ralph Yarborough introduced in January 1967. In that same year, over 35 similar bills were introduced into the House. The original bill was intended to provide assistance to agencies in setting up bilingual programs for Spanish-speaking children for whom English was a foreign language. The final Senate bill, however, included all low-income, non-English-speaking groups within the scope of the bill's funding. Nonetheless, the legislative history of the law indicates that programs were intended to be primarily directed toward Spanish-speaking groups. A report issued by the Department of Housing, Education and Welfare (HEW) stated:

> Let us make clear that in administering such a program benefits must go to those areas where the problem is most severe. Clearly the bulk of the assistance would be made available to assist persons of Spanish-speaking background. (PL 90–247, Legislative History, 2780)

The final legislation recognized the "problems of those children who are educationally disadvantaged because of their inability to speak English" (PL 90–247, Legislative History, 2779). Section 702 of the law defined bilingual education as a federal policy, which would be "to provide financial assistance to local educational agencies to carry out new and imaginative elementary and secondary school programs designed to meet these special educational needs" (PL 90–247, Sec. 702). As the intention was to encourage varied and innovative programs, rather than mandate a strict policy, the law neither defined nor prescribed types of programs needed. However, it recognized that bilingual programs need not be limited to only language arts and noted that possible programs for grants included "programs to impart to students a knowledge of the history and culture associated with their languages" (PL 90–247; Title VII, Sec. 704[a][2][e]).

The BEA was an important piece of legislation in that it defined bilingual education programs as falling within federal educational policy. In doing so, it marked a change of policy toward language minorities and undermined the English-only laws that were still on the books in many states (Laosa, 1984). More important, perhaps, it suggested that *equal education* was not the same as *identical education*, even when there was no difference in location or teacher.

Title VI and HEW Interpretive Guidelines

Although the BEA had no power of prescription or enforcement, the HEW published Title VI regulations and guidelines regarding the schooling of language minority children. The guidelines stated that "school systems are responsible for assuring that students of a particular race, color, or national origin are not denied the opportunity to obtain education generally obtained by the students in the system" (33 *Fed. Reg.*, 4956, 1968). In 1970, J. Stanley Pottinger, the director of the Office of Civil Rights, sent a memorandum to school districts that served language minority students. The memorandum, published in the *Federal Register* as guidelines, specifically interpreted Title VI as it related to language minority students. These interpretive guidelines became the basis for subsequent court action. The memorandum noted that a Title VI compliance review had found "a number of practices which have the effect of denying equality of educational opportunity to Spanish-surnamed pupils" and that these practices "have the effect of discrimination on the basis of national origin." The 1970 guidelines specified that "where inability to speak and understand English excludes national origin minority group children from effective participation in the educational program ... the district must take affirmative steps to rectify the language deficiency" (35 *Fed. Reg.*, 11595). The memorandum further noted that schools could not assign national origin minority groups to special programs for the mentally retarded on the basis of English language skills. The new guidelines, however, did not specify what the "affirmative steps" should be and said nothing about instructing LEP students in their native language (Levin, 1983).

Lau v. Nichols:
The New Federal Policy Is Tested

Although the guidelines were published in 1970, the legal obligation of school districts to provide bilingual education programs was not tested until the 1974 Supreme Court ruling in *Lau v. Nichols*, which established the legal obligation for public schools receiving federal funds to comply with the HEW regulations and the interpretive guidelines. In addition, it established the guidelines that have been used for the past 15 years to evaluate and guide compliance with the regulations. Finally, it contributed strongly to the Equal Education Opportunity Act of 1974.

When the BEA did not provide the widespread solution its supporters had hoped for, parents of minority language students gradually turned toward the courts in hopes of finding a constitutional right to bilingual education (Mc-

Fadden, 1983). *Lau v. Nichols* was a class action suit brought by Chinese public school students against the San Francisco Unified School District in 1970. The district had identified 2,856 limited-English-proficient students, less than half of whom were receiving English as a second language (ESL) instruction. The district did not dispute the number of students involved, and it had made some attempt to address the situation. The issue, then, was whether non-English-speaking children receive an equal educational opportunity in a mainstream classroom, and whether the school district was under a legal obligation to provide special services. The federal District Court and the Ninth Circuit Court of Appeals found that, because all students were receiving the same curriculum in the same classes, the non-English-speaking children were being treated *no differently* and were not being discriminated against. The school district was, therefore, under no legal obligation to provide special services to these students. The court reasoned that "every student brings to the starting line of his educational career different advantages and disadvantages caused in part by social, economic and cultural background, created and continued completely apart from any contribution by the school system" (487 F.2d 797).

The same constitutional issue, however, was answered differently by a federal District Court for New Mexico in 1972. In *Serna v. Portales Municipal Schools*, the court held that Mexican American children were being treated *differently* when they received the same curriculum given to English-proficient students and that their constitutional right to equal protection had been violated. The District Court ordered bilingual education as a remedy.

The 1974 Supreme Court ruling in *Lau v. Nichols* avoided the constitutional question altogether. The Court's opinion relied entirely on legislative grounds, citing violations of both Title VI and the 1970 HEW guidelines. The Court held that the HEW interpretive guidelines "clearly indicate that affirmative efforts to give special training for non-English speaking pupils are required by Title VI as a condition to federal aid to public schools" (414 U.S. 569). The Supreme Court found that the requirement to know English that is implied in the California educational system is such that students who do not understand English are "effectively foreclosed from any meaningful education" (414 U.S. 566). The Court found that Title VI was violated when there was the *effect* of discrimination, although there was no *intent*.

As the plaintiffs had not requested any specific remedy, the Court stayed clear of prescribing one. In a concurring opinion, Justice Blackmun stated that numbers were "at the heart of this case," suggesting that his decision would have been different had fewer children been involved. Although Title VI and the HEW guidelines protect the rights of the "individual," and do not specify that a certain number is required, this opinion set the precedent for regarding numbers involved in future cases.

In the aftermath of *Lau*, courts followed the guidelines established by the Supreme Court. They tended to avoid the constitutional issue, to rely on "discriminatory effect" application of Title VI, to choose a remedy case by case, and to take into account the number of children involved. Shortly after the *Lau* decision, the Tenth Circuit Court ruled in the appeal in the *Serna* case. The court followed the formula set down by the Supreme Court, stating that "in light of ... *Lau* ... we need not decide the equal protection issue" (McFadden, 1983).

REGULATION AND ENFORCEMENT OF FEDERAL POLICY

The Equal Education Act: Section 1703f

Several months after the *Lau* decision was handed down, Congress codified the Supreme Court ruling into the Equal Educational Opportunity Act (EEOA) of 1974. This new piece of legislation extended the *Lau* decision to all public school districts, and not just those receiving federal funding. The EEOA required school districts to "take appropriate action to overcome language barriers that impede equal participation by its students in its instructional programs" (20 U.S.C. Sec. 1703f). In 1975, a federal Court of Appeals ruled that simply the failure to take "appropriate action" in the absence of discriminatory intent was a violation of Section 1703f (*Morales v. Shannon*, 1975). However, the EEOA did not specify what constituted an "appropriate action" and courts varied in their interpretation, in line with the case-by-case remedy approach.

In 1981, the Fifth Circuit court finally interpreted Section 1703(f) of the EEOA in the case of *Castaneda v. Pickard*. In essence, the court took on the task of deciding what Congress had in mind in passing Section 1703(f). The federal court rejected the policy of the courts deferring to local school boards in evaluating whether an appropriate remedy had been implemented, stating that Congress had "deliberately placed on federal courts the difficult responsibility of determining whether that obligation had been met" (648 F.2d 989). The court established three criteria the implemented remedial program had to meet to be considered appropriate:

(1) It should be considered legitimate by experts in the field;

(2) the program should be implemented in a reasonable manner; and

(3) the program must produce results indicating that "the language barrier is being overcome."

However, the court stopped short of prescribing an "appropriate action," and, in particular, between choosing between an ESL and a transitional program. This decision, the court held, Congress "intended to leave [in the hands of] state and local education authorities" who "were free to determine" how they wished to discharge their obligation.

In the late 1970s and early 1980s, lawyers pressing the interests of language minority students relied increasingly on the EEOA rather than on the *Lau* decision, which had been threatened by subsequent discrimination cases. The issue lay with whether a "discriminatory effect" in the absence of deliberate intent was enough to violate Title VI (McFadden, 1983). In 1981 the *U.S. v. Texas* decision, the district court found that the Texas Educational Agency (TEA) had violated Section 1703(f), although it was not in violation of Title VI. The court, citing earlier cases, found that a substantiation of "discriminatory *intent*" was necessary to violate Title VI (McFadden, 1983). However, because the state and the TEA had failed to take "appropriate action" they had violated Section 1703(f). Two other decisions make this case notable. First, the district court spoke to the type of program that should be implemented by the state and the TEA. The court recognized that bilingual education was not required by any law, and the TEA could have implemented another "appropriate action." However, the evidence demonstrated that a violation of Section 1703(f) had occurred. Summarizing the court's argument, August and Garcia (1988) note:

> The evidence also demonstrated that bilingual instruction is uniquely suited to meet the needs of the state Spanish-speaking students. Therefore, the defendants would be required to take further steps, including additional bilingual instruction, if needed, to satisfy their affirmative obligations.

In the course of the trial, Texas had passed new minority language education legislation that addressed many of the issues in the court's decision. In 1982, the Fifth Circuit Court of Appeals overturned the verdict on several grounds. The most compelling ground was that the new Texas legislation had made the previous case moot (McFadden, 1983). However, more damaging was the finding that "no local district may be subjected to remedial orders" without first having the opportunity to be heard individually. Thus each district would have to be sued in individual actions before a court could order a remedial action in that district (McFadden, 1983).

The Lau *Remedies and the NPRM*

After the *Lau* decision, HEW appointed a task force to establish guidelines in implementing the *Lau* decision. The guidelines, known as the "*Lau* Remedies," were issued in 1975. These guidelines directed school districts to identify and evaluate non-English-proficient students and to provide a transitional bilingual-bicultural program. As the guidelines were only applied to districts found to be out of compliance with Title VI or the EEOA, they were applied piecemeal across the nation.

Although the *Lau* Remedies were never formally established as regulations, HEW began to treat them as such. Between 1975 and 1980, over 500 cases were negotiated on the *Lau* Remedies (Levin, 1983). In 1980, the Department of Education eventually issued a Notice of Proposed Rulemaking (NPRM) in the *Federal Register*. This publication followed a 1978 suit filed by the State of Alaska and several of its school districts in an attempt to prevent enforcement of the *Lau* Remedies (Levin, 1983). The plaintiffs claimed that HEW was in violation of the Administrative Procedures Act for not publishing the "regulations" for public comment. The court approved a consent decree in which HEW would publish the *Lau* Remedies as regulations.

The NPRM received a very political and divided reception (see Levin, 1983, for a detailed analysis). At the hearings, the majority of the testimony was in favor of the rules; those in opposition were so because the rules did not go far enough. However, the written testimony was largely opposed to the rules because they went *too* far. The major education organizations attacked both the rules and the Department of Education (Levin, 1983). In general, the NPRM was far less stringent than the *Lau* Remedies. Most notably, the NPRM weakened the bicultural requirement, introduced a panoply of possible waivers, and increased the number of students required before full services had to be provided from 20 LEP students in a district to 25 within two grades in a school. In addition, the NPRM provided that the exit criterion from the program (30th percentile) would be lower than the entrance cutoff criterion (40th percentile). That is, students scoring below the 40th percentile would be eligible for services, but students scoring above the 30th percentile would be exited from the program. The NPRM also provided for a diminished requirement for bilingual education in high school.

The NPRM was short-lived. Congress made several attempts to limit the NPRM prior to its publication. In late 1980, Congress passed a resolution prohibiting the Department of Education from publishing the final regulations until June 1981. One of the Reagan administration's first acts was to withdraw the NPRM, thus there was no final regulation of the rights of language minority students. However, the irony is that, in eliminating NPRM, the Reagan administration left the old enforcement system, the *Lau* Remedies, in place. Thus school districts are now under greater constraint than had the NPRM become final (Levin, 1983).

TYPES OF PROGRAMS

Although the first bilingual program at the Coral Way School was a two-way enrichment program, this model for bilingual education spread to very few public schools. Following the passage of the BEA, a number of states passed legislation either mandating or permitting bilingual education programs. Massachusetts was the first state to pass a mandatory bilingual education law with the Transitional Bilingual Education Act of 1968 (Laosa, 1984). Where legislation exists, it generally follows the *Lau* Remedies: that is, transitional bilingual programs when there are more than 20 students in a district. In the absence of this critical mass, pullout ESL is provided.

Different types of programs, however, have evolved over the years. August and Garcia (1988) distinguished six models for bilingual education, which are best seen as prototypes within which considerable variation and combination can occur:

(1) transitional bilingual education,

(2) maintenance bilingual education,

(3) submersion model,

(4) English as a second language,

(5) U.S. immersion or sheltered English, and

(6) the immersion model.

Transitional bilingual education. The transitional bilingual education models are the most common in U.S. public schools. These programs are intended to provide both English language instruction and grade-appropriate subject content prior to mainstreaming into a regular English-speaking class. During the period of English acquisition, the native language is used to cover other subjects. Native language arts may or may not be taught; the teacher may or may not be fluent in both languages.

Maintenance bilingual education. The original Dade County bilingual education program, on the other hand, followed the maintenance model. The program targeted students from two distinct groups, and the goal was for all students to achieve proficiency in both languages. Instruction is provided in both languages. Frequently the school day is divided into two language periods, that is, subjects taught in the morning are in one language, and those taught in the afternoon are in another. There are few public school maintenance bilingual programs in the United States.

Submersion and ESL models. The submersion model is, in fact, the absence of any special program: It is the "sink or swim" method. Students are placed in regular classrooms and are offered no special help or English language instruction. The ESL model provides special English instructional activities on a pullout basis, and the remainder of school day is similar to a submersion model. That is, LEP students are pulled out of the regular classroom on a regular schedule and given special instruction in English language arts. This model is frequently used when there are LEP students from different language backgrounds in the same school. In New York City, the majority of non-Spanish-speaking LEP students are in ESL programs (New York City Board of Education, 1988).

Canadian immersion. The Canadian immersion programs were first developed to produce French-English bilinguals among the English-speaking community in and around Montreal. These programs emphasize the second language in the first few grades, that is, the children are "immersed" in French, and English language arts are introduced in second or third grade. By sixth grade, the day is divided equally between the two languages. This model has been extended to three-way immersion, adding a third ethnic group language to French and English. It is important to note that this model, while successful, was largely implemented with majority language, middle-class children who faced no pressure to abandon their native language.

U.S. immersion or sheltered English. U.S. immersion, or sheltered English, is a variant on the Canadian model with a major difference: It is designed to develop proficiency in English only. LEP students are grouped together in special classrooms staffed by bilingual teachers. Instruction is carried out in English, and the native language is used only to enhance communication. However, no knowledge of English is assumed and the vocabulary and instructional materials are modified to suit the students' English language ability.

Of these six types of programs, the majority are designed to help students make the transition from one language to another; that is, they take monolinguals and produce monolinguals. In this sense, they are considered "subtractive." Immersion programs and maintenance bilingual education, on the other hand, are "additive" in that they develop and *maintain* proficiency in two languages.

In 1988, 12 states and Guam had legislation mandating bilingual education, and 12 states had legislation permitting it. West Virginia is the only state
still prohibiting special services (August & Garcia, 1988). The remaining 26
states have no legislation relevant to bilingual education. The legislation in
each state covers different aspects: 22 states allow or require instruction in
another language—that is, transitional bilingual programs—including the 12
states mandating bilingual education; 28 states require special certification
for bilingual education teachers, and 15 states require parental consent for
enrollment in bilingual programs.

In 1984, Developmental Associates carried out a nationwide study of language minority instruction for the Department of Education. They sampled
programs in kindergarten through fifth grade in 335 schools, covering 191
public school districts and 19 states. The study relied on local school district
definitions of LEP students and data reported by these districts. The authors
suggest that their estimates may be conservative because of the tendency for
some districts to underestimate their language minority LEP populations. The
study found that schools reported three to four times as many LEP students in
grade one as in grade five. On average, the schools mainstreamed 20% of the
students each year, and schools with smaller percentages of LEP students
mainstreamed a greater percentage. Only half of the teachers responsible for
teaching language minority students reported being able to speak a second
language (in addition to English), and only 28% had received bilingual education certification. In general, use of the native language was deemphasized
in favor of English: 93% reported that English was the key ingredient in the
program, while only 7% reported that the native language was emphasized.
However, 60% reported that both languages were used to some extent.

RESEARCH ON PROGRAM EFFECTIVENESS

In part due to complex legislative, judicial, and regulatory activities, a vast
array of programs to meet the language needs of minority students has
emerged. The task of evaluating whether or not any particular approach is
effective is a truly difficult endeavor. Summative evaluations of Title VII
transitional bilingual education programs with control groups are difficult
due to a variety of reasons. For example, Baker and de Kanter (1983), in
attempting such a comparison across a large number of evaluations, found
numerous problems with inappropriate controls, inadequate dependent measures, and other methodological flaws. Indeed, from an initial pool of "several hundred studies" (they do not cite the exact number), they were able to

use the results of only 39. Willig (1985) used the same pool of evaluations as Baker and de Kanter and arrived at similar conclusions with respect to methodology (although her conclusions about the effectiveness of bilingual education were quite different):

> The overwhelming message of these findings reflects on the quality of research and evaluation in bilingual education. The unacceptable quality of the major portion of this research is substantiated not only by the information contained in the studies, but also by that *not* contained in the studies. Information crucial to understanding the research very often was not included in the reports. Documentation of the nature and characteristics of the programs being studied was frequently missing as well as information on the characteristics of the students, teachers, and contexts of the programs. Even the kinds of information most basic for any reputable research report were frequently missing. This is exemplified by the number [of studies that even fail to report] means, standard deviations, and/or sample sizes. These study characteristics ... add up to one glaring message: It is imperative that the quality of research and evaluation in bilingual education be upgraded. (Willig, 1985, p. 311)

An alternative approach to a summative evaluation would be to identify effective schools and to describe their characteristics (Carter & Chatfield, 1986; Garcia, 1987; Tikunoff, 1983). In reviewing these studies, August and Garcia (1988) noted that an important instructional variable in "effective" programs was the cultural appropriateness of the teaching practices used by the teacher, that is, the extent to which there was overlap between the classroom and the home culture. In general, studies have found that the quality of teacher-student interaction and peer interaction played an important role in the development of English proficiency. Such identification and description of success stories can be quite useful as role models for other programs, as well as for boosting the morale of a stressed educational system.

Citing the highly political and volatile nature of evaluation studies, in addition to their empirical inadequacies, Hakuta and Snow (1986) proposed the use of information from basic research on bilingualism and second-language acquisition in assessing the theoretical soundness of bilingual education programs. They proposed the following principles that are supported by basic research:

- Bilingualism is a good thing for children of all backgrounds—when bilingual children are compared with monolingual children on different kinds of skills, bilingual children are superior.
- To be "proficient," "to be fluent," "to know" a language means many different things: You can have good conversational skills, but that is different from being

able to use the language in other settings, such as in school. Bilingual children are often informally evaluated in their conversational skills but not in how they can use English in school.

- The two languages of the bilingual child are interdependent—they do not compete for limited space and resources.
- The stronger the native language of the children, the more efficiently they will learn English.
- Knowledge and skills learned in one language transfer to the other language—they do not have to be relearned.
- It is a myth that children are like linguistic sponges; they may take anywhere from two to seven years to acquire a second language, especially to master the academic uses of English.
- It is a myth that the younger the children are, the faster they learn a second language. For example, 10-year-olds are faster learners than 5-year-olds.

They urge policymakers to pay more attention to what basic research says is possible to develop in bilingual children rather than being limited to programmatic comparisons. One limitation of this model of the "ideal" bilingual is that practical limitations such as teacher availability and the general issue of program implementation are not considered.

Another useful type of research from the practitioner's and policymaker's perspectives are studies of learning conducted in the context of actual programs. Chamot (1988) provides an excellent summary of recent works that fit this description, including those conducted under the auspices of the Center for Language Education and Research (CLEAR). These studies would be particularly useful to the extent that the original research questions are addressed from the research consumer's perspective and, preferably, in a collaborative setting. As we attempt to rescue bilingual education research from its fatefully political predicament, while paying attention to its legacy of divisiveness, it would be most constructive to design research programs that avoided the drawing of battle lines and that attempted to truly design a pragmatic model of bilingual functioning in the school setting.

REFERENCES

Anderson, T., & Boyer, M. (1970). *Bilingual schooling in the United States.* Austin: Southwest Educational Laboratory.

August, D., & Garcia, E. E. (1988). *Language minority education in the United States: Research, policy and practice.* Springfield, IL: Charles C Thomas.

Baker, K. E., & de Kanter, A. A. (1983). Federal policy and the effectiveness of bilingual education. In K. A. Baker & A. A. de Kanter (Eds.), *Bilingual education: A reappraisal of federal policy* (pp. 33–86). Lexington, MA: Lexington.

Carter, T. P., & Chatfield, M. L. (1986). Effective bilingual schools: Implementation for policy and practice. *American Journal of Education, 95*, 200–234.

Chamot, A. U. (1988). Bilingualism in education and bilingual education: The state of the art in the United States. *Journal of Multilingual and Multicultural Education, 9*, 11–35.

Developmental Associates. (1984, December). *LEP students: Characteristics and school services* (Final report, descriptive phase study of the National Longitudinal Evaluation of the Effectiveness of Services for Language Minority Limited English Proficient Students). Arlington, VA: Author.

Easterlin, R. A., Ward, D., Bernard W. S., & Rueda, R. (1982). *Immigration.* Cambridge, MA: Harvard University Press.

Garcia, E. E. (1987). Effective schooling for language minority students. In *New focus: Occasional papers in bilingual education.* Wheaton, MD: National Clearinghouse for Bilingual Education.

Glenn, C. L. (1988) *The myth of the common school.* Cambridge, MA: University of Massachusetts Press.

Hakuta, K. (1986). *Mirror of language.* New York: Basic Books.

Hakuta, K., & Snow, C. (1986). *The role of research in policy decisions about bilingual education.* Washington, DC: U.S. House of Representatives, Education and Labor Committee.

Laosa, L. M. (1984). *Social policies toward children of diverse ethnic, racial, and language groups in the United States.* In H. W. Stevenson & A. E. Siegel (Eds.), *Child development research and social policy.* Chicago: University of Chicago Press.

Lerea, L., & Kohut, S. (1961). A comparative study of monolinguals and bilinguals in verbal task performance. *Journal of Child Psychology, 27*, 49–52.

Levin, B. (1983). An analysis of the federal attempt to regulate bilingual education: Protecting civil rights or controlling curriculum. *Journal of Law and Education, 12*(1), 29–60.

Lewis, H. P., & Lewis, E. R. (1965). Written language performance of sixth-grade children in low socio-economic status from bilingual and from monolingual backgrounds. *Journal of Experimental Education, 35*, 237–242.

Mackey, W. F., & Beebe, V. N. (1977). *Bilingual schools for a bicultural community: Miami's adaptation to the Cuban refugees.* Rowley, MA: Newbury House.

McFadden, B. J. (1983). Bilingual education and the law. *Journal of Law and Education, 12*(1), 1–27.

New York City Board of Education. (1988). *Facts and figures. Brooklyn: NYC Board of Education, Office of Bilingual Education.*

Peal E., & Lambert, W. E. (1962). The relation of bilingualism to intelligence. *Psychological Monographs: General and Applied, 76*, 1–23.

Sears, D. O., & Huddy, L. (1987, September 1). *Bilingual education: Symbolic meaning and support among non-Hispanics.* Paper presented at the annual meeting of the American Psychological Association, New York City.

Teitelbaum, H., & Hiller, J. R. (1977). The legal perspective. In *Bilingual education: Current perspectives* (Vol. 3). Washington, DC: Center for Applied Linguistics.

Tikunoff, W. (1983). *Significant bilingual instructional features study.* San Francisco: Far West Laboratory.

Willig, A. C. (1985). A meta-analysis of selected studies on the effectiveness of bilingual education. *Review of Educational Research, 55*, 269–317.

PART II

Research Perspectives in Bilingual Education

Part II provides a generally nontechnical review of the major issues involved in conducting research on language education. These issues range from the basic research questions of the relationship between language, bilingualism, and cognition to the more focused topics of native language instruction and African American dialects and the learning process.

Kenji Hakuta, in "Language and Cognition in Bilingual Education" (Chapter 3), recognizes the important theoretical issues—in linguistics, education, and cognition—that are involved in bilingual education. Hakuta also reveals the social-cultural context of research in bilingual education by illuminating the racially motivated assumptions that bilingualism is a cognitive handicap and that bilingual individuals are intellectually inferior.

In contrast, the more recent research tradition in bilingualism shows a number of cognitive and/or intellectual benefits: enhanced cognitive flexibility and the early development of "metalinguistic" skills (i.e., the ability to think in the abstract about the nature of language). In addition, bilingual proficiency is associated with enhanced nonverbal IQ and better than average academic achievement scores. Hakuta's conclusion calls for an emphasis on native language instruction as well as the "holistic development" of the linguistic minority child's language and education.

Catherine E. Snow, in "Rationales for Native Language Instruction: Evidence from Research" (Chapter 4), presents a more focused review of the pros and cons of using language minority children's native language in initial education and literacy training.

According to Snow, four arguments are articulated against the use of native language instruction: (a) The history argument points to the success of certain European immigrant groups in the absence of federally sponsored bilingual education; (b) the "ghettoization" of linguistic minority children results in segregation, stigma, and the maintenance of intergroup differences; (c) the amount of "time-on-task" is reduced by bilingual education; and (d) the inevitable attrition of native languages makes for a "hopeless cause" in bilingual education.

In contrast, Snow identifies three arguments in favor of native language instruction: (a) to enhance the cultural-social identity of linguistic minority children (i.e., increasing the match between the culture of the teacher/school and the culture of the student/home); (b) to take advantage of the cognitive and social benefits of bilingualism; and (c) to enhance the development of early literacy skills, which occurs most readily in young children's first language. Snow concludes by strongly supporting the use of native language instruction in order to maximize achievement in both the children's native language and in English.

Halford H. Fairchild and Stephanie Edwards-Evans, in "African American Dialects and Schooling: A Review" (Chapter 5), present an overview of the research and teaching issues pertinent to the topic of African American dialects. Fairchild and Edwards-Evans note that research on this topic has been embedded in an ideological climate of White racism, and, as a result, the early research tended to degrade these dialects as inferior or deficient.

Focusing on the attitudes and behaviors of teachers, Fairchild and Edwards-Evans review the literature on teacher effects and offer a number of general principles for pedagogical practice. They conclude that a more fundamental revolution in American education is needed if the problems of academic underachievement on the part of African Americans is to be redressed.

As a group, the three chapters that compose Part II cover a variety of issues in language education: the relationship between language and thinking; the role of using children's native language in their early education; and the issues pertinent to dialect minorities (e.g., speakers of African American dialects).

3

Language and Cognition in
Bilingual Children

KENJI HAKUTA

There are many negative myths about bilingualism in children (see Cummins, 1984). Some educators have cautioned against the use of two languages in children, claiming that bilingualism causes cognitive, social, and emotional damage. Although few scholars today would claim that bilingualism could cognitively harm children, this view was strongly advocated in the past and it can be occasionally witnessed in the popular press and among some educators today.

This topic is of great concern to those interested in foreign language education and to practitioners of bilingual education. Any decision about the soundness of pedagogical approaches involving two languages should be informed by the body of research on the issues of bilingualism and cognitive development.

THEORETICAL ISSUES

Of fundamental importance in conceptualizing this area of research are the theoretical tensions concerning the development of language and thought (Hakuta, 1986). The claim that bilingualism would have any effect on cognitive ability, be it positive or negative, is based on the assumption that language is a central part of cognitive activity. However, the influential developmental theory of Jean Piaget, for example, places a minimal role on language in cognitive development, and, therefore, Piaget's theoretical approach would maintain that bilingualism should have little or no effect on cognition. On the other hand, theorists such as Lev S. Vygotsky emphasize the importance of language in guiding thought processes, viewing it as a process of social shaping through language; so, according to this theory, bilingualism can have profound effects on cognitive processes—they could be negative or positive, depending on society's attitudes and actions toward the phenomenon.

Another related tension is the question of whether or not the mind should be thought of as a "limited capacity container." The claim that bilingualism can cause a cognitive slowdown is based on the assumption that there is only so much information that can be processed by the child at any given time, and, therefore, attempting to learn two languages would, so to speak, blow some cognitive fuses. Theoretical issues such as these continue to be debated in the behavioral sciences, and they have influenced, and will continue to influence, the research on bilingualism and cognitive ability.

HISTORICAL BACKGROUND

In addition to theoretical concerns, there have been societal concerns influencing research on bilingualism that need to be considered. Indeed, the literature on the negative consequences of bilingualism on mental development can be traced back to social concerns at the turn of this century about the intellectual quality of immigrants who happened to be bilingual (see Hakuta, 1986). The debate in those days centered not so much on issues of mental development and psychology but on social issues concerning the new wave of immigrants from southern and eastern Europe that began in the late nineteenth century. Social scientists and educators reflected the concern of the public that these new immigrants were not adapting well in mainstream American society. As evidence, they pointed to the fact that the new immigrants were performing poorly on IQ tests and that their children were doing poorly in the schools.

Two opposing camps of psychologists advanced "explanations" for the cause of this adjustment failure. They are essentially the same two camps who are still debating the determinants of IQ, even though the tests themselves have changed considerably since those early days. The hereditarians believed that IQ is determined primarily through heredity and, therefore, could not be modified by experience. The environmentalists, on the other hand, believed that IQ could be developed through experience. A factor that came to play a central role in this debate was bilingualism, where a bilingual individual is not necessarily proficient in two languages but comes from a language background other than English and is proficient in English to varying degrees.

The hereditarians argued that bilingualism was not a factor in the low IQ scores. The environmentalists, in contrast, argued for the position that the bilingual experience delayed the mental development of children. This was consistent with the then-prevalent views of development that stressed the role of experience in learning. Ironically, neither camp was willing to admit that perhaps IQ tests administered in English simply were not good measures of intelligence for people who were not comfortable in English. The legacy of this early research is the view that bilingualism causes cognitive retardation.

Research with "True" Bilinguals

More recent studies of bilingualism, a tradition begun by Elizabeth Peal and Wallace Lambert (Peal & Lambert, 1962) at McGill University in Montreal, have tended to look at what would be considered "real" bilingualism in children. These studies examine children who are roughly equal in their abilities in two languages. In these studies, a variety of mental performances are measured, often of the same types of abilities as those measured in IQ tests. The results of these studies indicate that, when these children are compared with a group of monolingual children (with equivalent socioeconomic backgrounds), the bilingual children perform better. These results have been replicated in over 30 studies in different cultural settings (Hakuta, 1986, 1987).

Among the abilities in which bilingual children seem to be superior is a skill that has been called *metalinguistic ability*, which refers to the ability to think flexibly and abstractly about language (in adults, this can be seen, for example, in poetry, where language must be carefully controlled and chosen to fit the governing "rules"). In children, this can be seen in the ability to make judgments about the grammar of sentences and to appreciate plays on words in jokes. The theory is that, while all children, both monolingual and bilingual, develop metalinguistic ability, the bilingual experience attunes children to better control their mental processes. In the research literature with monolingual children, metalinguistic ability has been linked with the development of early reading skills. By extension, it follows that bilingual children should, all other things being equal, have an edge in learning the basics of reading.

Research with Students in Bilingual Education Programs

There are now data to suggest that even language minority students in bilingual education programs, who are in the process of learning English, can benefit from some of the cognitive advantages of bilingualism. In one study we conducted with Puerto Rican elementary school students in New Haven (Diaz, 1985; Hakuta, 1987; Hakuta & Diaz, 1985), the students who became more bilingual also showed superior metalinguistic ability in their native language as well as in nonverbal intelligence. This relationship was found even though the students were in the bilingual education program and, therefore, had not yet attained a very high degree of bilingualism.

Educational Implications

These studies should allay the common fear that bilingualism per se might cause cognitive confusion on the part of the child. If anything, bilingualism can lead to higher levels of metalinguistic awareness and cognitive ability. Having established that bilingualism is a desirable goal on cognitive and linguistic grounds, the question then becomes one of understanding the specific nature of bilingual cognition. We have recently conducted studies in New Haven in two areas that shed light on this question.

THE NATURE OF THE CROSS-LANGUAGE
TRANSFER OF SKILLS

Bilingual education is founded on the principle that knowledge and skills in one language will transfer to the other. The important question for research to address is *not* the obvious one of *whether* transfer occurs from one language to another. Rather, research needs to generate a better understanding of *how* this process occurs, and under what circumstances it occurs most efficiently. Although considerable research exists to show that transfer between the first language (L1) and the second language (L2) is commonplace, we do not have a detailed understanding of the process. The purpose of the current research was to provide such a detailed picture.

In the course of our discussions with teachers, a number of them expressed concern about kindergarten children's mastery of spatial terms not just in English but in Spanish as well. Expression of spatial concepts is an important aspect of language development. In fact, many speech specialists believe that early control of spatial concepts is a good predictor of later language development. Thus, for example, the *Boehm Test of Basic Concepts* (1986) looks primarily at spatial concepts in assessing the verbal and conceptual ability of children. In response to observations about this important issue, we conducted a small pilot study in order to assess the children's knowledge of spatial terms.

The Pilot Study

For our pilot study, we drew up a list of 40 crucial spatial concepts, both the Spanish terms and their (rough) English equivalents, drawing on the IDEA curriculum. We then developed a set of simple pictures representing each of the terms. Children were given pairs of pictures and asked to choose the one that showed the spatial concept in question. The pictures were constructed to ensure that the children's answers would reflect their understanding of the concepts and to minimize confusion from the pictures themselves.

We gave this test to 16 kindergartners in New Haven. The results reflected the children's knowledge at the end of a year of kindergarten in the bilingual program. In general, contrary to the claims of some of the teachers about the deprived state of the language of the students, they did quite well with the Spanish terms; only a few items posed serious difficulties. Their performance on the English tasks, too, was quite good. The students with a stronger grasp of the concepts in Spanish tended to do better in English. Another interesting finding was that, contrary to common belief, there were no differences between boys and girls. We also found that the mother's level of education did not seem to matter in how well the children performed on this test. These results indicated to us that by the end of a year of kindergarten most children can use many Spanish spatial terms in simple tests with pictures, and that they have begun to develop knowledge of their English equivalents. Armed with this information, we decided to conduct a rigorous experiment to look at the transfer of specific concepts from Spanish to English.

An Experiment on Transfer

One goal of the experiment was to be as specific as possible about the area of conceptual space over which transfer occurred. As we developed and refined this experiment, indeed, we thought about it more and more as a study testing the limits of detailed specificity in terms of what we mean when we say that there is transfer between L1 and L2. What we decided to ask was at the level of specificity of the following sort: If children are made highly aware and conscious of a particular concept, such as that expressed by *alrededor* ("around") in Spanish, would they be better at learning and using *around* in English? Notice that this is quite a different way of thinking about transfer than asking if stronger Spanish skills lead to stronger acquisition of English. The former is a specific way of looking at transfer, the latter is more global and general.

The logic of the experiment was as follows. We decided to train two different groups of children in two different sets of concepts in Spanish. Following this differential training, all children would be taught a common set of words in English. Some of these English words would cover the same conceptual space as that trained in Spanish for one group of children; other English words would cover the conceptual space trained in Spanish in the other group of children. The question, then, could be asked whether children are better in learning and using the English words for which they had been cognitively "primed" in the Spanish training. If this could be shown, then we would have solid evidence for the specificity of transfer from L1 to L2.

In particular, we decided to train one group of students on *spatial concepts* in Spanish, and another group on *temporal concepts*. We concentrated on terms that our pilot study suggested would cause difficulty. The spatial terms selected were *alrededor/sobre* (around/over), *centro/esquina* (middle/corner), *cerca/lejos* (near/far), *hacia-adelante/para-atras* (forward/backward), *derecha/izquierda* (right/left), *primero/segundo/tercero* (first/second/third), and *invertido* (inverted). The temporal terms were *primero/ultimo* (first/last), *antes/ahora/despues* (before/now/after), *ayer/ hoy/mañana* (yesterday/today/tomorrow), *pasado/presente/futuro* (past/ present/future), *nunca/algunas-veces/siempre/durante* (never/sometimes/ always/during). In addition to these two groups who received training on specific Spanish concepts, a third group was selected as a control group and received no linguistic training. Rather, this group received a self-concept development program.

In terms of specific transfer, then, we predicted that those students who received training on Spanish temporal concepts would learn and use English temporal terms better than those who received training on spatial concepts. Also, we predicted that students receiving training on Spanish spatial concepts would do better on English spatial terms than the temporal group. Finally, both groups were expected to do better than the control, who received no training.

A total of 68 first graders participated in our study. The children were selected from two pairs of classrooms in two different schools. Within each class, students were divided randomly into the three experimental groups:

one that received spatial training, another that received temporal training, and a third that received the self-concept, nonlinguistic training (control).

Prior to the actual training, we also administered a pretest to determine the children's levels in Spanish and English vocabulary and their use of spatial and temporal concepts in Spanish in a variety of tasks. One purpose of the pretest was to see if the three groups, though randomly selected, might differ in their basic abilities in the two languages. They did not. Another purpose was to determine the extent to which English and Spanish abilities influenced posttreatment scores in English.

The spatial and temporal training component in Spanish had three major goals: first, to review the concepts themselves, that is, to focus on those particular conceptual categories of time and space relations; second, to review the L1 terms that express those concepts; and third, to teach the children to recognize these terms in written form. The second two goals, vocabulary development and word recognition, were aimed at developing aspects of the children's "metalinguistic awareness," that is, utilizing the distinction between linguistic form and meaning, highlighting the word as a linguistic unit, and demonstrating that written language conveys the same kind of meaning as spoken language. Training was conducted in 30- to 45-minute sessions in small groups by Margarita Rodriguez Lansberg, a research assistant for the Center for Language Education and Research project. Each session covered one set of contrasting concepts. Thus one session, for example, covered *primero/ultimo* (first/last), another covered *antes/ahora/despues* and so forth. At the end of each session, an informal assessment was conducted to ensure that the students were in control of the concepts and their written form. The entire training phase covered a period of approximately three weeks.

After the training phase came the English training phase. Here, all children were exposed to the same materials. They were taught the full set of English words corresponding to the Spanish spatial and temporal concepts. The classes were taught, more or less, in a traditional ESL-type context by two research assistants. Assessment of learning and use of the English terms was conducted in a group-administered paper-and-pencil test.

Findings

From the viewpoint of the advocate of a specificity-oriented view of transfer, the results were disappointing. That is to say, there was very little evidence of the specific transfer of training from Spanish to English. There was one exception having to do with the cognates (*presente*-present/*pasado*-past/*futuro*-future) used in this study. There was good evidence that students transferred training in these cases from Spanish to English. This was particularly true for students whose English level was low. However, in terms of overall results, it is safe to conclude that transfer on the specific level did not occur. We feel confident in making the claim that it did not, because we used a relatively sophisticated experimental design in which we excluded a lot of contaminants that could have muddied our results.

The results, however, were quite encouraging for the advocate of a global view of transfer. Regardless of the training condition, the level of control of Spanish was an excellent predictor of how well the students did on the posttraining test in English. This fact held true even after the students' initial level of English was taken into account. Thus the study once again turned up evidence for transfer occurring at a global level but not at the specific level.

Educational Implications

The study clearly showed that students with high levels of development in Spanish also developed high levels of ability in English. What we failed to demonstrate was that specific development of concepts in Spanish was tied to the learning of those specific concepts in English. Thus the findings are not consistent with a view of transfer that proceeds step-by-step, skill by skill, from Spanish to English. Clearly, this finding comes from limited observation of a limited arena of academic learning in these children. Nevertheless, the most obvious implication of this study is that academic programs for these children should be geared toward the holistic development of their native language skills. The general native language base then would result in transfer to English. The study argues against a myopic view of transfer, where each concept in the native language is taught aimed at its transfer to English. To take an analogy from writing instruction, much in the same way that attention to details such as spelling can lead instruction astray from the overall goal of literacy development, we believe that too much attention to specific transferable skills can detract from the overall goal of developing a strong and integrated language arts base in bilingual instruction.

TRANSLATION AS A METALINGUISTIC SKILL

The second set of studies conducted in New Haven have to do with the ability of bilingual children to *translate* (we use this term generically to cover both translation and interpretation abilities) between Spanish and English. This ability was first called to our attention in one of our brainstorming workshop sessions by Steve Strom, an elementary school teacher in New Haven, who pointed out that he used children who could translate as instructional assistants by pairing them up with monolingual Spanish-speaking children when using English materials. Translation interested us (my collaborators in these studies include Marguerite Malakoff, Laurie Gould, Marcus Rivera, Margarita Rodriguez Lansberg, and Jose Capuras) for two reasons. First, it is a valued skill that offers international job opportunities. And, second, the ability to translate well implies a high degree of awareness about the interrelatedness as well as distinctiveness of the languages involved.

In our first study, we decided to explore the psycholinguistic properties of translation. As subjects, we selected a small group of fourth and fifth graders who had had some experience translating for their relatives and friends (by parental report). We constructed tasks in which they were to translate words, sentences, and stories from English to Spanish and from Spanish to English (in all of these cases, we provided the source in written form on a computer screen, and the children provided the responses orally). Ability to translate was assessed by measuring the time it took to provide the translation and by analyzing the types of errors made in translation. We also gave them a written story to translate into written form. Finally, we made assessments of their proficiency levels in English and Spanish.

Overall, the results showed that these children were very good translators. We were interested in the extent to which they made intrusion errors, that is, where vocabulary or grammatical structures from the source language intrude into the translation. Here are some examples:

Source sentence: *La luna blanca brilla en la noche.*
Translation: The moon white shines in the night.
Source sentence: *Es redonda la mesa y las cuatro sillas son azules.*
Translation: It's round the table and the four seats are blue.

Such intrusion errors were infrequent, even when there were ample opportunities for them to occur.

We note that this low incidence of intrusion errors strongly supports the contention of sociolinguists who have studied code-switching (e.g., Zentella, 1981) and argued against the belief that it is the result of language confusion. Our subjects amply demonstrated that they could code-switch whenever the situation so warranted, that is, when they were with other Spanish-English bilinguals, but almost categorically separated the languages in the translation tasks.

We also discovered some interesting properties about translation efficiency. For example, we were interested in finding out how well the proficiencies in the two languages could predict translation speed. It turns out that what matters in translation efficiency is the proficiency in the language into which the translation is being made. Thus, when translating from English to Spanish, Spanish proficiency is more important, and when translating from Spanish to English, English proficiency matters more. In addition to proficiency in the languages, though, we found that performance on another kind of task mattered even more. In this task, the subjects were asked to make a determination as to whether words projected on the computer screen were English or Spanish (we used only words that could not be judged on superficial features such as accents and letter combinations unique to either language). The speed with which subjects could perform this task was an even better predictor of translation efficiency. We believe that this task reflects what specialists in translation have called a "translation proficiency," different from the proficiency in the two languages independently. Translation proficiency, we believe, is related in important ways to various metalinguistic skills and is an ability that can be trained through practice and experience.

An Experiment on Translation

Having found some interesting properties, we then moved to the question of how widespread this ability might be. In our initial experiment, we did not sample from a random population of bilingual children but on the basis of what parents told us about their children's abilities. In the next study, we tested 52 fourth and fifth graders from bilingual classrooms, not being particularly selective, and choosing all students who were able, on the judgment of the teachers, to write minimally in both languages. For this study, we did not give them the full battery of tests as in the first study but a simple story translation task going in both directions. Below are some examples of translations that we received:

SOURCE: *Los tres niños jugaban bajo el arbol viejo en la casa de su abuela. Cerca del jardin estaba un perro enorme. El perro salió corriendo y los niños lo siguieron. Llegaron todos a una vieja casa abandonada. Entraron silenciosamente para buscar al perro. Dentro de la casa oscura, se abri una puerta con un ruido extraño. Uno de los niños salto un grito porque tenia miedo. Pero otro de los niños corrio hacia la puerta abierta. Allí descubrieron al perro y se fueron todos a su casa.*
TRANSLATION: The three boys were playing under an old tree in they're grandmothers house. Near the back hard there was a big dog. The dog came out

running and the children ran after him. Then they all got to an old house that was empty. They entered the house silenlli to find the dog. In the old dark house a door opend with a strange noise. One of the boys scrimed because he was scared. But one of the boy's ran to the door that was open. There they discovered the dog and went home.

SOURCE: *A lonely cat was looking for something to play with. He suddenly saw a baseball. He began to play with it. After a while he got bored, though, and went outside. In a garage he discovered a whole bunch of paper boxes and began climbing them. Inside one of the boxes was his old friend, Fido the dog! Together the two animals played all afternoon. They realized afterwards that they had lost track of time and that it was very late. When the cat got home, he washed up and ate his dinner.*

TRANSLATION: un gato solo estaba mirando a algo para jugar. El derepente vio un juego de pelota. El comenso a jugar, despues un tiempo el se amorinno, penso, y se fue afuera. en un garage el descubrio un bonche de cajas de papel y comenso a treparse por el. Adentro uno de las cajas fue el mayor amigo, Fido el perro! juntos los dos animales jugando al mediodia. Ellos se dieron cuenta despues aqueyo ellos fuero perdidos atrapado el tiempo y despues fue ·vastante tarde. cuando el gato se fue a casa, el vano ariba y el comio.

There is no doubt that, overlooking minor details of spelling, these are excellent translations, certainly products you would be proud of had these been produced by your foreign language students.

As in the first experiment, we conducted various analyses of errors in the written translation task. We found that errors were roughly comparable in both quantity and quality between the subjects in the two experiments. For example, in the above stories going from Spanish to English, in the first experiment, there were an average of 1.79 errors attributable to source language intrusions per story, and an average of 2.17 errors in the second experiment. Going from English to Spanish, there was an average of 3.23 errors per story for the first experiment, and 2.18 for the second experiment. In general, then, we can conclude that translation skills may be readily developed within the population of bilingual youngsters found in this bilingual education program.

Our comparison of the two populations on this translation task is noteworthy on a further point, which is that, in going from English to Spanish, the second group (those in the bilingual program) made fewer grammatical errors overall than did those subjects in the first group (many of whom had been mainstreamed or had never been in bilingual programs). This pattern, combined with other information on language use obtained from this population (Hakuta, Ferdman, & Diaz, 1987), suggests a rather rapid decline of Spanish language skills within this school population.

Educational Implications

The studies summarized herein suggest that by as early as fourth or fifth grade—probably even earlier—bilingual students are very capable of translation in both directions. We believe that the ability to translate is related to a variety of metalinguistic skills, the delineation of which constitutes our future agenda. We furthermore believe that translation skills can be developed and can serve as an effective method of developing metalinguistic skills in bilingual youngsters, and that this would have a positive effect on their literacy skills. Equipped with these observations, we have made some preliminary attempts to develop programs for the training of translation skills, one such effort being reported in Padilla, Fairchild, and Valadez (1990, chap. 14).

CONCLUSIONS

Our research on the cognitive bases of bilingualism suggests that true, additive bilingualism can be a valuable part of the educational enrichment of linguistic minority students. Bilingualism is positively associated with higher levels of cognitive functioning. Bilingual students are adept at translation—a skill that is truly enviable from the monolingual perspective. It appears that one way to achieve this would be through the holistic development of the native language early on in the child's education, followed by an aggressive effort to maintain the native language and develop metalinguistic skills (such as translation training) once bilingualism is attained.

REFERENCES

Boehm Test of Basic Concepts. (1986). New York: Harcourt Brace Jovanovich.

Cummins, J. (1984). *Bilingualism and special education*. San Diego: College Hill.

Diaz, R. (1985). Bilingual cognitive development: Addressing three gaps in current research. *Child Development, 56*, 1376–1388.

Hakuta, K. (1986). *Mirror of language: The debate on bilingualism*. New York: Basic Books.

Hakuta, K. (1987). Degree of bilingualism and cognitive ability in mainland Puerto Rican children. *Child Development, 58*, 1372–1388.

Hakuta, K., & Diaz, R. M. (1985). The relationship between degree of bilingualism and cognitive ability: A critical discussion and some new longitudinal data. In K. E. Nelson (Ed.), *Children's language* (Vol. 5, pp. 319–344). Hillsdale, NJ: Lawrence Erlbaum.

Hakuta, K., Ferdman, B. M., & Diaz, R. M. (1987). Bilingualism and cognitive development: Three perspectives. In S. Rosenberg (Ed.), *Advances in applied psycholinguistics* (Vol. 2, pp. 284–319). Cambridge: Cambridge University Press.

Padilla, A. M., Fairchild, H. H., & Valadez, C. M. (Eds.). (1990). *Foreign language education: Issues and strategies.* Newbury Park, CA: Sage.

Peal, E., & Lambert, W. E. (1962). The relation of bilingualism to intelligence. *Psychological Monographs, 76*(546), 1–23.

Zentella, A. (1981). Language variety among Puerto Ricans. In C. A. Ferguson & S. B. Heath (Eds.), *Language in the USA* (pp. 218–238). Cambridge: Cambridge University Press.

4

Rationales for Native Language Instruction

Evidence from Research

CATHERINE E. SNOW

The purpose of this chapter is to review evidence relevant to one aspect of educational policy for language minority children, in particular, the choice of whether to include native language instruction as part of the educational program. Clearly, the decision whether or not to use native language instruction is not the only challenge to educational policymakers; one must also decide, if the choice is in favor of native language use, *how* it should be included, *how much* native language instruction is optimal, and what constitutes the best quality instruction, either in the native language or in English. Decisions about these crucial matters become necessary, though, only if we

AUTHOR'S NOTE: I am grateful to the Spencer Foundation and to the U.S. Department of Education for support of research reported in this chapter. N.I.E. provided research support (to Jeanne S. Chall and Catherine Snow, principal investigators) for "Families and Literacy: The Contribution of Out-of-School Experiences to Low-Income Children's Development of Literacy," the study that is reported in Snow, Barnes, Chandler, Goodman, and Hemphill, in press. The Spencer Foundation supported the collection and initial analysis of data from the U.N. International School, and O.E.R.I., through the Center for Language Education and Research, supported further analysis of those data as well as further data collection in New Haven. The opinions expressed in this chapter are, of course, those of the author alone.

can offer clear and convincing arguments in favor of the use of native language instruction for language minority children. The evidence to be reviewed below is organized in terms of the major arguments that can be made either for or against native language use.

There are many familiar arguments *against* using native languages in educational programs for language minority children. I have come to think of the most frequently encountered of these as the "history argument," the "ghettoization argument," the "time-on-task argument," and the "hopeless cause argument." Each of these arguments has some currency in the public debates about the optimal educational environment for language minority children, so it may be helpful to describe each of them clearly, prior to discussing four of the arguments *in favor of* native language maintenance programs for language minority children. The arguments in favor of native language use and the arguments against it can then be directly compared and evaluated.

THE ARGUMENTS AGAINST NATIVE LANGUAGE INSTRUCTION

The History Argument

A frequently encountered argument against the need for native language instruction for language minority children invokes the successes of European immigrants of the late nineteenth and early twentieth centuries, who arrived in this country knowing no English, who received no bilingual education or specific educational programs, and who nonetheless became successful and productive members of American society. What's wrong with the immigrants of today, goes the argument, that they require special educational plans, native language teachers, and bilingual programs? Why can't they just learn English like previous generations of immigrants?

The Ghettoization Argument

Bilingual education programs typically involve total or near-total separation of language minority children from the other children in the school. It seems paradoxical to try to teach children English by isolating them from the large numbers of native English speakers available in the mainstream classrooms of their schools and provide them instead with a single English model, the teacher. Furthermore, the teacher who is responsible for instruction in English is frequently a native speaker of the children's home language and may, therefore, be a less than perfect model in English. Bilingual programs can thus have precisely the opposite of their intended effect, by contributing to the isolation of the language minority community and the postponement of the integration of language minority children into the mainstream English-speaking society.

The Time-on-Task Argument

A reliable conclusion from a large body of educational research is that children learn more if they spend more time-on-task (Rosenshine & Berliner, 1978). Children in classes that spend an hour a day in uninterrupted reading instruction make greater gains in reading than children in classes with shorter, less frequent, or less concentrated reading periods. If time-on-task is an important predictor of learning, it seems obvious that children would learn English more quickly if they spent more time—the whole day—at it rather than spending half their school days in native language instruction. The time-on-task studies would suggest that, if fluency in English is the goal of bilingual education programs, time spent in learning, speaking, and hearing English should be maximized.

The Hopeless Cause Argument

The first three arguments against the use of native language instruction for language minority children derive from the view that the only goal of educational programs for these children is proficiency and school achievement *in English*. An alternative view is that preservation of the native language is a goal that is almost as important as the acquisition of English, and that language minority children constitute a resource of potential bilinguals for the society. Even those who value multilingualism, though, can argue that bilingual programs do not function effectively to preserve or enhance native language proficiency. The demographic data on heritage language use by members of the second and third generation in the United States lead unequivocally to the conclusion that these languages are not maintained (see, for example, Veltman, 1980). Why should the society invest resources in bilingual education if it only postpones by a few years the inevitable loss of native languages by language minority children?

THE ARGUMENTS IN FAVOR OF
NATIVE LANGUAGE EDUCATION

Four arguments in favor of the use of native language instruction in educational programs for language minority children have evolved: the social-cultural identity argument, the cognitive consequences argument, the linguistic skills argument, and the academic achievement argument. The arguments in favor of native language instruction (unlike the arguments against it) rest on recent research concerning the development of bilingual and language minority children. Accordingly, each of these arguments will be discussed at somewhat greater length than the ones presented above.

Social-Cultural Identity

A basic fact we must emphasize in discussing educational policies for language minority children is that, in addition to not being English speakers, these children are minority group members. There is extensive evidence that members of minority groups show poorer achievement in school than White, middle-class majority group members, whether or not they are English speakers. For example, the 1985 NAEP report on reading shows that Black and Hispanic children were comparable to one another in reading proficiency, but both groups scored at levels of proficiency considerably lower than White, non-Hispanic children. Educational policy must confront the problem that schools are alien institutions for many of these children. In schools, the rules that govern behavior, the goals of the actors, and the messages that are conveyed are often mysterious.

It is very difficult to present hard data to document the degree to which the strangeness of the school environment affects the achievement of language minority children, but there are ample data from ethnographic studies of classrooms and from classroom discourse analyses to conclude that children from different cultural groups have very different expectations about how classrooms should be organized (see, for example, Au, 1980; Shultz, Florio, & Erickson, 1980; and the papers in Trueba, Guthrie, & Au, 1981). For example, Shultz, Florio, and Erickson (1980) described the classroom of a Chicana teacher in contrast to that of an Anglo teacher. The Anglo teacher operated in a way familiar to us all: Children were encouraged to work independently, individual achievement was rewarded by the adult, a slight distance was maintained in the teacher-child relationship, and competition among the children was utilized to motivate success. The Chicana teacher adopted a much more maternal relationship with the children in her class-room, calling them by pet names, often hugging and kissing them, and hold-ing them on her lap during lessons. She also fostered a much less competitive atmosphere in the classroom by encouraging student appreciation of each other's accomplishments, involving the entire class in rewarding achieve-ment, and organizing fewer individual activities.

The contrast between the Anglo and the Chicano teaching style does not imply that one is better than the other—but clearly one is closer to what Chicano children arrive at school expecting. It seems very possible that a Chicano child would view the classroom of the Anglo teacher as cold, un-friendly, and threatening. Many studies have shown that academic achieve-ment improves when children are provided with teachers (or even teacher aides) from their own language and cultural groups—adults whose expecta-tions about how the classroom should be organized match the children's, adults who understand and correctly interpret the children's ways of express-ing themselves, and adults whose structuring of relationships and of learning contexts re-creates what the children are familiar with (Au & Jordan, 1981; Diaz, Moll, & Mehan, 1986; Duran, 1983; Erickson, 1986; Tharp & Gallimore, 1988). Interactions within classrooms, like interactions within families, show enormous cultural variation, and one way to ensure that we are not violating the cultural norms and expectations of minority children is to ensure that there are adult comembers from the children's culture in their classrooms.

Proscription on the use of the home language at school is no longer en-dorsed as official educational policy, although the practice of forbidding Spanish in schools is not so distant in American history. It is important to recognize, though, that by failing to show sensitivity to children's cultural norms and expectations, we may be devaluing their cultural identity and threatening their sense of self-worth as effectively as by posting notices say-ing "No Spanish spoken here." Schools should be operated in ways that maximize the self-esteem of their students—because that is a worthy goal in itself, but also because students with high self-esteem work harder, learn better, and achieve more. The official recognition of the value of the home language and home culture, through native language instruction, constitutes a major contribution to the maintenance of the self-esteem of language minor-ity children.

Cognitive Consequences of Bilingualism

Much research has now confirmed that children who grow up bilingual, or who become bilingual at an early age, enjoy an advantage in a number of areas of cognitive functioning over children who are monolingual (see Cummins, 1976; Hakuta, 1986, for reviews). One particular advantage that bilingual children have is in the area of metalinguistic awareness—the ability to analyze the form as well as the content of language, knowledge of how to talk about language, and control over nonliteral uses of language like puns, irony, and figures of speech. Certain kinds of metalinguistic skills—such as recognizing that words have no intrinsic connection to the objects they refer to—typically emerge several years earlier in bilingual than in monolingual children. Nor is it surprising that the process of learning a second language or of switching back and forth between two languages would heighten one's likelihood of becoming aware of the formal aspects of the linguistic system and one's understanding of the arbitrariness of the linguistic code.

Metalinguistic skills relate strongly in young children to the emergence of reading. Indeed, in order to learn the rules that govern phoneme-grapheme correspondence, it is crucial to attend to the form rather than the content of speech. Similarly, in order to function well in writing, in many language arts exercises, and in planned oral discourse, a certain level of metalinguistic awareness is very helpful. In many ways the successful school learner draws upon metalinguistic skills that, for monolingual children, are most likely to develop in intensely verbal homes that offer an enriched linguistic environment.

The advantages in metalinguistic skills that are usually available only to children from extremely verbal homes are, however, also accessible to children from families of low income and low educational attainment if they are bilingual. Bilingualism—as long as it involves a reasonable level of proficiency in both languages—provides language minority children with academically relevant skills that their low-SES monolingual peers lack. The only way to let these advantages operate, though, is to ensure that the language minority children actually are bilingual, at least for some period of time. The classic *subtractive bilingual model*, in which the home language disappears as the school language is acquired, does not provide for any period of stable bilingualism during which the positive cognitive consequences of being bilingual can emerge.

Linguistic Skills

There are direct linguistic advantages to native language instruction—advantages that children enjoy in their acquisition of English if they have received language and literacy instruction in their native language. This may seem paradoxical, but it is true because some language skills are *not* limited to the language in which they were acquired. Clearly, many language skills are language specific—vocabulary and specific rules of grammar must be learned anew in each language one acquires. But other aspects of language proficiency, such as how to organize a paragraph and how to make an argument, are usable in any language one knows.

Evidence in favor of the claim that some language skills are transferable from one's first to a second language derives from an analysis by Lanauze and Snow (in press) of writing samples produced by third- and fourth-grade Puerto Rican children attending a bilingual program in the New Haven Public Schools. The children had been rated by their teachers as "good" or "poor" on their oral proficiency and reading ability in Spanish (the children's first and dominant language) and in English (the language they were learning at school). Because New Haven operates a split-day bilingual program, with different teachers for the Spanish and the English programs, the ratings of the children in Spanish and English were done independently by two different teachers. Three groups of children emerged from the ratings: those rated as good in English and in Spanish by their English and Spanish teachers, respectively (GG); a second group rated as poor both in English and in Spanish (PP); a third group, and the one of greatest interest, rated as good in Spanish but poor in English (GP). These were the children who had solid academic skills in Spanish but were still in the early stages of acquiring English. All the children carried out a writing task in both English and Spanish that involved describing a picture of a beach scene. Because there had been very little emphasis on writing in the New Haven curriculum, this was a challenging task for the children in both languages.

We wished to assess the quality of the children's writing both in Spanish and in English, but also to compare the quality of the writing products of the three groups. Obviously, one would expect that the GG group would produce better writing in both Spanish and English, that the PP group would produce poor writing in both languages, and that the GP group would look like the GG group in Spanish but like the PP group in English. However, on all of the measures of quality examined (including total length, complexity of sentences, and use of specific descriptive sentences), the GP group's English descriptions looked more like those of the GG than those of the PP group. In other words, the children who wrote better in Spanish also wrote better in English regardless of their oral proficiency in English. The implications of these findings are that certain language skills—those that enabled the children to produce better, more specific, and more complex descriptions—were transferable from Spanish to English. The children who were most at risk, then, of failure in writing development in English were those whose native language skills were deficient.

Needless to say, the GP group did not produce written descriptions in English that were indistinguishable from those of the GG group. They made more errors in English, and they made many more references to colors—presumably because the color vocabulary was one they had mastered, whereas they did not yet know how to refer to other aspects of the picture in English. Nonetheless, they were saying more about the picture, being more specific in their descriptions, and using more complex syntax than one would have expected from their oral proficiency in English, thus demonstrating the value to their English performance of what they had acquired in Spanish.

Another source of evidence about the value of native language skills in second-language achievement derives from our study of children attending the U.N. International School (UNIS), a private school that serves the children of U.N. employees, of those working at missions to the United Nations, of the international community of Manhattan, as well as of many American families seeking a high-quality multicultural education for their children.

In an extensive study carried out at UNIS of the oral language skills that relate to academic achievement, we found that children's abilities to give formal definitions related strongly to their scores on the language and reading subtests of the California Achievement Test (Snow, Cancino, Gonzalez, & Shriberg, 1989). Giving a good formal definition involves skills that are available to support performance in any language one knows (e.g., analysis of one's own knowledge about word meaning, understanding taxonomic relations, identifying definitional features, and avoiding personal associations to the word).

When looking at the effects of the children's home language backgrounds on their scores on the definitions task and on the California Achievement Test, we found that children from monolingual, non-English-speaking homes performed as well as children from monolingual English-speaking homes, indicating that being bilingual constituted no obstacle to high academic achievement. However, children from homes in which English was spoken but was not the native language of either parent performed worse on both formal definitions and on the California Achievement Test. In other words, having had more exposure to English constituted a detriment to performance in English *if* that exposure did not come from native speakers and if it took the place of the higher-quality interaction that would have been possible in another language.

Academic Achievement

The most convincing argument in favor of the use of native languages in the educational programs designed for language minority children would be evidence that it causes better academic achievement. For reasons that have to do with the complexities of carrying out evaluation research, it is very difficult to find unambiguous evidence that bilingual education programs produce greater academic achievement than alternative programs without native language instruction. Willig's (1985) meta-analysis of evaluations of bilingual education programs, however, provides the most convincing evidence available that incorporating native language instruction improves achievement for language minority children.

Why might we expect that academic achievement in English should be enhanced by native language instruction? One major reason has to do with the difficulties language minority children often have with the acquisition of literacy. Learning to read is the major task to be accomplished during the first couple of years of schooling, and the ability to read is prerequisite to almost all the instruction that goes on thereafter. Many children from families where the parents' literacy skills are low, and where reading and writing activities are not frequently engaged in by adults, arrive at school at considerable risk for poor literacy development because the methods used to teach reading in the primary grades typically presume children already know what reading is for. Reading instruction thus fails to provide sufficient opportunities for learning the various functions or the value of literacy. For low-SES children who are not native English speakers, the difficulties of achieving a relatively remote skill like literacy are greatly exacerbated by having to acquire it in a language they do not speak very well. Even for highly literate adults, learning to control a new orthography is very difficult until some oral capacity in the related language has been achieved; accordingly, successful foreign language programs in Hebrew, Arabic, and Japanese do not typically teach reading independent of oral skills.

Learning to read in a language one does not speak well can have long-term negative consequences for academic achievement (Collier, 1987; Collier & Thomas, 1988). Collier studied the test outcomes of non-English-speaking children in a school system that provided only ESL programs for its population of (largely middle-class) foreign children. Although children who arrived at ages 7 to 9 scored at the 50th percentile in reading (still not at a level comparable to their English-speaking peers in this school system) after three to five years, children who arrived at age 5 or 6 (before having had native language schooling) still showed deficits five and six years later on academic achievement tests. Collier argued that these deficits can be related to the children's receiving initial reading instruction in a language they controlled only very poorly.

It is possible to make the same argument about reading as was made in the previous section about language—that some reading skills are language-specific, but others are not. Language-general reading skills include the metacognitive and strategic skills that have been implicated in the performance of good readers (Brown, 1980), as well as reliance on world knowledge, which, once acquired, is available to support top-down processing of reading material in the second language (L2) as well as in the first language (L1) (Goodman, Goodman, & Flores, 1979). Thus it is not surprising that children who have developed some effective metacognitive strategies to support their reading, and who have acquired more world knowledge, can learn to read in L2 more easily than younger children who do not benefit from any L1 reading skills (see also Cummins, 1981).

In a study on the determinants of reading achievement in a sample of low-income children who were from English-speaking families (Snow, Barnes, Chandler, Goodman, & Hemphill, in press), we found that four instructional factors were strongly related to children's gains in reading comprehension: teacher-parent contacts, practice, structure, and enrichment. Children made greater gains in reading comprehension during years when their parents and teachers had more contacts with one another (independent of who initiated the contacts), when they had the opportunity to practice reading a lot, when their instruction in reading included specific attention to comprehension strategies and the sorts of homework or workbook exercises that structure the acquisition of such strategies, and when their classrooms provided rich and varied language and literacy environments. It is interesting to contemplate the implications of these findings from English-speaking children for language minority students. On the assumption that the same factors would prove facilitative, how could they be implemented in educational programs for language minorities?

It is clear that parent-teacher contacts are unlikely to occur unless there is a native language teacher available who feels comfortable approaching the families and with whom the family members feel they can communicate effectively. Practice in reading is possible only if children are willing to sit down and read, which is not likely if they are expected to read in a language they do not yet understand, or if they have to read material much below the level that interests them because of limitations on their language proficiency. A rich and challenging variety of literacy materials and of language experiences can only occur in a language the children speak well—that is, at least during the first couple of years of instruction in English, enrichment must happen in the native language. Of the four factors we found related to gains in reading, then, only one can be implemented in an English-only instructional program for language minority children—structure. Enjoying the positive consequences of the other three factors requires that the native language be a part of the educational program provided to language minority children.

RECONSIDERING THE ARGUMENTS AGAINST
NATIVE LANGUAGE INSTRUCTION

In light of this presentation of four arguments in favor of the use of the native language in educating language minority children, we can now reconsider the four arguments introduced above against its use.

The History Argument Reconsidered

The history argument takes as a premise the success of earlier generations of immigrants, generations that did not enjoy special educational programs. A more careful analysis of the historical record reveals, however, three facts that must be taken into account:

(1) Many immigrants in earlier generations were not educationally successful, and the existence of large immigrant communities made it possible for many to survive without achieving high levels of proficiency in English. Although the success stories of immigrants who went to college and assimilated fully are more likely to be transmitted, we cannot assume that they represent the majority of the immigrant's generation.

(2) Educational success was much less crucial to economic viability in an era of great demand for physical laborers, in an expanding economy, and at a time when a much smaller proportion of the total population finished high school or entered college.

(3) The levels of literacy skill required to function in even the lowest-level jobs are much higher today than 100 years ago, so levels of academic success that would have been sufficient to provide employability for our grandparents would no longer be sufficient.

In light of the fact that the majority of high school graduates today must seek employment in service positions rather than in higher-paying blue-collar jobs with lower literacy demands, we can no longer be satisfied with the degree of success achieved by the schools of the 1890s in teaching immigrant children English and literacy skills. Accordingly, we must exploit the native language skills children bring to school in order to enhance their achievement in English.

Ghettoization Reconsidered

The isolation of language minority children in bilingual programs is a serious problem, especially because evidence suggests that it can take as many as five years for children to achieve sufficient proficiency in a second language to be effective school learners (Collier, 1987). One approach that improves the language minority child's access to native English speakers, by allowing for the placement of language minority and mainstream children in the same classroom from the start, is the "two-way" bilingual program, in which half the children are native English speakers who thus have the opportunity to learn the other language while the language minority children learn English. While two-way bilingual programs are operating effectively in many school systems, they receive parental endorsement from English speakers only if they offer "useful" languages (Spanish or Chinese, not Khmer or Hmong) and thus cannot be a universal solution to the ghettoization problem. Policies for ensuring that the bilingual program is not a separate entity but a resource for the entire school where it is located need to be actively pursued, and mechanisms for ensuring contact between the language minority and the mainstream children that do not disadvantage the non-English speakers need to be developed.

Time-on-Task Reconsidered

The arguments presented above, that many language and literacy skills can be acquired in a native language and transferred readily to English, undercut the presumption of the time-on-task argument, that the child's "task" must be defined exclusively as learning English. The child's task is to become a successful school learner, and that means that all the time devoted to learning—in whatever language the learning takes place—can be considered time on task. In addition to the learning of the language and literacy skills discussed above, much of what goes on during instruction in the native language constitutes learning of content material. The knowledge about mathematics or social studies acquired in Spanish or Gujarati will be available to the child in English as well, and should not be considered irrelevant to the child's school success just because it was taught in the native language.

Hopeless Cause Reconsidered

The ultimate loss of the home language is likely to be the long-term consequence for most children in bilingual programs. That loss is regrettable, but the arguments presented above suggest that there are advantages to initial instruction in the native language and to a period of active bilingualism that by themselves can motivate bilingual programs. In addition, of course, educational programs that help bilingual children to continue to develop their native language skills (e.g., junior high native language literature and language arts classes instead of foreign language instruction for these children) should be initiated. Under normal circumstances, knowledge of a first language continues to develop throughout the school years; language minority children in the United States, however, typically start to experience attrition of native language skills as soon as they exit from bilingual programs. An optimal educational policy would provide opportunities for bilingual children to become stronger bilinguals throughout their school years; in the absence of such a policy, we can only hope that some of these children are able to retain enough proficiency to recover native language skills through study in high school or college.

SUMMARY AND CONCLUSIONS

The arguments that are typically offered against the use of the native language in instructional programs for language minority children are, unfortunately, arguments that may initially make good sense. It is not surprising that many intelligent citizens, who see the assimilation of language minorities as one goal of the American educational system, are of the opinion that current immigrants should be treated much like the successful immigrants of 100 years ago, and that keeping them in separate classrooms promotes isolation rather than integration. Concern for the ultimate educational success of language minority children might well lead thoughtful people to suggest that time spent studying in the native language is time lost to the mastery of English. And it is undeniable that most members of immigrant groups lose mastery of their native language within a generation, so it is not unreasonable to see educational support for native language instruction as a waste of resources.

Nonetheless, despite the surface sensibility of the arguments against the use of native language instruction with language minority children, research evidence and a deeper consideration of the factors impinging on educational success shows that they are wrong. Native language instruction for language minority children promotes their educational success *in English* in a variety of ways, while at the same time preventing the alienation from the school culture that can undermine their educational achievement. Understanding why native language instruction promotes achievement in English involves abandoning traditional simplistic models of language proficiency to recognize that many aspects of performance on language tasks draw upon skills that are not language-specific, skills that may be more efficiently acquired in one's first language.

This is not to suggest that introducing native language into instructional programs for language minority children would automatically solve all their educational problems. Poor quality bilingual programs do not work any better than poor quality ESL or submersion programs. Language minority children are typically at considerable educational risk for reasons that have nothing to do with their bilingualism, so they need the best quality instruction available to ensure their continued progress. Lengthy stays in bilingual programs can isolate language minority children from the English-speaking majority, and special efforts have to be made to address this problem. For children from many of the recent immigrant groups, sufficient numbers of qualified native language teachers are unavailable, and well-designed native language curricular materials are often equally inaccessible. Such problems require creative solutions and professional dedication; we cannot expect that the simple presence of a nonspecialist, adult native speaker in the classroom will, by itself, constitute a solution to the problems Haitian or Hmong immigrants have in American schools. Nonetheless, though many challenges remain in ensuring academic success for members of language minority groups, we can be confident that including instruction in their native languages as part of their educational programs will promote, not impede, their progress.

REFERENCES

Au, K. H. (1980). Participation structures in a reading lesson with Hawaiian children: Analysis of a culturally appropriate instructional event. *Anthropology and Education Quarterly, 11*(2), 91–115.

Au, K., & Jordan, C. (1981). Teaching reading to Hawaiian children: Finding a culturally appropriate solution. In H. Trueba, G. Guthrie, & K. Au (Eds.), *Culture and the bilingual classroom: Studies in classroom ethnography* (pp. 139–152). Rowley, MA: Newbury House.

Brown, A. L. (1980). Metacognitive development and reading. In R. K. Spiro, B. C. Bruce, & W. F. Brewer (Eds.), *Theoretical issues in reading comprehension* (pp. 53–481). Hillsdale, NJ: Lawrence Erlbaum.

Collier, V. P. (1987). Age and rate of acquisition of second language for academic purposes. *TESOL Quarterly, 21*, 617–641.

Collier, V. P., & Thomas, W. P. (1988, April). *Acquisition of cognitive-academic second-language proficiency: A six-year study.* Paper presented at AERA, New Orleans, LA.

Cummins, J. (1976). The influence of bilingualism on cognitive growth: A synthesis of research findings and explanatory hypotheses. *Working Papers on Bilingualism, 9*, 1–43.

Cummins, J. (1981). The role of primary language development in promoting educational success for language minority students. In *Schooling and language minority students: A theoretical framework* (pp. 3–49). Los Angeles: California State University, National Evaluation Dissemination and Assessment Center.

Diaz, S., Moll, L., & Mehan, H. (1986). Sociocultural resources in instruction: A context-specific approach. In *Beyond language: Social and cultural factors in schooling language minority students* (pp. 187–230). Sacramento: California State Department of Education, Bilingual Education Office.

Duran, R. (1983). *Hispanics' education and background: Predictors of college achievement.* New York: College Entrance Examination Board.

Erickson, F. (1986). Qualitative methods in research on teaching. In M. C. Wittrock (Ed.), *Handbook of research on teaching* (pp. 119–158). New York: Macmillan.

Goodman, K., Goodman, Y., & Flores, B. (1979). *Reading in the bilingual classroom: Literacy and biliteracy.* Rosslyn, VA: National Clearinghouse for Bilingual Education.

Hakuta, K. (1986). *Mirror of language: The debate on bilingualism.* New York: Basic Books.

Lanauze, M., & Snow, C. (in press). The relation between first- and second-language writing skills: Evidence from Puerto Rican elementary school children in the mainland. *Linguistics and Education.*

Rosenshine, B. U., & Berliner, D. C. (1978). Academic engaged time. *British Journal of Teacher Education, 4*(1), 43–46.

Shultz, J., Florio, S., & Erickson, I. (1980). Where's the floor: Aspects of the cultural organization of social relationships in communication at home and at school. In P. Gilmore & A. Glatthorn (Eds.), *Ethnography and education: Children in and out of school.* Philadelphia: University of Pennsylvania Press.

Snow, C. E., Barnes, W., Chandler, J., Goodman, I., & Hemphill, L. (1989). *Unfulfilled expectations: Family and school effects on literacy.* Cambridge, MA: Harvard University Press.

Snow, C. E., Cancino, H., Gonzalez, P., & Shriberg, E. (in press). Giving formal definitions: An oral language correlate of school literacy. In D. Bloome (Ed.), *Classrooms and literacy.* Norwood, NJ: Ablex.

Tharp, R., & Gallimore, R. (1988). *Rousing minds to life: Teaching, learning and schooling in social context.* Cambridge, MA: Harvard University Press.

Trueba, H. T., Guthrie, G. P., & Au, K. H. (Eds.). (1981). *Culture in the bilingual classroom: Studies in classroom ethnography.* Rowley, MA: Newbury House.

Veltman, C. (1980). *The retention of minority languages in the United States.* Washington, DC: National Center for Education Statistics.

Willig, A. (1985). A metaanalysis of selected studies on the effectiveness of bilingual education. *Review of Educational Research, 55*, 269–317.

5

African American Dialects and Schooling

A Review

HALFORD H. FAIRCHILD
STEPHANIE EDWARDS-EVANS

African American dialects (variously known as "nonstandard English," "nonstandard Black English," "Black Vernacular English," "Vernacular Black English," "Standard Black English," "Negro Speech," and so on) constitute a controversial issue in American education. This chapter reviews the research debates about the nature of African American dialects, with an emphasis on the attitudes and behaviors of teachers in shaping the achievement behaviors and school adjustments of African American pupils.

Because the issues surrounding African American dialects are so vast, and because the state of knowledge concerning appropriate interventions is so limited, our focus is on providing practitioners with a general introduction that highlights the key principles in teaching children who speak an African American dialect. Our focus is also limited to the situation in the United States, because the relationship between schooling and African American dialects outside of the United States (e.g., the Caribbean, Central America, South America) is beyond our expertise.

It is important to contextualize this discussion, however, within the broader reality of the educational crises confronting the nation concerning the education of African Americans and other ethnolinguistic minority groups. Namely, African Americans and other linguistic minorities (particularly the Spanish-speaking) are plagued by a number of grim statistics in scholastic achievement. These include low test scores, high dropout rates prior to the completion of high school, low college entry, and high college attrition (see Comer, 1985; Fairchild, 1984a; Fisher, 1981; White, 1984). These educational failures, then, have been linked with vulnerabilities to poor self-concepts (Fairchild, 1988a, 1989; Macias, 1973), unemployment (Banks, 1982; Comer, 1985), the reproduction of economic inequality (Apple, 1978), and a plethora of "social plagues" of the African American community, including crime, drug abuse, homicide/suicide, intergenerational poverty, and threats to physical and mental well-being (Fairchild, 1989). Although African American dialects play a role in these broader social, cultural, and economic realities, they are only a part of a complex matrix of factors that create and sustain the victimization of African American communities.

Note also that we select the phrase, *African American dialects,* in favor of the other terms in order to avoid the unfortunate color symbolism associated with racial labeling in the United States (see Fairchild, 1985, 1988a). In addition, *African American dialects* conveys the fact that the subject of our chapter falls on a continuum, and that discrete categorizations (e.g., "Black English") are inevitably misleading. This latter point also applies to any operational definition of *Standard English,* which we view as an "idealized standard" that masks tremendous regional diversity even within this "standard."

This chapter presents an overview of the research controversies surrounding African American dialects and a review of research on teacher attitudes, behaviors, and outcomes. The chapter presents a number of emerging principles concerning teaching pupils who speak African American dialects and concludes with a call for the total restructuring of American education.

RESEARCH CONTROVERSIES

Racial Biases

Because of the omnipresence of White racism (see Bowser & Hunt, 1981), much of the social sciences, including education, linguistics, and psychology, has revealed clear White racial biases concerning studies of African Americans (see Fairchild & Gurin, 1978). These biases were revealed, for example, in theories that concluded that Africans were genetically inferior to "Whites" (e.g., Jensen, 1985).

In the context of language, early researchers concluded that African American dialects were reflective of a simplistic cognitive style and of low intelligence (for reviews, see Baratz, 1970; Baugh, 1983; Jenkins, 1982; White, 1984). Linguists and educational psychologists, prior to the 1950s, were generally convinced that Africans were inherently inferior to Europeans, and this inferiority was reflected in their patterns of thinking and language.

These biases, as absurd as they may seem, were consistent with the complex ideological system that supported racial inequality in the United States (see Akbar, 1985; Persell, 1981). Unfortunately, these biases remain well-entrenched in the public and educational arenas today. The contemporary entrenchment of these ideological biases are revealed, for example, by (a) the public's willingness to "blame the victim" (Ryan, 1971) for failure in school and in life, and (b) researchers' focus on individual-level predictors (such as motivation or self-esteem) and the well-established tradition of "controlling for race and class" in studies of educational production (see Fairchild, 1984a).

Rejoinders

In response to the biased conclusions that endorsed racial inequality, researchers have generated a great deal of evidence and critiques in debunking those conclusions (see Baugh, 1983).

It is now generally accepted, for example, that although African American dialects differ from "Standard English" in vocabulary, grammar, and pronunciation, they operate according to the same sorts of structural rules as any other language or dialect. Wolfram (1969, 1970) and Fasold and Wolfram (1970), for example, provided exhaustive examples of the complex linguistic features of African American dialects. This research in *descriptive linguistics* has concluded that African American dialects are not deficient or defective and should be accorded an equal status relationship with "Standard English" or any other language.

A number of researchers have enumerated the varieties of African American dialects. Although frequently classified in different ways, most researchers recognize that African American dialects fall on a continuum with a vast range of similarity or difference with "Standard English" (see Baugh, 1983). Region and urbanicity are also strong determinants of specific African American dialectical characteristics.

Researchers have also identified the "bidialectical" nature of the African American population (Hilliard, 1983). That is, many speakers of African American dialects speak both "Standard English" (or close approximations thereof) and one or more varieties of African American dialects (Torrey, 1983). These "varieties" of African American dialects are closely tied to socioeconomic level, region, urbanicity, and level of residential integration and mobility (see Baugh, 1983, concerning dialect diversity; see Fairchild & Tucker, 1982, concerning constraints on residential mobility).

In some respects, it could be argued that some African American dialects "meet or exceed" the sophistication of "Standard English" by the use of intonation, syllable stress, and nonverbal cues to modify meaning. White (1984), in emphasizing the rich oral tradition of Africans and African Americans, recounted in some detail the verbal and nonverbal rituals that may be found in many African American communities. Others have noted the importance of nonverbal cues in conveying or modifying the meaning of the spoken word (Baugh, 1983; Cooke, 1980). A final illustration of the complexity of African American dialects is revealed in the recent (mid- to late 1980s) cultural phenomenon known as "Rap," where African American language forms are created in sharply syncopated rhythms and rhymes.

In sum, research on African American dialects has concluded that they are a legitimate variant of English that operate according to their own rules of syntax, grammar, and the derivation of meaning. As such, they should be accorded an equal status relationship with "Standard English." Yet, studies indicate that teachers, and the public, continue to harbor negative attitudes and beliefs about the nature of African American dialects and their role in schooling.

TEACHER ATTITUDES

Manifestation

The attitude that a teacher has for a student demonstrably affects the student's attitudes and behaviors. After years of research and scores of studies, educational researchers have documented the processes underlying the "self-fulfilling prophecy" (see Eder, 1981, 1983; Jenkins, 1982).

In essence, the self-fulfilling prophecy is a process where a teacher's expectation of a student's performance is communicated to the student in a way that affects the attitudes and behaviors of both student and teacher. The result is that the teacher's expectation (for example, "Johnnie can't read") becomes true. Teachers who expect failure typically demand less, provide less information and feedback, and generally engage in conscious and unconscious behaviors that produce failure. Teachers who expect success typically have high standards and demands, provide a great deal of input, and give students consistent feedback and positive rewards.

Most of the research in this area has demonstrated negative expectations, and related behaviors, based on race. The expectation of lower academic achievement potential for African Americans is so pervasive, it might be considered an axiom of American education (see, for example, Washington, 1982). Some evidence also suggests that African American males are the most at risk of these pessimistic teacher attitudes and behaviors. Simpson and Erickson (1983), for example, reported that teachers in their sample gave the least amount of praise, and the most amount of verbal and nonverbal criticism, to African American males.

Some studies have also demonstrated that teachers have generally more negative attitudes toward *linguistic* minority children (see DeStefano, 1978; Freeman, 1982). Politzer and Hoover (1976), for example, showed that teachers demonstrated lower expectations for speakers of "Vernacular Black English" than for speakers of "Standard Black English" (the differences between these two dialects are also strongly related to social class). It is easy to imagine that African American dialectical styles are a contributing factor to the generally negative attitudes and expectations that teachers have for African American students. It is also easy to imagine that race and dialect may interact in their relationship with teachers' attitudes.

The most troubling aspect of teachers' attitudes and behaviors is the effect these attitudes may have on students. According to one theoretical formulation (Murray & Fairchild, 1989), African American children develop a sense of "conditioned failure" as a result of negative scholastic experiences (especially interactions with teachers who harbor negative expectations) and become willing participants in their own failure syndrome. Research indicates that performance deteriorates in response to failure (Weisz, 1981), which may account for the increasing achievement disparities between Whites and African Americans with increasing grade levels. It is worth noting, as well, that many of these negative expectations and behaviors are characteristic of African American teachers as well as White teachers (Washington, 1982).

In a landmark Supreme Court decision, it was found that the Ann Arbor, Michigan, school district failed to provide an equal educational opportunity to African American students because of their failure to take into account the pedagogical implications of African American dialects (see Freeman, 1982; Jenkins, 1982; Vaughn-Cooke, 1980; Whatley, 1980; White, 1984; Whiteman, 1980). Indeed, it was found that the teachers explicitly degraded the legitimacy of the children's dialects, and this was harmful to their academic achievement and self-esteem.

PEDAGOGICAL IMPLICATIONS

The foregoing review of literature suggests a number of principles for the education of African American children. These principles apply, usually, to the education of all children.

Expectations

Teachers must consciously monitor their attitudes and behaviors toward racial and linguistic minorities. A long history of prejudice and discrimination against African Americans has deeply embedded racist ideologies within American culture. It is our perspective that few if any individuals can live in the United States and not be affected by racism. Unfortunately, racism is generally manifested in the belief in White racial superiority and the inferiority of other groups on a sliding scale that corresponds to skin color (see Fairchild & Gurin, 1978; Fairchild & Tucker, 1982). Others have also demonstrated the effects of dialect or native language on teachers' attitudes (Ovando, 1983). Thus, unless these negative attitudes are consciously acknowledged and combated, they are likely to invade the classroom in ways that re-create racial and ethnic inequality (see Freeman, 1982; Gere & Smith, 1979; Lewis, 1980).

Teachers must presume academic success for all students. Teachers' expectations work in both directions: Negative expectations may produce failure; positive expectations may produce success. Teachers must not assume, for example, that dialect or native language differences are tied in any systematic way to academic achievement potentials (Lewis, 1980). Due to the variety of African American dialects, and due to the dialect-switching that characterizes many of the speakers of African American dialects, it is inappropriate to assume *anything* based on dialect differences alone.

Behaviors

Teachers must accept each child's language or dialect as legitimate (Freeman, 1982). In so doing, teachers must use teaching techniques that meaningfully communicate with children in ways that provide for academic enrichment. Berdan (1980), for example, showed that teachers who reject African American dialects tended to "hypercorrect" the oral reading of children who speak an African American dialect. These corrections, however, were often rigidly applied to pronunciation and other dialect differences, rather than the actual content or meaning of reading passages. As a result, students engaged in a number of "survival strategies," such as withdrawal and acting out behaviors, in order to escape the pejorative treatment that teachers directed toward their native linguistic styles. Berdan (1980) concluded with the identification of a general principle for reading instruction: Teachers should accept oral pronunciations that are appropriate for each student's normal speech (unless an obvious error related to meaning is made). Thus teachers should avoid interrupting students while reading for the purposes of minor corrections; they should not force adherence to an idealized standard that is inappropriate when universally applied.

Teachers must *condition* academic success. They can do this by structuring the classroom in a way that engenders involvement and academic success. This includes meaningful communication that ensures understanding (Goodlad, 1979), by providing opportunities for students to experience success (Slavin, 1983, 1987), providing rewards and other incentives (Goodlad, 1979), varying tasks and the length of instructional segments (Boykin, 1982), and directing learning activities toward topics that are germane to the students themselves (Barona, 1986; Peyton, this volume; Shuy, 1970).

Curriculum Content

The educational community must combat ethnic, racial, and linguistic biases in the curriculum (see Akbar, 1985). In this regard, the content of curriculum must recognize multicultural education as a part of basic education (Fortune, 1979). The curriculum must demonstrate its relevance to various cultural groups (Edmonds, 1981; Macias, 1973) and accurately reflect cultural pluralism. Teachers must aggressively seek curricular materials and resource persons that provide this relevance.

More fundamentally, the content of education should "empower" students to solve problems in their lives and communities (see Graman, 1988; Smitherman & McGinnis, 1980; Stewart, 1970). In this regard, the purpose of education should be geared toward helping students be *generators* of knowledge rather than passive *receivers* of information (Graman, 1988). In this sense, the classroom becomes a microcosm of the world, with the world's problems and perils and with a mandate to seek problem resolution.

School Administration

School administrators must recognize the role of school environments in enhancing academic achievement. Research has concluded that the climate of the school, including curricular supports, adequacy of materials, and the role of the principal, are keys to academic achievement (see Cuttance, 1980; Purkey & Smith, 1983; Wynne, 1981).

Social Culture

Inasmuch as general racial and ethnic attitudes underlie the attitudes of teachers, efforts must be made to generate alternative representations of these groups in the mass media. Fairchild (1984b, 1988b), for example, has articulated a creative effort to develop "prosocial television" programming that reverses ethnic and gender stereotypes. His educational program, *Star Crusaders*, portrays African Americans in cooperative leadership roles with other ethnic groups, demonstrates gender equality, and advances the tenets of the peaceful resolution of conflict (Fairchild, 1984b, 1988b).

More fundamentally, a need exists for the broader American social culture to accept linguistic and dialect diversity as a national resource and asset (see Kochman, 1987; Padilla, this volume; Tucker, 1990). Part of this recognition, then, must be translated into the involvement of the citizenry and communities in enhancing the learning opportunities of all of the nation's children (Goodlad, 1979; Wilson, 1983). The general citizenry can act, for example, as resources of multicultural education and as professional role models for students.

Public Policy

In the area of public policy, the guiding principle must continue to be the provision of equal educational opportunities for all children. This means, without doubt, the ultimate development of a national policy on language education (see, in this connection, Ovando, 1983).

More fundamentally, we are concerned with evidence of the continuing denial of equal educational opportunities. Fairchild (1984a), for example, documented large disparities in the amount of instructional funding provided to predominantly Black, Hispanic, and White schools. Moreover, instructional expenditures and school size were significantly related to standardized measures of academic achievement. Other studies have shown the benefits of small class sizes, which naturally involve a commitment for much greater resources to the educational arena (e.g., Day, 1979; Smith & Glass, 1980). In addition to higher achievement, small classes are also conducive to teacher/student verbal interactions (Asher & Erickson, 1979).

CONCLUSIONS

The debates concerning African American dialects are likely to continue into the foreseeable future. Both the African American community and the public at large must address fundamental pedagogical questions about the nature of language, and language education, in order to redress the cycles of educational failure that characterize a disturbingly large proportion of African American children.

This search for a transformation in American education is likely to benefit the whole of society. As we recognize the special perils confronting African American children, we expand our curriculum to include multicultural content and, we hope, multicultural understanding. As we pursue the development of language competence on the part of linguistic or dialect minorities, we enhance our understanding of the processes of language acquisition and the education of special populations.

Most important, as we address the individualized needs of our students, we transform education into a purposeful activity that provides students with skills that will enable them to pursue productive economic lives, and to assist in the empowerment of their communities.

REFERENCES

Akbar, N. (1985). Our destiny: Authors of a scientific revolution. In H. P. McAdoo & J. L. McAdoo (Eds.), *Black children: Social, educational, and parental environments* (pp. 17–32). Beverly Hills, CA: Sage.

Apple, M. (1978). The new sociology of education: Analyzing cultural and economic reproduction. *Harvard Educational Review, 48,* 495–503.

Asher, K. N., & Erickson, M. T. (1979). Effects of varying child-teacher ratio and group size on day care children's and teachers' behavior. *American Journal of Orthopsychiatry, 49*(3), 518–521.

Banks, J. A. (1982). Educating minority youths: An inventory of current theory. *Education and Urban Society, 15*(1), 88–103.

Baratz, J. C. (1970). Educational considerations for teaching Standard English to Negro children. In R. W. Fasold & R. W. Shuy (Eds.), *Teaching Standard English in the inner city* (pp. 20–40). Washington, DC: Center for Applied Linguistics.

Barona, A. (1986). Non-linguistic factors in second language learning. In E. E. Garcia & B. Flores (Eds.), *Language and literacy research in bilingual education* (pp. 21–31). Tempe: Arizona State University, Center for Bilingual Education.

Baugh, J. (1983). A survey of Afro-American English. *Annual Review of Anthropology, 12,* 335–354.

Berdan, R. (1980). Knowledge into practice: Delivering research to teachers. In M. F. Whiteman (Ed.), *Reactions to Ann Arbor: Vernacular Black English and education* (pp. 77–78). Washington, DC: Center for Applied Linguistics.

Bowser, B. P., & Hunt, R. G. (Eds.). (1981). *Impacts of racism on White Americans.* Beverly Hills, CA: Sage.

Boykin, A. W. (1982). Task variability and the performance of Black and White schoolchildren: Vervistic explorations. *Journal of Black Studies, 12*(4), 469–485.

Comer, J. P. (1985). Empowering Black children's educational environments. In H. P. McAdoo & J. L. McAdoo (Eds.), *Black children: Social, educational and parental environments* (pp. 123–138). Beverly Hills, CA: Sage.

Cooke, B. G. (1980). Nonverbal communication among Afro-Americans: An initial classification. In R. L. Jones (Ed.), *Black psychology* (2nd ed., pp. 139–160). New York: Harper & Row.

Cuttance, P. (1980). Do schools consistently influence the performance of their students? *Educational Review, 32*(3), 267–280.

Day, C. W. (1979). Are small schools better? *School Business Affairs, 45*(7), 32–33.

DeStefano, J. S. (1978). Register: A concept to combat negative teacher attitudes toward Black English. In J. S. DeStefano (Ed.), *Language, society and education: A profile of Black English.* Worthington, OH: Charles A. Jones.

Eder, D. (1981). Ability grouping as a self-fulfilling prophecy: A micro-analysis of teacher-student interaction. *Sociology of Education, 54,* 151–162.

Eder, D. (1983). Ability grouping and students' academic self-concepts: A case study. *Elementary School Journal, 84*(2), 149–161.

Edmonds, R. R. (1981, September/October). Making public schools effective. *Social Policy, 12,* 56–60.

Fairchild, H. H. (1984a). School size, per-pupil expenditures, and school achievement. *Review of Public Data Use, 12,* 221–229.

Fairchild, H. H. (1984b). Creating, producing, and evaluating prosocial TV. *Journal of Educational Television, 10*(3), 161–183.

Fairchild, H. H. (1985). Black, Negro, or Afro-American: The differences are crucial! *Journal of Black Studies, 16*(1), 47–55.

Fairchild, H. H. (1988a). Glorification of things White. *Journal of Black Psychology, 14*(2), 73–74.

Fairchild, H. H. (1988b). Creating positive television images. In S. Oskamp (Ed.), *Applied social psychology annual: Vol. 8. Television as a social issue* (pp. 270–279). Newbury Park, CA: Sage.

Fairchild, H. H. (1989, March 16). *African American self esteem: Issues and perspectives.* Statement read to the California Task Force to Promote Self Esteem and Personal and Social Responsibility, California State University, Los Angeles.

Fairchild, H. H., & Gurin, P. (1978). Traditions in the social-psychological analysis of race relations. *American Behavioral Scientist, 21*(5), 757–778.

Fairchild, H. H., & Tucker, M. B. (1982). Black residential mobility: Trends and characteristics. *Journal of Social Issues, 38*(3), 51–74.

Fasold, R. W., & Wolfram, W. (1970). Some linguistic features of Negro dialect. In R. W. Fasold & R. W. Shuy (Eds.), *Teaching Standard English in the inner city* (pp. 41–86). Washington, DC: Center for Applied Linguistics.

Fisher, S. (1981). Race, class, anomie, and academic achievement: A study at the high school level. *Urban Education, 16*(2), 149–173.

Fortune, R. C., Jr. (1979). Multicultural education: A part of basic education? *Cross Reference, 2*, 118–128.

Freeman, E. B. (1982). The Ann Arbor decision: The importance of teachers' attitudes toward language. *Elementary School Journal, 83*(1), 41–47.

Gere, A. R., & Smith, E. (1979). *Attitudes, language and change.* Urbana, IL: National Council of Teachers of English.

Goodlad, J. I. (1979). Can our schools get better? *Phi Delta Kappan, 60*(5), 342–346.

Graman, T. (1988). Education for humanization: Applying Paulo Freire's pedagogy to learning a second language. *Harvard Educational Review, 58*(4), 433–448.

Hilliard, A. G., III. (1983). Psychological factors associated with language in the education of the African-American child. *Journal of Negro Education, 52*(1), 24–34.

Jenkins, A. H. (1982). *The psychology of the Afro-American: A humanistic approach.* New York: Pergamon.

Jensen, A. R. (1985). The nature of Black-White difference on various psychometric tests: Spearman's hypothesis. *Behavioral and Brain Sciences, 8*(2), 193–218.

Kochman, T. (1987). The ethnic component in Black language and culture. In J. S. Phinney & M.-J. Rotheram (Eds.), *Children's ethnic socialization: Pluralism and development* (pp. 219–238). Newbury Park, CA: Sage.

Lewis, S. A. R. (1980). Teacher attitude change: Does informing make a difference? In M. F. Whiteman (Ed.), *Reactions to Ann Arbor: Vernacular Black English and education* (pp. 85–92). Washington, DC: Center for Applied Linguistics.

Macias, R. F. (1973). Developing a bilingual culturally-relevant educational program for Chicanos. *Aztlan, 4*, 61–78.

Murray, C. M., & Fairchild, H. H. (1989). Models of black adolescents academic underachievement. In R. L. Jones (Ed.), *Black adolescence.* Berkeley, CA: Cobb & Henry.

Ovando, C. J. (1983, April). Bilingual/bicultural education: Its legacy and its future. *Phi Delta Kappan, 64*, 564–568.

Persell, C. H. (1981). Genetic and cultural deficit theories: Two sides of the same racist coin. *Journal of Black Studies, 12*(1), 19–37.

Politzer, R. L., & Hoover, M. R. (1976). *Teachers' and pupils' attitudes toward Black English speech varieties and Black pupils' achievement.* Stanford, CA: Stanford Center for Research and Development in Teaching.

Purkey, S. C., & Smith, M. S. (1983). Effective schools: A review. *Elementary School Journal, 83*(4), 427–452.

Rosenholtz, S. J., & Cohen, E. G. (1983). Back to basics and the desegregated school. *Elementary School Journal, 83*(5), 515–527.

Ryan, W. (1971). *Blaming the victim.* New York: Random House.

Shuy, R. W. (1970). Teacher training and urban language problems. In R. W. Fasold & R. W. Shuy (Eds.), *Teaching Standard English in the inner city* (pp. 120–141). Washington, DC: Center for Applied Linguistics.

Simpson, A. W., & Erickson, M. T. (1983). Teachers' verbal and nonverbal communication patterns as a function of teacher race, student gender, and student race. *American Educational Research Journal, 20*(2), 183–198.

Slavin, R. E. (1983). When does cooperative learning increase student achievement? *Psychological Bulletin, 94*(3), 429–445.

Slavin, R. E. (1987). Developmental and motivational perspectives on cooperative learning: A reconsideration. *Child Development, 58*, 1167.

Smith, M. L., & Glass, G. V. (1980). Meta-analysis of research on class size and its relationship to attitudes and instruction. *American Educational Research Journal, 17*(4), 419–433.

Smitherman, G., & McGinnis, J. (1980). Black language and Black liberation. In R. L. Jones (Ed.), *Black psychology* (2nd ed., pp. 131–138). New York: Harper & Row.

Stewart, W. A. (1970). Foreign language teaching methods in quasi-foreign language situations. In R. W. Fasold & R. W. Shuy (Eds.), *Teaching Standard English in the inner city* (pp. 1–19). Washington, DC: Center for Applied Linguistics.

Torrey, J. W. (1983). Black children's knowledge of Standard English. *American Educational Research Journal, 20*(4), 627–643.

Tucker, G. R. (1990). Second language education: Issues and perspectives. In A. M. Padilla, H. H. Fairchild, & C. M. Valadez (Eds.), *Foreign language education: Issues and strategies.* Newbury Park, CA: Sage.

Vaughn-Cooke, F. B. (1980). Evaluating the language of Black English speakers: Implications of the Ann Arbor decision. In M. F. Whiteman (Ed.), *Reactions to Ann Arbor: Vernacular Black English and education* (pp. 24–54). Washington, DC: Center for Applied Linguistics.

Washington, V. (1982). Racial differences in teacher perceptions of first and fourth grade pupils on selected characteristics. *Journal of Negro Education, 51*(1), 60–72.

Weisz, J. R. (1981). Learned helplessness in Black and White children identified by their schools as retarded and nonretarded: Performance deterioration in response to failure. *Developmental Psychology, 17*(4), 499–508.

Whatley, E. M. (1980). Black English: Implications of the Ann Arbor decision for the classroom. In M. F. Whiteman (Ed.), *Reactions to Ann Arbor: Vernacular Black English and education* (pp. 61–76). Washington, DC: Center for Applied Linguistics.

White, J. L. (1984). *The psychology of Blacks.* Englewood Cliffs, NJ: Prentice-Hall.

Whiteman, M. F. (Ed.). (1980). *Reactions to Ann Arbor: Vernacular Black English and education.* Washington, DC: Center for Applied Linguistics.

Wilson, S. H. (1983). Strengthening connections between schools and communities: A method of improving urban schools. *Urban Education, 18*(2), 153–177.

Wolfram, W. A. (1969). *A sociolinguistic description of Detroit Negro speech.* Washington, DC: Center for Applied Linguistics.

Wolfram, W. (1970). Sociolinguistic implications for educational sequencing. In R. W. Fasold & R. W. Shuy (Eds.), *Teaching Standard English in the inner city* (pp. 105–119). Washington, DC: Center for Applied Linguistics.

Wynne, E. A. (1981, January). Looking at good schools. *Phi Delta Kappan, 62*, 377–381.

PART III

Program Design and Evaluation

Part III includes three chapters that (a) offer suggestions for the development of bilingual immersion programs, (b) trace the development of a bilingual education "master plan" in a metropolitan school district, and (c) report the results of an evaluation of a two-way bilingual immersion program.

Kathryn Lindholm, in "Bilingual Immersion Education: Criteria for Program Development" (Chapter 6), recalls many of the demographic projections of earlier chapters and emphasizes the increasing need to address linguistic diversity in American schools. She notes that the current thrust is to simultaneously meet the language education needs of linguistic minority and majority students by the use of bilingual immersion programs. Bilingual immersion programs, particularly when designed for "two-way" or "interlocking" teaching strategies, use two languages for the purposes of content instruction. For example, native Spanish-speaking and native English-speaking students receive content instruction in both English and Spanish. In this way, students from the two groups serve as linguistic role models for each other.

Lindholm notes four critical features of bilingual immersion: dual language immersion (both languages used for instruction); language isolation (the two languages are used in distinctly different periods and the proportion of one language or the other may vary over the grade levels); student mixing (language minority and language majority students mixed in roughly equal proportions); and the integration of language arts curriculum with the traditional academic content areas (using a second language to teach math, science, or social studies).

Lindholm then enumerates the "criteria" for the successful implementation of bilingual immersion programs: (a) programs must be planned for a period of from four to six years at a minimum; (b) language/content integration makes the instruction *purposeful*, thereby enhancing the communicative relevance of each student's second language; (c) second language input and output should be optimized through exciting language arts curriculum and instruction; (d) the strict separation of languages enhances students' attention to curriculum and facilitates language development; (e) the ratio of English-speaking to non-English-speaking students should probably be no less than about 50% at least at the beginning of the program; (f) an emphasis is on the maintenance of the language minority students' native language; (g) a program must have the unequivocal support of the school administration; (h) classroom heterogeneity enhances bilingual communicative proficiency and intercultural relations; (i) teachers should focus on reciprocal dialogues about the content material rather than relying solely on teacher-to-student transmission of knowledge; (j) qualified teachers with native or near-native ability in the languages being used in the classroom are essential; and (k) a partnership must be formed between parents and the school in the implementation of an immersion education program.

Concepción M. Valadez and Clementina Patiño Gregoire, in "Development of a Bilingual Education Plan" (Chapter 7), present a detailed description of a school district's response to its changing student population. Their focus is on the conversion of a school district from one with low achievement scores among its Spanish- and Portuguese-proficient students and low morale among its staff to one that has gained a national reputation for its orientation to limited-English-proficient students. The authors present a brief demographic history of the ABC Unified School District in Southern California, and how the district responded to legislation concerning language education. Valadez and Gregoire include a discussion of staff development, training, contributions from abroad, and staff morale. Their chapter illustrates an exemplary response of a metropolitan school district to the changing demography and language education needs of its students. They conclude that strong and unequivocal leadership is the most important factor in the success of the district's language education programming.

Kathryn Lindholm and Halford H. Fairchild, in "Evaluation of an Elementary School Immersion Program" (Chapter 8), describe the implementation of a model program in Santa Monica, California, and report the results of a preliminary evaluation. According to Lindholm and Fairchild, the goals of the Edison School Program were to produce normal to superior academic achievement in both English and Spanish, age-appropriate bilingual oral proficiency and literacy, enhanced feelings of self-competence on the part of the children, and positive cross-cultural attitudes and relationships.

They compared 112 kindergarten and first-grade bilingual immersion students with students enrolled in regular classrooms. Lindholm and Fairchild report that the bilingual immersion students demonstrated significant achievement gains and had higher scores on every measure than the comparison group (although only the math scores were statistically significant). Self-competence scores for the bilingual immersion students were comparable to those reported for a middle-class sample. The authors conclude that the interaction of the language groups was beneficial to both groups and that bilingual immersion programs produce average to better than average achievement levels.

As a whole, the chapters in Part III compose a collection that covers curriculum development for classrooms, schools, and school districts. Implementation and evaluation strategies are highlighted.

6

Bilingual Immersion Education
Criteria for Program Development

KATHRYN J. LINDHOLM

The dynamics of population change indicate that the United States is becoming an increasingly multiethnic and multilingual society. The major factors contributing to this change include sizable immigration and the fact that the average age of ethnic minorities is about five years less than the national average. This means that a larger percentage of ethnic minorities are in, or are entering, the most active childbearing years (Cortés, 1986).

According to data from the Census Bureau, between 1970 and 1980, the U.S. population increased by 11.6%. However, the Black population grew by 17.8%, Hispanics by 61%, Native Americans by 71%, Asian Americans by 233%, and the remaining Americans by only 7% to 8%. Schools have, and will have, therefore, a major challenge in dealing with the large number of limited-English-proficient students who are in need of special services. It has been estimated that currently at least 3.4 million children are limited in the English language skills needed to succeed in school programs designed for native English speakers.

Nationally, the academic performance of minority students is considerably below majority norms, and the gap grows wider with each school year (Kagan & Zahn, 1975). Reading is critical to student achievement in all subjects, yet the achievement gap is greatest in reading. By the eighth grade, 39.9% of Mexican American children are two or more years behind in reading compared with 12.8% of Whites (Carter & Segura, 1979). As society moves further into the technological age of computers, with jobs requiring literacy- and computer-based skills, low educational attainment will be even more detrimental. These findings show that "the United States's public school system is failing with regard to the achievement of minority children" (Kagan, 1986, p. 223).

However, the public education system is generally not meeting the educational needs of many majority students either (U.S. Department of Education, 1987): About 20% of all American 17-year-olds are functionally illiterate, unable to comprehend simple written instructions (Lerner, 1981); nearly half of our graduating high school students do not know the basics of how our government works (Johnson, Johnson, & Tiffany, 1984); and "Americans' incompetence in foreign languages is nothing short of scandalous and is becoming worse" (President's Commission on Foreign Language and International Studies, 1979). At the same time, the great national language resource represented by immigrant and native, non-English groups is being rapidly eroded, as second and third generations are not learning their native languages.

Special educational programs for language minority students have caused tremendous controversy among educators, lawmakers, and the general public. Many current bilingual education programs grew out of the civil rights movement of the 1960s, in which there was a call for a system of education where the language minority student would receive equal access to education. Bilingual education was to provide a setting in which the student's native language and culture would be valued; students would be able to develop a positive self-image; opportunities for academic success would be enhanced; and solidarity with the community would be strengthened (Hernández-Chávez, 1984).

After a decade and a half of bilingual education, however, the controversy has grown instead of diminished (e.g., Baker, 1987; Secada, 1987; Willig, 1987). Many research studies have been inadequately designed to provide educators and policymakers with information about the effectiveness of bilingual education and thus they have fueled rather than cooled the fires of controversy. A carefully conducted analysis of the bilingual education research (Association for Supervision and Curriculum Development, 1987; U.S. General Accounting Office, 1987; Willig, 1985) demonstrated that bilingual education programs can be successful in improving the academic performance of limited-English-proficient students. Unfortunately, bilingual education has not been as effective in its implementation as it could have been if there had been policies defining the implementation of programs that were designed to promote educational achievement rather than merely the learning of English. The tragedy of many American Indian groups, who have lost their native language without gaining any educational advantage, is stark evidence that learning English is neither a necessary nor sufficient condition for enhanced educational achievement.

For a variety of sociopolitical, economic, as well as pedagogical reasons, many educators have supported short-term "quick fix" solutions that move limited-English-proficient students into mainstream English-only classes as quickly as possible. Monolingual English immersion education is being increasingly cited as a possible option to bilingual education.

Traditional immersion programs use, in part, a non-English language as a medium of instruction for subject matter classes (Lambert, 1984). However, the term *immersion* is often used incorrectly with reference to language minority students (Dolson, 1985a). While the model has been successful with language majority children, its appropriateness with language minority children has been strongly called into question by most knowledgeable researchers (e.g., Hernández-Chávez, 1984).

A submersion program refers to a curriculum designed for and populated by native English speakers but inappropriately used with non-English-speaking students. A considerable amount of research documents the failure of submersion approaches to meet the educational needs of language minority students (California State Department of Education, 1982; National Assessment for Educational Progress, 1982). Many educators who are aware of this research readily reject submersion as an appropriate educational treatment for language minority students. Most educators agree that an educational program designed for limited-English-proficient students needs to promote adequate language development, academic achievement, and psychosocial adjustment for students from non-English language backgrounds.

When it is applied to the proper target group under appropriate conditions, immersion education can have very successful results. Evaluation of Spanish immersion programs in the United States and French immersion programs in Canada (Campbell, 1984; Genesee, 1985; Swain, 1984) show that immersion education can be highly effective for English-speaking students, both majority and ethnic/racial minority students. These students eventually demonstrate high levels of proficiency in the second language (i.e., French, German, Spanish) in addition to high academic achievement, without any loss to the development of their English skills.

Currently, evaluation and research studies suggest that education programs can be designed to simultaneously meet the needs of language minority and majority students by combining the best features of immersion programs with the best features of bilingual education. Bilingual immersion is based on the premise that a second language is best acquired by language minority students when their first language is firmly established (see Hakuta & Gould,

1987), and that a second language is best developed by language majority children through immersion in that language (Genesee, 1985). It is felt that the immersion of fluent-English-proficient (FEP) students in non-English instruction is beneficial for their acquisition of true communicative proficiency in the second language. Their English language skills, meanwhile, develop unimpeded due to the dominance of English in their social/cultural environment. For limited-English-proficient (LEP) students, instruction in their native language provides the necessary linguistic foundation for the later acquisition of English and the further development of full proficiency in both languages.

The rationale for this apparent inconsistency in native versus second-language instruction is twofold. First, English is the dominant societal language, and the non-English language is in jeopardy of attrition without early intensive exposure to the less dominant language. Second, a critical theoretical and societal distinction exists between second-language immersion for language majority versus language minority students: This distinction is between enrichment, or additive bilingualism, and assimilation, or subtractive bilingualism (Lambert, 1987; Skuttnabb-Kangas, 1981). *Additive bilingualism* refers to language education programs that offer language enrichment and enable children to add one or more foreign languages to their accumulating skills and benefit immediately without fear of native language loss. In contrast, *subtractive bilingualism* exists in language education programs in which the learner must put aside or subtract out their ethnic language for a more necessary, useful, and prestigious national language (Lambert, 1987). Research indicates that additive bilingualism is associated with high levels of proficiency in the two languages, whereas subtractive bilingualism is associated with lower levels of second-language attainment and scholastic performance.

Thus, in bilingual immersion programs, while language minority children are taught primarily in their native language for the first few years of schooling, language majority children are instructed primarily in their second language (Genesee, 1985). Students from the two language communities serve as peer tutors for their mutual language development. Bilingual immersion programs are, therefore, equally concerned with the language and academic development of both language minority and language majority children (Lindholm, 1987). Thus another major assumption underlying bilingual immersion education is concerned with the relationship between language and thought: It is expected that knowledge learned through one language paves the way for knowledge acquisition in the second language. Thus students who learn content in one language are expected to demonstrate content knowledge in the second language once they acquire the language skills to

express that knowledge (Cummins, 1987). Finally, another underlying premise is built on the threshold hypothesis (Cummins, 1987), which states that
students need to reach a certain level of native language proficiency in order
to facilitate second-language development. Furthermore, long-term cognitive
advantages of bilingualism will not accrue until the student has sufficiently
developed both languages.

Although bilingual immersion programs vary in terms of the proportion of
instruction in one language or the other, the duration of the immersion, and
the subject matter that is taught in the two languages (Lindholm, 1987), all
bilingual immersion programs offer fluent-English-proficient (FEP) and limited-English-proficient (LEP) students the opportunity to share the first years
of elementary school primarily immersed in the non-English language. This
integrative approach is expected to improve intergroup attitudes, and attitudes toward the target language and culture, of both language minority and
language majority children (Baecher & Coletti, 1986; Lindholm, 1987).

Bilingual immersion programs address the needs of both native English
speakers and native speakers of other languages, and potentially result in
high levels of language proficiency in both the other language and English,
academic achievement at or above grade level as measured in both languages, and enhanced psychosocial development and cross-cultural skills and
attitudes. In doing so, these programs can help to develop citizens who will
be better prepared to strengthen mutual bonds of our national unity in a time
of growing ethnic and linguistic diversity, and who will at the same time be
better able to meet the mounting demands of international collaboration in a
multilingual world, where the knowledge of languages other than English are
essential to our national well-being.

DEFINITION OF BILINGUAL IMMERSION EDUCATION

Bilingual immersion education combines the most significant features of
bilingual education for language minority students and immersion education
for language majority students. Academic and language arts instruction is
provided to native speakers of two languages using, alternatively and sequen-
tially, both languages; one of the languages is a second language for each
group of students. Thus, for language minority students, academic instruction
is presented through their first language and they receive English language
arts and, depending on the particular program, portions of their academic
instruction in English. For language majority students, academic instruction
is provided through their second language and they receive English language

arts and, depending on the program design, some portion of their academic instruction in English. The academic curriculum provides the same high-quality content as in non-bilingual immersion programs, focusing on state and local curriculum requirements.

The definition of bilingual immersion education encompasses four critical features: (a) The program essentially involves some form of dual language instruction, where the non-English language is used for a significant portion of the students' instructional day; (b) the program involves periods of instruction during which only one language is used; (c) both native English speakers and nonnative English speakers (preferably in balanced numbers) are participants; and (d) the students are integrated for most content instruction.

CRITICAL FEATURES OF SUCCESSFUL LANGUAGE EDUCATION PROGRAMS

Over the last several years, a number of comprehensive reviews have been conducted of research and evaluation studies concerning bilingual and immersion education (Baker & de Kanter, 1981; Crawford, 1989; Cummins, 1979, 1983; Diaz, 1983; Dolson, 1985a; Fisher & Guthrie, 1983; Swain & Lapkin, 1985; Troike, 1978, 1986; Willig, 1985). An examination of these investigations points to certain sociolinguistic and instructional factors that tend to contribute to successful dual language programs. The importance of these factors is evident from the frequency and consistency with which they are found in programs that promote high levels of first- and second-language competencies, academic achievement in both languages, and high self-esteem and positive cross-cultural attitudes. Thus these factors form the core criteria for successful bilingual immersion education.

The first eight criteria are essential for successful *language* education programs. The last three apply to educational programs in general, but have special relevance to dual language settings. These last criteria are mentioned here because they are important elements in an educational program and the presence of these criteria cannot be assumed but must be carefully considered in designing and implementing a successful bilingual immersion program.

(1) *Duration of instructional treatment.* The instructional treatment is provided to the participating students for a period of *at least* four to six years. This is the amount of time required, on average, to reach second-language or bilingual proficiency, but not necessarily nativelike proficiency, as confirmed by a number of evaluation studies on immersion and bilingual programs (Cummins, 1981; Krashen & Biber, 1988; Swain, 1984; Troike, 1978). In its review of foreign language programs, the National Commission on Excel-

lence in Education (1983) has concluded that achieving proficiency ordinarily demands from four to six years of study.

(2) *Focus on academic curriculum.* The programs are designed to focus on subject matter as well as language development. Students are exposed to the same high-quality, academic core curriculum as students in regular programs. For native English speakers, academic achievement is attained primarily through second-language (L2) content instruction and interactions in the first language (L1) at home and in the community. Academic achievement is further bolstered by content taught through English. For language minority students, instruction in and through the native language forms the basis for initial academic advancement. Academic achievement and English language proficiency are further developed through English language arts and content instruction through English.

(3) *Optimal language input and output.* Optimal input has four characteristics: (a) It is adjusted to the comprehension level of the learner, (b) it is interesting and relevant, (c) there is sufficient quantity, and (d) it is challenging. This is accomplished through communicatively sensitive language instruction and subject matter presentation. In the early stages of second-language acquisition, input is made more comprehensible through the use of slower, more expanded, simplified, and repetitive speech oriented to the "here and now" (Krashen, 1981; Long, 1980); highly contextualized language and gestures (Long, 1980; Saville-Troike, 1987); comprehension and confirmation checks (Long, 1980); and communication structured so that it provides scaffolding for the negotiation of meaning by L2 students by constraining possible interpretations of sequence, role, and intent (Saville-Troike, 1987).

Balanced with the need to make the second language more comprehensible is the necessity for providing stimulating language input (Swain, 1987), particularly for the native speakers of each language. There are two reasons why students need stimulating language input. First, such input serves to facilitate continued development of language structures and skills. Second, when students are instructed in their first language, the content of their lessons becomes more comprehensible when they are then presented with similar content in the second language.

Optimal language input also involves the need to provide language arts instruction in *both* the English and the non-English languages and to design the instruction so that it is integrated with the academic curriculum. There has been controversy in the area of second-language education about the importance of second-language instruction in second-language learning (e.g., Krashen, 1981; Long, 1983; Swain, 1987). Many immersion programs, in fact, neglect language arts in the immersion language, assuming that the students will learn the language through the subject matter instruction and will achieve more nativelike proficiency if they receive the kind of language exposure that is similar to first-language learning (see Swain, 1987). As some immersion researchers have discovered (e.g., Harley, 1984; Swain, 1985; Swain & Lapkin, 1985), though, the fluency and grammar ability of most immersion students is not nativelike and there is a need for formal instruction in the second language.

However, it is best if this formalized language instruction does not follow the traditional foreign language instructional practices consisting of translation and memorization of grammar and phrases. It is important to develop a language arts curriculum that specifies which linguistic structures should be mastered (e.g., conditional verb forms) and how these linguistic structures should be incorporated into the academic content (e.g., including the preterit and imperfect verb forms of the verb *ser*—"to be"—in history subject matter and the conditional, future, and subjunctive tenses of the verb *ser*—"to be"—in mathematics and science content). The language arts class can then focus on specific linguistic skills, utilizing the content that was used to introduce the linguistic skill. This integrative and content-based approach reinforces both the content taught during subject matter presentation and the linguistic skill.

Language output is also important to monitor. As noted earlier, immersion students, and foreign language students in general, have difficulty in producing nativelike speech in the second language. Part of this difficulty stems from an absence of the opportunity to talk with fluent speakers in the language they are learning. According to Swain (1985, 1987), students in traditionally designed immersion programs get few opportunities to produce extended discourse in which they are required to make their language coherent, accurate, and sociolinguistically appropriate. Thus promoting highly proficient oral language skills necessitates providing both structured tasks and unstructured opportunities for oral production as well as aural comprehension.

(4) *Separation of languages for instruction.* Studies of bilingual education programs indicate that monolingual lesson delivery (i.e., different periods of time devoted to instruction in and through each of the two languages, respectively) is superior to designs that rely on language mixing during a single lesson or time frame (Baker & de Kanter, 1981; Dulay & Burt, 1978; Legaretta, 1979, 1981; Swain, 1983). This is not to say that language mixing itself is harmful; rather, it appears that sustained periods of monolingual instruction in each language require students to actively attend to the instruction and result in improved language development and subject matter attainment.

(5) *Ratio of English to the non-English language use.* Immersion education was designed to promote high levels of second-language proficiency while maintaining first-language proficiency. Although there are several program variations, many traditional full immersion programs utilize the non-English language for 100% of the instructional day and English is not used at all for at least the initial stages of the program. Other partial immersion programs involve equal amounts of English and the non-English language. No research has yet determined the best ratio of English to non-English instruction for both language minority and majority students. However, research comparing FLES (Foreign Language in the Elementary School) and immersion programs that utilize different amounts of instruction in the non-English language shows that students with greater exposure to the second language have higher levels of second-language proficiency (Campbell, Gray, Rhodes, & Snow, 1985) and that these students also maintain their English and perform at or above grade level in tests of English achievement (Campbell, 1984; Genesee, 1985). Furthermore, research in bilingual education shows that students with greater amounts of native language instruction achieve at higher levels than students with lesser amounts of native language instruction, at least in the early years of schooling (Krashen & Biber, 1988; Willig, 1985).

From studies of bilingual and immersion students, then, it appears that a minimum of 50% non-English language instruction is necessary to promote high levels of the non-English language proficiency among language majority students and to promote language proficiency and academic achievement among language minority students. Furthermore, although studies have not addressed the minimal level of English necessary, it seems prudent to suggest a minimum allocation of 10% of the instructional time for dedication to English in the early grades to promote English language development for the nonnative speakers of English. Also, to develop a high level of academic English language skills among the language minority students, the amount of content instruction in English should be about 50% for the late elementary school years (grades four to six) (ESEA Title VII Bilingual Demonstration Project, 1982).

(6) *Additive bilingual environment.* All students are provided the opportunity to acquire a second language at no cost to their home language and culture. This "enrichment bilingualism" results in high levels of proficiency in the two languages (Hernández-Chávez, 1984; Skuttnabb-Kangas, 1981), adequate self-esteem, and improved cross-cultural attitudes (Lambert, 1987). Conversely, subtractive bilingual contexts, in which the native language is replaced by a second language, seem to have negative effects on the school performance of many language minority students. Native language loss is

often associated with lower levels of second-language attainment, scholastic underachievement, and psychosocial disorders (Lambert, 1984). Successful language development programs seem not only to prevent the negative consequences of subtractive bilingualism but also to effectively promote the beneficial aspects of additive bilingualism.

(7) *A positive school environment.* Research indicates that the success of bilingual education programs is dependent on the level of support the program receives from the school administration (Cortés, 1986; Troike, 1978). Drawing on this research, then, a successful bilingual immersion program should have the support of the principal, other administrators, and nonbilingual immersion staff. This support is based on a knowledge of the program and is demonstrated through a desire for the program to succeed by an expenditure of resources that is comparable to other educational programs in the school, by devoting attention to promoting acceptance of the program among the community and other school staff, and by closely integrating the structure and function of the bilingual immersion program with the total school program (Troike, 1978).

(8) *Classroom composition.* Little research has been conducted to determine the best classroom composition for bilingual education programs. To maintain an environment of educational and linguistic equity in the classroom, and to promote interactions among native and nonnative English speakers, the most desirable ratio is 50% English speakers to 50% nonnative English speakers. However, the ratio of English speakers to nonnative English speakers may exceed this ratio in the early grades to ensure that there are enough language models of each language to allow for attrition and the almost impossible replacement of native speakers of English.

(9) *Positive interdependence and reciprocal interactive instructional climate.* Promotion of positive and interdependent interactions between teachers and students, and between language minority and majority student peers, is an important instructional objective. When teachers use positive social and instructional interactions in equal amounts with both minority and majority students, both groups perform better academically (California State Department of Education, 1982; Kerman et al., 1980). In addition, teachers should adopt a reciprocal interaction model instead of adhering to the traditional transmission model of teaching (Cummins, 1986). The basic premise of the transmission model is that the teacher's task is to impart knowledge or skills to students who do not yet have these abilities. In the reciprocal interaction approach, teachers participate in genuine dialogue with pupils and facilitate rather than control student learning. This model encourages the development of higher-level cognitive skills rather than just factual recall (Cummins, 1986).

The achievement of language minority pupils is affected not only by the status perceptions of teachers but also by the status perceptions of majority peers. Allowing only unplanned or incidental contact between majority and minority students may only reinforce negative expectations. Kagan (1986) and others have proposed ways in which contacts between minority and majority students can be organized so that the achievement of both groups can be maximized. These studies suggest that, when minority and majority students work interdependently on school tasks with common objectives, students' expectations and attitudes about each other become more positive and their academic achievement improves. A number of strategies under the rubric of "cooperative learning" have been developed that utilize these principles (e.g., Kagan, 1986). Finally, language development is facilitated by extensive interactions among native and nonnative speakers (Long & Porter, 1985).

(10) *High-quality instructional personnel.* Students receive their instruction from certified teachers. Over the course of the program, students are exposed to a number of teachers who have native or nativelike ability in either or both of the language(s) in which they are instructing. Teachers, although bilingual, may assume monolingual roles when interacting with students. It is important that the teacher be able to understand the child's mother tongue in the initial stages of language learning. If the teacher does not understand the native language, then he or she cannot respond appropriately in the second language to the children's utterances in their native language. In this case, comprehensible input may be severely impaired (Swain, 1985). Further, teachers should be knowledgeable with regard to the curriculum level and how to teach it.

(11) *Home-school collaboration.* Another important feature is parental involvement and collaboration with the school. When parent-school partnerships are formed, parents often develop a sense of efficacy that communicates itself to children, with positive academic consequences, especially in the case of language minority children (Met, 1987; Tizard, Schofield, & Hewison, 1982). In fact, most parents of minority students have high aspirations for their children and want to be involved in promoting their academic success (Lindholm, 1988; Wong Fillmore, 1983). Often parents of language minority children are able to fulfill this role more effectively through their native language (Dolson, 1985b) in interactions involving literacy- and other academically-related topics.

Dramatic changes occur in children's academic progress when parents interact with their children at home in certain ways. Activities such as reading and listening to children read are feasible, practical, and contribute to improved scholastic achievement (Ada, 1986; Cummins, 1986). Effective programs tend to incorporate a variety of home-school collaboration activities. The general outcome on the part of students is an increased interest in schoolwork and improved achievement and behavior.

In summary, a number of important instructional features have been discussed that are based on evaluation of successful bilingual education and immersion education programs and also on research on effective schools and teaching. The extent to which these features are incorporated into a bilingual immersion program may affect the program's success in achieving its goals.

REFERENCES

Ada, A. F. (1986). Creative education for bilingual education teachers. *Harvard Educational Review, 56,* 386–394.

Association for Supervision and Curriculum Development. (1987). *Building an indivisible nation: Bilingual education in context.* Washington, DC: Author.

Baecher, R. E., & Coletti, C. D. (1986). Two-way bilingual programs: Implementation of an educational innovation. *NABE Journal, 2*(1), 42–58.

Baker, K. (1987). Comment on Willig's "A meta-analysis of selected studies in the effectiveness of bilingual education." *Review of Educational Research, 57*(3), 351–362.

Baker, A. K., & de Kanter, A. (1981). *Effectiveness of bilingual education: A review of the literature.* Washington, DC: Office of Planning, Budget and Evaluation, U.S. Department of Education.

California State Department of Education. (1982). *Basic principles for the education of language minority students, an overview.* Sacramento: Office of Bilingual Bicultural Education.

Campbell, R. N. (1984). The immersion education approach to foreign language teaching. In *Studies on immersion education: A collection for U.S. educators* (pp. 114–143). Sacramento: California State Department of Education.

Campbell, R. N., Gray, T. C., Rhodes, N. C., & Snow, M. A. (1985). Foreign language learning in the elementary schools: A comparison of three language programs. *Modern Language Journal, 69,* 44–54.

Carter, T. P., & Segura, R. D. (1979). *Mexican Americans in school.* New York: College Entrance Examination Board.

Cortés, C. E. (1986). The education of language minority students: A contextual interaction model. In *Beyond language: Social and cultural factors in schooling language minority students* (pp. 3–33). Los Angeles: California State University, Evaluation, Dissemination and Assessment Center.

Crawford, J. (1989). *Bilingual education: History, politics, theory and practice.* Trenton, NJ: Crane.

Cummins, J. (1979). Linguistic interdependence and the educational development of children. *Review of Educational Research, 49,* 222–251.

Cummins, J. (1981). The role of primary language development in promoting educational success for language minority students. In *Schooling and language minority students: A theo-*

retical framework. Los Angeles: California State University, Evaluation, Dissemination, and Assessment Center.

Cummins, J. (1983). *Heritage language education: A literature review.* Toronto: Minister of Education.

Cummins, J. (1986). Empowering minority students: A framework for intervention. *Harvard Educational Review, 56,* 18–36.

Cummins, J. (1987). Bilingualism, language proficiency, and metalinguistic development. In P. Homel, M. Palij, & D. Aaronson (Eds.), *Childhood bilingualism: Aspects of linguistic, cognitive and social development* (pp. 57–73). Hillsdale, NJ: Lawrence Erlbaum.

Diaz, R. M. (1983). "Through two languages: The impact of bilingualism on cognitive development." In *Review of Research in Education* (pp. 23–54). Washington, DC: American Educational Research Association.

Dolson, D. (1985a). Bilingualism and scholastic performance: The literature revisited. *NABE Journal, 10,* 1–35.

Dolson, D. (1985b). The effects of Spanish home language use on the scholastic performance of Hispanic pupils. *Journal of Multilingual and Multicultural Development, 6,* 135–155.

Dulay, H., & Burt, M. (1978). From research to method in bilingual education. In J. Alatis (Ed.), *International dimensions of bilingual education.* Washington, DC: Georgetown University Press.

ESEA Title VII Bilingual Demonstration Project. (1982). *An exemplary approach to bilingual education: A comprehensive handbook for implementing an elementary-level Spanish-English language immersion program* (Publication #I-B-82–58). San Diego, CA: San Diego Unified School District.

Fisher, C. W., & Guthrie, L. F. (1983). *Executive summary: Significant bilingual instructional features study* (Document SBIF-83-R.14). San Francisco: Far West Laboratory for Educational Research and Development.

Genesee, F. (1985). Second language learning through immersion: A review of U.S. programs. *Review of Educational Research, 55,* 541–561.

Hakuta, K., & Gould, L. J. (1987, March). Synthesis of research on bilingual education. *Educational Leadership, 44,* 38–45.

Harley, B. (1984). How good is their French? *Language and Society, 10,* 55–60.

Hernández-Chávez, E. (1984). The inadequacy of English immersion as an educational approach for language minority students. In *Studies on immersion education: A collection for U.S. educators* (pp. 144–183). Sacramento: California State Department of Education.

Johnson, D. W., Johnson, R., & Tiffany, M. (1984). Structuring academic conflicts between majority and minority students: Hindrance or help to integration. *Contemporary Educational Psychology, 9,* 61–73.

Kagan, S. (1986). Cooperative learning and sociocultural factors in schooling. In *Beyond language: Social and cultural factors in schooling language minority students.* Los Angeles: California State University, Evaluation, Dissemination, and Assessment Center.

Kagan, S., & Zahn, G. L. (1975). Field dependence and the school achievement gap between Anglo- and Mexican-American children. *Journal of Educational Psychology, 67,* 643–650.

Kerman, S. et al. (1980). *Teacher expectations and student achievement.* Downey, CA: Office of Los Angeles County Superintendent of Schools.

Krashen, S. (1981). Bilingual education and second language acquisition. In Office of Bilingual Bicultural Education, California State Department of Education, *Schooling and language minority students: A theoretical framework* (pp. 51–70). Los Angeles: California State University, Evaluation, Dissemination, and Assessment Center.

Krashen, S., & Biber, D. (1988). *On course bilingual education success in California.* Sacramento: California Association for Bilingual Education.

Lambert, W. E. (1984). An overview of issues in immersion education. In *Studies in immersion education: A collection for U.S. educators* (pp. 8–30). Sacramento: California State Department of Education.

Lambert, W. E. (1987). The effects of bilingual and bicultural experiences on children's attitudes and social perspectives. In P. Homel, M. Palij, & D. Aaronson (Eds.), *Childhood bilingualism: Aspects of linguistic, cognitive and social development* (pp. 197–221). Hillsdale, NJ: Lawrence Erlbaum.

Legaretta, D. (1979). The effects of program models on language acquisition by Spanish-speaking children. *TESOL Quarterly, 8*, 521–534.

Legaretta, D. (1981). Effective use of the primary language in the classroom. In Office of Bilingual Bicultural Education, California State Department of Education, *Schooling and language minority students: A theoretical framework* (pp. 83–116). Los Angeles: California State University, Evaluation, Dissemination, and Assessment Center.

Lerner, B. (1981). The minimum competence testing movement: Social, scientific, and legal implications. *American Psychologist, 27*, 1057–1066.

Lindholm, K. J. (1987). *Directory of bilingual immersion programs* (Monograph No. 8). Los Angeles: University of California, Center for Language Education and Research.

Lindholm, K. J. (1988). *Edison Elementary School Bilingual Immersion Program: Student progress after one year of implementation* (Technical report no. 9). Los Angeles: University of California, Center for Language Education and Research.

Long, M. H. (1980). *Input, interaction, and second language acquisition.* Unpublished Ph.D. dissertation, University of California, Los Angeles.

Long, M. H. (1983). Native speaker/non-native speaker conversation in the second language classroom. In M. Clarke & J. Handscombe (Eds.), *On TESOL 82: Pacific perspectives on language, learning and teaching* (pp. 207–225). Washington, DC: TESOL.

Long, M. H., & Porter, P. A. (1985). Group work, interlanguage talk, and second language acquisition. *TESOL Quarterly, 19*, 207–228.

Met, M. (1987). *Parent involvement in foreign language learning.* Unpublished manuscript, Montgomery County Public Schools, Rockville, MD.

National Assessment for Educational Progress. (1982). *Students from homes in which English is not the dominant language: Who are they and how well do they read.* Denver: Education Commission of the States.

National Commission on Excellence in Education. (1983). *A nation at risk: The imperative for educational reform.* Washington, DC: U.S. Department of Education.

President's Commission on Foreign Language and International Studies. (1979). *Strength through wisdom: A critique of U.S. capability.* Washington, DC: Government Printing Office.

Saville-Troike, M. (1987). Bilingual discourse: The negotiation of meaning without a common code. *Linguistics, 25*, 81–106.

Secada, W. G. (1987). This is 1987, not 1980: A comment on a comment. *Review of Educational Research, 57*(3), 377–384.

Skuttnabb-Kangas, T. (1981). Bilingualism or not: The education of minorities. *Multilingual Matters, 7*, 121–135.

Swain, M. (1983). Bilingualism without tears. In M. A. Clarke & J. Handscombe (Eds.), *On TESOL '82: Pacific perspectives on language learning and teaching* (pp. 35–46). Washington, DC: TESOL.

Swain, M. (1984). A review of immersion education in Canada: Research and evaluation studies. In *Studies on immersion education: A collection for United States educators* (pp. 87–112). Sacramento: California State Department of Education.

Swain, M. (1985). Communicative competence: Some roles of comprehensible input and comprehensible output in its development. In S. M. Gass & C. G. Madden (Eds.), *Input in second language acquisition* (pp. 235–253). Rowley, MA: Newbury House.

Swain, M. (1987). *The case for focussed input: Contrived but authentic—Or, how content teaching needs to be manipulated and complemented to maximize second language learning.* Plenary paper presented at TESOL 1987 Conference, Vancouver, BC.

Swain, M., & Lapkin, S. (1985). *Evaluating bilingual education: A Canadian case study.* Avon, England: Multilingual Matters.

Tizard, J., Schofield, W. N., & Hewison, J. (1982). Collaboration between teachers and parents in assisting children's reading. *British Journal of Educational Psychology, 52*, 1–15.

Troike, R. C. (1978). Research evidence for the effectiveness of bilingual education. *NABE Journal, 3*, 13–24.

Troike, R. C. (1986). *Improving conditions for success in bilingual education programs.* Washington, DC: U.S. House of Representatives, Committee on Education and Labor.

U.S. Department of Education. (1987). *Japanese education today* (Vol. 1). Washington, DC: Government Printing Office.

U.S. General Accounting Office. (1987). *Bilingual education: A new look at the research evidence.* Washington, DC: Program Evaluation and Methodology Division.

Willig, A. (1985). A meta-analysis of selected studies on the effectiveness of bilingual education. *Review of Educational Research, 55*, 269–317.

Willig, A. C. (1987). Examining bilingual education research through meta-analysis and narrative review: A response to Baker. *Review of Educational Research, 57*(3), 363–376.

Wong Fillmore, L. (1983). The language learner as individual: Implications of research on individual differences for the ESL teacher. In M. A. Clarke & J. Handscombe (Eds.), *On TESOL '82: Pacific perspectives on language learning and teaching* (pp. 157–171). Washington, DC: TESOL.

7

Development of a Bilingual Education Plan

CONCEPCIÓN M. VALADEZ
CLEMENTINA PATIÑO GREGOIRE

In the 1960s, a growing recognition emerged that the public schools were particularly ineffective for large numbers of language minority students, and that new ways of offering educational services for these groups were needed. This recognition culminated with the Bilingual Education Act of 1968, which was an amendment to the Elementary and Secondary Education Act of 1965 (see Malakoff & Hakuta, this volume). This act was to be the vehicle for federal participation in promoting bilingual education. Subsequently, in 1974, the Supreme Court decision *Lau vs. Nichols* was interpreted in a way that mandated compensatory bilingual education programs that would facilitate the integration of non-English and limited-English-speaking students into the regular curriculum in the nation's schools. This legislation and Supreme Court ruling provided the bases for a continuing focus on language minority students.

In the last few years, the increased number of immigrants has magnified the discussion over bilingualism and bilingual-bicultural education. The current "English-only movement" sweeping the country has also contributed to the close attention given to these alternative educational approaches. Nevertheless, the ever-increasing proportion of cultural and linguistic diversity among our students necessitates the redevelopment of an innovative educational strategy for these special populations.

In determining the efficacy of bilingual education programs, researchers must determine the characteristics of implementation (including school climate and administrative leadership) that contribute to the effectiveness of these instructional programs. Gregoire (1985) indicated that evaluation research must focus on the specific implementation strategies and a variety of contextual components that compose the program.

Further, research has also demonstrated that bilingual education is not a uniform, undifferentiated whole, and that the *process* of instruction contributes to student participation, which ultimately becomes reflected in student achievement (Gregoire, 1985). An ecological model of contextual inputs and outcomes, therefore, has been proposed (see Sarason, 1971). This model suggests that bilingual-bicultural program outcomes cannot be separated from the sociocultural contexts in which they operate. That is, bilingual education may be the result of a constellation of contextual variables rather than independent variables in their own right. The particular combination of people in a school setting, including administrative and school-site leadership, and the circumstances that surround them, create situation-specific demands that produce interactional differences between one teaching-learning situation and another (Valadez, 1986).

PURPOSE

This study examines the curriculum, broadly defined, of a school district and traces the way the school district has responded to changing curriculum needs during the past 10 to 15 years, as the number of language minority students increased and legislation to address the educational needs of these students has been mandated. The study focuses on key junctures where decisions were made on instructional goals, staff development, teaching materials, and evaluation methods. Hence, a major focus of this study is on the "process" of instruction.

SIGNIFICANCE OF THE STUDY

This inquiry into curriculum design models in bilingual education provides information that is important for understanding the participation of limited-English-proficient (LEP) students in the instructional process. We know of schools that are effectively serving language minority students and we know of others where the administration and teaching staff feel over-whelmed by the educational needs of these students.

Educational research has yielded a literature on effective schools, with useful lists of features to look for (see Purkey & Smith, 1983). The present study is unique in that it focuses on the process of *how an effective school district got there*. The study of curriculum design models must address the *process* as well as the *content* involved. We expect this study to raise aware-ness of the various ways in which competent student participation and achievement is accomplished. Hence, this report provides a basis for policy decisions regarding instruction, teacher training, and curriculum develop-ment. Additionally, this study may serve as a reference for those interested in the dynamics of the process of an effective change strategy in meeting partic-ular instructional goals.

RATIONALE

Most educators, government officials, parents, and community members would agree that the goal of educational programs is to promote students' highest possible development of language, academic, and social skills neces-sary to participate fully in all aspects of life. For language minority students, additional goals include (a) high levels of English language proficiency, (b) normal cognitive and academic achievement, (c) adequate psychosocial and cultural adjustment, and (d) sufficient levels of primary language develop-ment to promote normal school progress (California State Department of Education, 1981). Bilingual curriculum design models, as well as properly designed and adequately implemented bilingual education programs, are means to achieve such goals.

Principles of curriculum design for language minority students and cultur-ally diverse populations should focus on determining those educational expe-riences that are likely to attain the goals stipulated above; the effective orga-nization of these experiences, including methodology, instructional person-nel, support material, and implementation strategies; and, finally, the determi-nation of goal achievement.

RESEARCH OBJECTIVE

The goal of this research was to identify and examine the development of curricular design models that are particularly successful with the academic achievement of children who begin with little or no English proficiency. In particular, we wished to trace the way the selected school district has responded to curricular needs during the past 10-year period. Our emphasis is on the development of a prototype curriculum that is responsive to the goals discussed earlier and that can be used by curriculum specialists in this field.

METHODOLOGY

This study uses the framework of curriculum theory in its design. Data presented are exploratory and descriptive in nature. Data collection methods included questionnaires, observation (simple and participatory), document review, and interviews.

Site and Subject Selection

The collaborating district was chosen from those that met the following criteria:

(1) The proportion of language minority student population was to be at least 40% of the total district enrollment.
(2) The district was to have achieved some measure of recognition for effective educational services to students who begin school with limited or no English proficiency.
(3) The district was to have had bilingual education in place for at least 10 years.
(4) The district was to be interested in collaborating on this particular study.

One eligible district in Southern California (the ABC School District) was identified and the researchers entered into a collaborative agreement with that district regarding the study. District-level officials offered to facilitate access to classrooms, materials, documents, and personnel. Researchers, in turn, were to submit to the district any of the reports resulting from the study. In consultation with district-level officials, the individuals to interview were selected from the following list of personnel categories: principals, vice principals, teachers, resource personnel, and district-level administrators.

EDUCATIONAL PROGRAMS AT ABC

The following section summarizes information obtained from the interviews and review of the documents provided by district personnel.

Historical Perspective of District

Respondents were asked to relate a historical perspective on the district by providing a description of the area at the time the district was formed and how it had changed to its current description. They were asked to specifically comment on changes of the school population over the last 15 to 20 years.

The ABC Unified School District was formed in July 1965, when citizens voted to unify three elementary school districts (Artesia, Bloomfield, and Carmenita) and a portion of the Excelsior Union High School District. The district serves the cities of Artesia, Cerritos, and Hawaiian Gardens, portions of Lakewood and Norwalk, and parts of Long Beach. These are communities located within a 30-mile radius southeast of downtown Los Angeles.

Currently, the district has 22,000 kindergarten through twelfth-grade students enrolled in its 29 schools. An additional 6,000 students take classes at the ABC Adult School. The district employs approximately 2,100 staff members.

Twenty years ago, the largest minority group was Hispanic, with about 15% Hispanic students. Since then, both Hispanic and Asian students have continued to enter the district, with the Asian group growing at a faster rate. In 1987, both groups reached approximately the same level of representation in the district with about 26% each. The number of Black students had also increased although not in the same proportion as Hispanic and Asian students. The Hispanic population has begun to stabilize during the last 10 years. The dramatic growth of the district's student population as a whole, during the past 20 years, has resulted in many schools being built during this period.

When the ABC School District was formed, the northern part of the district was composed of middle-class, upwardly mobile people, whose children were academically inclined to succeed in school, as reported by José Ronquillo, Assistant Principal at Furgeson Elementary School. The southern end of the district, on the other hand, consisted of lower-working-class families, whose children often encountered difficulty in school. Teachers describe the focal difference between the students from the north and the south in terms of students' oral English language development. During the past 20 years, the district's population has grown but the factors that differentiated the district's population in the north and the south have become more accentuated.

District's Current Position on Bilingual/Bicultural Education

The review of documents obtained from the district offices indicates the commitment of the district to the philosophy that educational programs meet the individual needs of the students to be served. This goal is accomplished through the implementation of bilingual instructional alternatives to meet the diversified linguistic needs of students at the earliest possible date. These alternatives provide students and parents with program options that (a) facilitate mastery of English language skills, (b) allow for the development of pride in both the student's cultural heritage and the majority culture, (c) contribute to an improved self-image, and (d) facilitate academic skill development in the language best known to the student.

The board of education defines "bilingual education" as a process that uses a student's primary language and culture as the principal avenue for instruction while at the same time systematically teaching a second language. The board of education is, therefore, in agreement with the basic goals of federal- and state-legislated bilingual-bicultural education. Further, the board has expressed a commitment to bilingual education (in concept and practice) and to the allocation of available district, state, and federal funds for the development, implementation, and maintenance of bilingual instructional alternatives.

Master Plan for Bilingual Education

In 1979, the ABC School District developed a Master Plan for Bilingual Education. A group of community leaders, parents, administrators, and teachers worked together on a long-range, five-year plan. They looked at their existing needs and projected additional future needs. As stated above, this master plan was developed proactively, using the form of the "*Lau* Plan." They chose to use that model to document what they were already doing and to define what else needed to be done in the future. The district's Master Plan for Bilingual Education consists of the following components: (a) administration, (b) student language identification, (c) curriculum, (d) staff development, (e) community relations, (f) counseling and guidance, and (g) evaluation.

Administration. Administrative functions in support of educational services for LEP students include revising district policies and regulations; the employment and assignment of bilingual cross-cultural certificated and classified personnel; the proper allocation and budgeting of general, federal, and state funds; and the providing of direction and assistance in school-level educational plan development, program implementation, and evaluation. Specifically, it is the function of all levels of administrative management to ensure that the latest techniques of operational tasks be employed. The district's administrative philosophy is that no single department or functional level is completely independent in the development or implementation of programs, for it is the smooth functioning of the whole with interfacing parts that makes an organization totally skillful in carrying out operational tasks with measurable and successful results.

A system to monitor and review assists in this process at the ABC School District. To this end, the goals of the administrative component are as follows: (a) to identify and implement district educational policies that support the educational needs of LEP students; (b) to recruit, employ, and place staff that is linguistically and culturally knowledgeable to meet the educational needs of all students; and (c) to integrate educational programs designed for LEP students into the overall district educational program.

Student language identification. The goals of the student language identification component of the district's master plan are to establish and implement districtwide procedures for determining students' home language and to diagnose the English oral language proficiency of each student whose home language is other than English. The home language of all new enrollees is determined using the state-approved Home Language Survey forms.

The Language Proficiency Survey procedures are as follows: Upon student enrollment, parents complete the Home Language Survey. Within 30 days, students whose home language is other than English are tested by an ESL aide or bilingual teacher trained to administer the Language Assessment Scales (LAS) at the school site. The results of the Home Language Surveys and LAS are filed in the student's cumulative folder, which contains the student's academic material. If the student was identified as a limited-English-proficient student (LEP), the student is enrolled in bilingual classes or in an ESL program.

Curriculum. The ABC Unified School District's Master Plan for Bilingual Education describes programs for LEP students that meet their cognitive, affective, and linguistic needs. Bilingual education follows a regular course of study planned for all students in the district rather than being based on an isolated set of objectives. However, additional curricular innovations have been developed to better meet the LEP student's educational and affective needs.

The curriculum goals for the LEP students parallel the goals established for all students in the district. But an additional goal for LEP students is to offer bilingual instructional alternatives that meet the linguistic, cognitive, and affective needs of students with different language and cultural orientations, in order to permit them to

(1) develop English language skills to ensure effective participation in the English-speaking social, academic, and career environments;

(2) build language skills on a firm foundation, which includes a positive self-concept in the environments of the language and culture associated with each language;

(3) preserve and strengthen their self-image and sense of dignity through appropriate and meaningful instructional programs;

(4) utilize their primary language as a medium of learning in order to avoid premature experiences with the second language that could be detrimental to their academic progress;

(5) develop communication skills in two languages, one of which is English;

(6) develop incentives to remain in school, to succeed, and to prepare for future undertakings; and

(7) acquire the academic tools to pursue postsecondary education.

In articulating the above goals, a number of bilingual instructional alternatives are developed, which include (a) elementary bilingual/bicultural program; (b) elementary bilingual magnet program; (c) elementary bilingual individual learning program; (d) secondary bilingual/bicultural program; (e) secondary bilingual core program; (f) secondary bilingual individual learning program; (g) bilingual/bicultural preschool program; (h) bilingual MGM program; and (i) bilingual magnet program for LEP students with exceptional needs. Finally, within this connection, a goal of the district is the comprehensive assessment of language and academic achievement of students participating in any of the bilingual instructional alternatives.

Staff development. The ABC School District, in keeping with its philosophy to provide quality education to its students, provides in-service to personnel to meet the academic, linguistic, and cultural needs of the LEP students. The objective of the district's staff development is that of providing these students with the best possible education to meet their needs. The philosophy of the district relevant to staff development is analogous to its philosophy for ensuring educational excellence for its students. That is, it consists of matching educational programs for students with comparable training for certified and noncertified staff members.

The staff development component of the Master Plan for Bilingual Education includes the following long-range goal: to provide in-service to instructional and support staff to develop competencies required to meet the educational needs of the LEP students. Annually, a district staff development master calendar is developed to include a variety of activities to provide an ongoing in-service program for all staff. All in-service is systematically evaluated, and planning is on a continuous basis.

The thrust of staff development is to ensure that all staff members, aides, administrators, and classified staff have the opportunity to develop as proficient and effective members of an instructional and administrative team. The needs of the students are paramount, but continuing opportunities for career development and professional growth for the staff are also considered important.

Community relations. The community relations component of this plan is committed to encouraging the ongoing involvement of the community in the educational process and, more specifically, the parents of those students whose primary language is other than English. The district's community relations component includes the following goal statements: (a) to encourage the active participation of parents and other community members in the process of planning, implementing, and evaluating the instructional program, and (b) to continuously improve communication between home and school, and particularly with parents whose primary language is other than English.

Counseling and guidance. To meet the counseling and guidance needs of students, the district incorporates existing services as the basis for ongoing assessment and evaluation of LEP students. Pupil personnel staff assist students to grow emotionally, socially, academically, and vocationally by teaching them to solve problems in these areas.

The guidance and counseling component includes the following goal statements: (a) to provide a pupil personnel staff that has linguistic competence, cultural awareness, and positive attitude toward all students and their families, and (b) to provide counseling and guidance programs that promote a positive self-concept and ensure optimal learning, achievement, and motivation.

Evaluation. The district's philosophy is that all components be assessed and evaluated individually and as a whole for successful interfacing of the components of the system that constitutes the Master Plan for Bilingual Education. The overall goal of the evaluation component is to develop a comprehensive plan for evaluation including testing, acquisition/development of instrumentation, and a systematic evaluation of each component: administration, curriculum, staff development, community relations, and counseling and guidance.

In this scheme of things, their evaluation component must tell the system where it is in terms of reaching the goals and objectives, why it has or has not reached the criteria set forth, the reasons why the successes or failures are present, and what the data contain to substantiate the preceding. Hence, their evaluation task is to communicate to all concerned in the process how the system is performing and at what level of proficiency.

Responding to the Changing School Population

In its early years, teachers indicated that they individually responded to students' needs, particularly in the area of oral English language development, on a trial and error basis. That is, techniques that appeared to be fruitful in terms of student achievement were repeatedly implemented, with necessary modifications and improvements.

A difficulty that emerged in the early 1970s was that, in an effort to work efficiently with students having similar problems, students were set apart in groups with different teachers in different classrooms. This procedure was quickly identified as segregationist, and teachers had to find the way to eliminate this problem while at the same time serve the needs of language minority students. It occurred to teachers that fluent English-speaking students could be used as models for the limited-English-speaking students, and they proceeded to arrange their groups in this manner.

In the 1970s, the district made the decision to address not only their basic programs but also preschool programs, bilingual special education, and the need for a bilingual gifted and talented education (GATE) program. Since 1979, many of these programs have been implemented. The district, in 1987, had a Korean bilingual program in two schools and a Chinese bilingual program in one school in addition to Spanish and Portugese programs.

Hence, the district responded to the changing school population by instituting a variety of programs to serve the language minority students. Elementary programs included (a) preschool programs, (b) bilingual/bicultural programs, (c) magnet programs, and (d) diverse language programs. (These are at the elementary level, where teachers conduct English as a second language (ESL) classes and provide a sheltered environment for all LEP students in kindergarten. Students are provided with a monolingual teacher because there are diverse languages spoken.) Secondary programs included (a) a Portuguese and Spanish junior high school and (b) diverse language programs.

Effects of Federal and State Legislation

Several federal and state statutes had been enacted during the period in question. Respondents were asked to comment on the effects of the legislation on their educational programs.

Emergency School Aid Act. A salient turning point identified by one elementary school principal was the passage of the Emergency School Aid Act (ESAA) of 1970. Under the provisions of this legislation, a school district was able to apply for grants to institute programs to deal with diverse student populations. This act had many facets but its main goal was curbing low student achievement and student dropout.

In 1972, the district applied for funding under this grant. During this time, the alternative school movement was very strong, and the district was able to link the serving of the needs of language minority students with the alternative school concept. Although funding under this act subsequently ran out, the effects of the programs were lasting because people involved in these programs had developed the perspective that was conducive to effectively dealing with the language minority population.

Title VII. State statutes, such as Title VII, directing educational policy and programs for language minority students, have been very helpful. The state statutes, by virtue of having a concrete staffing requirement, have been of particular assistance. The staffing requirements provided the impetus to hire bilingual teachers, and the state statutes provided the guidelines for an organized program, including specific guidelines for identification, reclassification, and program requirements.

Seeking Assistance for New Instructional Needs

With new demands on their instructional services, where did the district look for trained personnel and staff development assistance?

In 1972, when the Spanish bilingual program began at ABC, there were only two certified bilingual teachers in the district; the rest of the teachers were on "waiver." The program had classroom settings with bilingual aides and monolingual teachers. In 1987, they had 80 certified Spanish bilingual teachers. In 15 years, this number increased dramatically. This increase was attributed to very aggressive recruitment and proactive approaches such as the development of the New Careers in Education Program (funded by the State of California).

New Careers in Education Program and aggressive recruiting. The New Careers in Education Program allowed the district to train bilingual teachers.

It consisted of taking students at the junior level at the neighboring California State University, Long Beach, and putting them into an internship program in ABC schools as paid assistants. Through this program, the district trained 20 bilingual teachers. However, in addition to this program, the district has aggressively recruited bilingual teachers and the district's reputation has attracted new teachers as well.

Staff development. Staff development was reported to be a very important part of ABC's program. Teachers normally have preservice staff development sessions at the beginning of the year to which all bilingual and monolingual teachers who are taking responsibility for conducting ESL classes for LEP students are invited. This preservice serves as a "kickoff" where new curricula are presented.

The district also has a team of bilingual resource teachers who are available to go to the schools and conduct demonstration lessons in the classroom. However, prior to presenting these demonstration lessons, resource teachers present content. ABC believes in Joyce's model (Joyce, Hersh, & McKibbin, 1983) of staff development, where there is follow-up after the presentation of content (also see Joyce & Showers, 1980, 1982).

Initially, staff development took the form of big workshops where teachers simply attended and listened. They then moved toward providing workshops for smaller numbers of people so there would be more interaction with one another and follow-up coaching. In essence, they were "miniconferences" in which teachers had the choice of attending different workshops. Many of the workshops were conducted by district teachers, and they evolved to help keep teachers from "burning out." Weekend retreats were another form of staff development practiced at ABC.

An additional form of staff development was the district's involvement in the development of the master's program. Thirty of the district's teachers went through this program in which California State University, Los Angeles, provided a Master of Arts Program at "satellite" district sites.

As a result of this program, teachers completed projects that have been a real benefit to the district. For example, three teachers developed a series of lessons that bring Spanish literature into the classroom. In addition, a literature guide in Spanish was developed and is continually being expanded. Hence, the district is moving beyond the home problems and providing leadership in the general education curriculum. Many other projects that have come out of the Master of Arts Program have also served for staff development.

District response to instructional materials needs. In terms of materials, teachers have developed criterion-referenced tests that cover the area of reading, language, and writing skills. Additionally, Korean and Chinese criterion-referenced tests have also been developed as well as social studies and science units.

Contributions from abroad. When the demand for teachers trained in languages appeared, the ABC School District went for help not only to local universities with teacher-training programs in bilingual education and ESL instruction but also to the Department of Education in Mexico (Secretaría de Educación Pública). Selected teachers attended summer classes in Mexico City at the Mexican Department of Education training center, where they were instructed in methods of teaching reading, mathematics, and social studies. Although the "trainer of trainers approach" was implemented using local staff who had previously been trained, the district also brought a group of Mexican trainers to their district to provide staff development for their teachers firsthand.

In sum, ABC went for help to its county Office of Education, the local state universities, the state Department of Education, and language scholars. They went out of the country, to Mexico, and they also found valuable resources among their own ranks.

District/Community Relationships

The question asked was whether the new developments in school programs had resulted in changes in the interactions between the schools and the community. In the early 1970s, the relationship with the community was not good. In 1970, a lawsuit concerning affirmative action was filed against the district. As a result, the district began to be more aggressive in recruitment of minorities and in developing an affirmative action plan and attempting to implement it. Hence, the district/community relationship has greatly improved.

Several advisory committees have been formed pertaining to issues relevant to Korean, Chinese, Portuguese, and Spanish-speaking populations. In addition, another committee pulls the chairs of all the separate committees together and provides in-service for parents as well as parent conferences. In addition, the district works with the University of California, Irvine, Cerritos College, and the California Assessment Program to form partnerships for parent conferences.

The diversity of instructional programs can be a source of concern with some parents. Sometimes this initially occurs with parents who do not understand the programs. In response, the district offers frequent meetings with parents both to answer questions and to build a trusting relationship with the community.

Staff Morale

The respondents were asked if the changes in population and resulting programs had affected the morale of the teaching staff. Initially, there seems to have been a great deal of dissension in terms of the innovative techniques that some teachers were implementing in an effort to deal with the instruction for the language minority population. Teachers recall that staffs were divided between teachers who had the students' interests uppermost in their minds and those who were reacting on a purely emotional level and resisting any change effort.

The margin between the two "camps" slowly began to narrow as those teachers who were philosophically in disagreement with innovative teaching practices, including what is now known as bilingual education and English as a second language instruction, began to leave the district.

In 1980, the California State Bilingual Education Office was seeking schools to participate in what was to become known as the bilingual "Case Studies Project." A computer search identified Furgeson Elementary along with 133 other schools that met the necessary criteria: (a) K–6 programs, (b) large concentrations of LEP children whose native language was Spanish, and (c) a "core group of certified bilingual teachers." Of the 30 schools that expressed interest, five were selected for the project in late 1981, including Furgeson Elementary School in this school district.

Although Furgeson staff was trying hard to make bilingual education work, their students' test scores were among the lowest in California. With the school's increase in LEP enrollments averaging 46% over the previous four years, its situation was rapidly getting worse.

For ABC, therefore, a key turning point was the selection of Furgeson Elementary to participate in the "Case Studies Project." "Teaming" was mandatory, which was not a popular idea at the outset, according to teachers and administrators. Under the new approach, a team typically made up of two bilingual teachers and one monolingual, English-speaking teacher consulted on the needs of each student, assigned children to various classes, and followed their progress. The collegial approach, along with growing indications of student progress, had a healthy effect on staff morale, according to one bilingual resource teacher at Furgeson.

A major benefit of the "Case Studies Project" was that it gave teachers a real mission—a vision of what it was they were trying to do. Teachers indicated that it really brought the staffs together. And by exposing the monolingual teachers to ESL techniques, the team approach helped them to understand what the children go through in the process of acquiring English and to develop empathy for these students.

The Outcomes

The benefits for ABC have been both affective and academic. According to one observer, students feel a lot better about themselves, feel that their language has some status and value, and feel that they represent a culture that is respected and has a place, that it is no longer something to be embarrassed about. Academically, test results have revealed substantial progress.

ABC is also learning about the cognitive development of children and how they can become better learners. They are making sure that students do not lose out on content acquisition in a sheltered English environment. Another benefit beyond language, cited by both teachers and administrators, is the conscious awareness on the part of teachers of the rationale buttressing bilingual education methodologies that they employ in their classrooms. This awareness increases teacher morale. Additionally, as a result of teacher involvement through staff development required for the implementation of the bilingual program, teacher isolation is less prevalent.

DISCUSSION AND CONCLUSIONS

One of the foci of this investigation was the identification of key junctures or turning points in the evolution of the ABC School District as it related to the education of language minority students. All subjects interviewed, including district and school-site administrators as well as classroom teachers, identified very similar events. Prominent among pivot points identified were *people and philosophies*. People in power base positions had the linguistic minority students' interests uppermost in their minds as well as the vision that an internal process and structure were needed to support and sustain the change effort. It was with this proactive philosophy that the district began to address the needs of this student population long before it was mandated by law.

The extent of this school district's openness to change encouraged teachers and administrators to candidly assess their own situation and to develop common understandings and mutual supports, which would increase willingness to take risks. While the district availed itself of "outside" assistance, they appeared to realize early on that their success was going to be due to their own efforts and abilities. District and school-site administrators began to encourage and implement behaviors conducive to responsible receptivity to change.

Among these behaviors were dialogue and interaction, which was continuing, pervasive, and substantive—a process referred to as "process orientation" that sought to promote instructional participation and leadership. Decision making at every level was based on staff involvement and participation, consideration of alternatives, weighing of evidence, and decisions made from alternatives discussed. Decisions were put into action, and actions were subsequently evaluated.

This type of proactive leadership encouraged interschool communications and dialogue, which prompted recognition and use of resources in sharing problems and solutions. This type of open communication not only brought teachers out of isolation but was the channel through which receptivity could be fostered and implemented. In this way, the peer group was strengthened by an increased communication among staff that was motivated toward finding more effective ways to share resources in solving common problems.

ABC's receptivity to change was conducive to (a) cooperative teaching arrangements, (b) more friendship networks among teachers, (c) more task-oriented communication networks among teachers, (d) teacher leadership and influence in decision making, (e) effective administrative leadership, and (f) a favorable school climate.

Basic Features of a Curriculum Design Model

What emerges from this discussion are basic features of a curriculum design model that meet the needs of language minority student populations. Although there is no single source of information that is completely adequate to provide a basis for wise and comprehensive decisions about the objectives of a district or school, it is evident that the observed curriculum at the ABC School District has given consideration to three crucial audiences: the student, the school, and the community.

The student. In considering the learner as a target of educational objectives, this district sought to identify needed changes in behavior patterns of the LEP student population that the district, through the school, would seek to produce. In studying its linguistically different student population, this district has been able to identify student needs and educational objectives for this group by determining students' language dominance, cultural customs and traditions, family structure, economic status, and school experiences. This information about the learner is compared with a desirable standard, so that the difference between the present condition of the learner and the acceptable norm can be identified. This difference, or gap, constitutes student needs.

The school. Interacting with the perception of student needs, obviously, is the basic educational philosophy of the district, including its policy position on bilingual education, its expectations for student achievement, and its posture vis à vis national, state, and local mandates. How the policies are implemented is the manifestation of the stated policies.

The community. Because the community is complex and continually changing, it is necessary to focus attention on this area as a source of educational objectives so that students learn what is relevant. Analyses made of the community by this school district have revealed important information as it related to language usage as well as other important external variables that suggested meaningful educational objectives for the LEP student population.

The curriculum design model that emerged as a result of the interplay and synergistic relationship of these three influences is an eclectic one, that is, one built out of the strengths and deficits of the three factions included in this model. In taking account of these three different perspectives, the district places itself in a unique position to be able to identify four fundamental questions. The first is a philosophical question that asks what educational *goals* their schools should seek to attain. The second is a curricular question of what educational *experiences* can be provided that are likely to attain these goals. The third is one of methodology, which asks how these educational experiences can be effectively *organized*. Finally, the fourth question is one of *evaluation*, asking how they can determine whether these goals are being attained (Tyler, 1949).

One of the goals of this investigation was to study the "process" of a school district that has been nationally recognized as being particularly successful with the academic achievement of children who begin school with limited or no English proficiency. Findings revealed that the ABC School District has followed a systematic process in dealing with a changing student population. In doing so, it adopted a way of thinking, an outlook, and an organized plan to ensure more effective student learning and to ensure that student learning was maximized.

Its curriculum consists of a planned, composite effort to guide student learning toward predestined learning outcomes. It focuses on the synergistic relationship among the learner, the school, and the community, and attempts to integrate the respective goals. On the basis of the integration of these goals, teachers and school-site and district administrators present options to their board of education, and together they orchestrate their curriculum effort.

It is evident from the findings that ABC's curriculum is not fixed; it is not final. Rather, it is continually searching for better goals and better procedures. Its curriculum is not static or fragmented but dynamic and holistic.

CONCLUSIONS

The assumptions about the nature of effective change strategies that appear to be operating at the ABC School District as revealed by structured interviews with administrators and teachers emanate from the school culture model, which assumes that changing schools require changing people, changing school organization and norms, in essence, a changing school culture.

Some of these assumptions include, but are not limited to, the following:

(1) Changes will not take place without the support and commitment of teachers who must adopt the change effort as their "own."

(2) Thus consensus around specific goals among teachers and staff is more powerful than overt control, although leadership is not ignored.

(3) Change strategy requires collaborative planning, collegial work, and an atmosphere conducive to experimentation and evaluation.

(4) Successful change efforts are more likely to be realized when the entire school culture is affected and involved.

(5) Leadership from the principal and administrative staff is crucial.

(6) Sensitivity to the importance of time in the change process is crucial.

Clearly, this school district uses an ecological approach in implementing its change strategy. This ecological approach suggests that all individuals in the school setting are viewed as elements of interaction. Hence, the life of a school is a continual interaction of structure, culture, and personalities. Changes in one area require changes in others, and stress can arise when changes occurring in one area are met by resistance to change in another.

Thus it would appear that, in planning changes or improvements of any kind, the ABC School District pays close attention to the requisite alterations in social structure, culture, and personal adjustments of the individuals concerned.

It is within this framework that effective changes and improvements have taken place in this district. This intervention strategy appears to have proven successful, because, in addition to focusing on goals and instructional procedures, it has devoted attention to major variables making up the character of schools.

This school district has put in place a process by which teachers and administrators think together, plan together, decide together, and act together in dealing with the problems inherent in the daily workings of their schools. That is, they have implemented an internal process and structure to support and sustain an effective change strategy.

Behaviors that make up this process include the following:

(1) *dialogue*: interaction—continuing, pervasive, substantive;
(2) *decision making*: based on staff involvement, consideration of alternatives, weighing of evidence, and ultimately selection made from among alternatives;
(3) *action*: implementation of decisions; and
(4) *evaluation*: staff's assessment of its own process.

This is the set of behaviors by which staffs at the ABC School District carry out the business of the school. It is the process by which they consider change or reject it.

A socialization process appears to have occurred that was conducive to maintaining openness to change in schools' staffs. This process included the development of common understandings and mutual supports, which appears to have increased individuals' willingness to take risks and recognize that failure in one attempt did not mean permanent disaster; the recognition that their success was due to their own efforts and abilities and not to outside expertise; openness to possibilities for change; and willingness to assess their own situation candidly.

Hence, it would appear that administrators and teachers in this school district recognize that they already possess enough resources and access to other resources to take care of a great part of the assistance and intellectual stimulation needed in order to make changes. Additionally, there appears to be sufficient interschool communications, which encourages recognition and use of resources in sharing problems and solutions.

It is evident that, through their "process orientation" approach, this district attempts to deal with fragmented fronts in faculties and staffs to the extent that administrators seek consensus of staff councils on how to proceed. But, most important, this district has developed a model for bilingual education programming that is maximally geared toward enhancing the achievement levels of its pupils.

REFERENCES

California State Department of Education. (1981). *Schooling and language minority students: A theoretical framework*. Los Angeles: California State University, Evaluation, Dissemination, and Assessment Center.

Gregoire, C. P. (1985). *Contextual features of bilingual/bicultural Chapter 1 programs yielding maximum and minimum academic results—A study of two programs*. Unpublished doctoral dissertation, University of California, Los Angeles.

Joyce, B., Hersh, R. H., & McKibbin, M. (1983). *The structure of school improvement*. New York: Longman.

Joyce, B., & Showers, B. (1980). Improving inservice training: The messages of research. *Educational Leadership, 37*(5), 379–385.

Joyce, B., & Showers, B. (1982). The coaching of teaching. *Educational Leadership, 40*(1), 4–10.

Purkey, S. C., & Smith, M. S., (1983). Effective schools—A review. *Elementary School Journal, 83*(4), 427–452.

Sarason, S. B. (1971). *The culture of the school and the problem of change* (2nd ed.). Boston: Allyn & Bacon.

Tyler, R. W., (1949). *Basic principles of curriculum and instruction*. Chicago: University of Chicago Press.

Valadez, C. M., (1986) Effective teachers for language minority students, national needs. *Compendium of papers on the topic of bilingual education*, Serial # 99-R (pp. 82–105). Washington, DC: U.S. Govrnment Printing Office.

8

Evaluation of an Elementary School Bilingual Immersion Program

KATHRYN J. LINDHOLM
HALFORD H. FAIRCHILD

Bilingual immersion education combines the most significant features of bilingual education (for language minority students) and immersion education (for language majority students). In typical immersion programs, academic and language arts instruction is provided to students using both languages. For language minority (i.e., non-English-dominant) students, academic instruction is presented through their first language and they receive English language arts and portions of their academic instruction in English. For language majority (i.e., English-dominant) students, academic instruction is through their second language and they receive language arts in both English and the non-English language, and they also may receive academic instruction in English (see Lindholm, this volume).

Bilingual immersion education, therefore, encompasses two key features: (a) The program essentially involves some form of dual language immersion, involving periods of instruction during which only one language is used; and (b) both English-dominant and non-English-dominant speakers are participants (preferably in balanced numbers). These programs, therefore, attempt

AUTHORS' NOTE: This chapter is condensed from a larger report titled *Edison Elementary School's Bilingual Immersion Program: Results after One Year of Program Implementation* (Technical Report No. 9), Center for Language Education and Research, University of California, Los Angeles (Lindholm, 1988).

126

to develop true bilingual academic competence in English and another language on the part of both groups of participating students.

This chapter summarizes the results of a study (see Lindholm, 1988), conducted by the Center for Language Education and Research (CLEAR) at the University of California, Los Angeles, of the bilingual immersion program at Edison Elementary School (a school within the Santa Monica-Malibu Unified School District in California). CLEAR's objective has been to work with Edison School to study and help improve their bilingual immersion program. This purpose was accomplished through student assessment, classroom observation, and professional development activities. The focus of this chapter is on the results of the student assessment.

The goals of the bilingual immersion program were to produce

(1) normal to superior academic achievement in Spanish and English;
(2) the development of proficient bilingual and biliterate skills in English and Spanish;
(3) high levels of self-competence; and
(4) positive cross-cultural attitudes.

The program was designed in concordance with the successful 10-year Spanish/English Bilingual Immersion Program in the San Diego City Schools. The specific instructional approach was developed in consultation with CLEAR, the California State Department of Education, the San Diego City Schools, and the Edison Task Force. Its instructional design was based on a careful review of the literature on successful bilingual and immersion education programs in the United States and Canada, as discussed in Lindholm (1987; also see Lindholm, this volume).

The specific articulation of the bilingual immersion program included four classrooms: two in each of the kindergarten and first-grade levels. In each grade, one class was a bilingual immersion classroom and the other was a non-bilingual immersion classroom. The program was administered by the school principal, with oversight and administrative assistance provided by the school's Title VII Program Specialist.

According to the instructional design, both native English-speaking and native Spanish-speaking kindergarten and first-grade students received 90% of their instructional day in Spanish. One teacher provided the Spanish instruction and used *only* Spanish with the students. For the remaining 10% of the instructional day, teaching was carried out in English by another teacher of the same grade. (For the English instruction, each class would move to the classroom of the English-speaking teacher.) Thus all academic subject matter was taught in Spanish except for English language arts and physical education, which were taught in English.

METHODOLOGY

Student Sample

In the first year, a total of 112 students participated in the bilingual immersion program. Of these 112 students, 58 were kindergartners and 54 were first graders. In the two kindergarten classes, 36 (62%) were native Spanish speakers, 18 (31%) were native English speakers, and 4 (7%) were Spanish/English bilinguals. The two first-grade classes contained 37 (69%) native Spanish-speaking students, 7 (13%) native English-speaking students, and 10 (18%) Spanish/English bilingual students.

Most of the students had attended preschool, with slightly more first graders than kindergartners having gone to preschool. In terms of their language ability, almost all of the English speakers were rated as having more English than Spanish abilities. Of the Spanish-speaking students, approximately 25% were rated as bilingual and the remainder were rated as having more Spanish than English language skills.

A sample of 39 limited-English-proficient (LEP) and English-only (EO) students not enrolled in the bilingual immersion program formed a control group on the English academic achievement test (CTBS-U). This group comprised 20 kindergartners and 19 first graders.

Procedures and Instrumentation

In November and December 1986, CLEAR individually administered the Perceived Competence Scale to all students in their native language. In May 1987, CLEAR individually administered the IDEA Proficiency Test (IPT) to all children in both Spanish and English. All students also participated in regularly scheduled achievement testing, using the Comprehensive Test of Basic Skills (CTBS-U). Students were administered the CTBS-U and the *La Prueba* tests in May and June 1987 by their teachers. In addition, the CTBS-Español test was group-administered in October 1986, and again in May 1987, by the students' teachers. Students were also individually tested on the Bilingual Syntax Measure (BSM) in Spanish and in English in September-October 1986, and again in May-June 1987, by Santa Monica-Malibu Unified School District staff. As with most longitudinal studies, missing data arose because of student attrition or absences on the days of data collection.

Teachers completed the Student Oral Language Observation Matrix (SOLOM) in January 1987. The SOLOM was completed in terms of Spanish proficiency only.

The *Pictorial Scale of Perceived Competence and Social Acceptance for Young Children* (*Perceived Competence Scale*) was a self-report instrument that measured the child's sense of competence across four domains (cognitive, physical, peer, and maternal), where each domain constituted a separate subscale of six items (Harter & Pike, 1983, 1984). Two overlapping versions of this individually administered scale were used, one for kindergartners and one for first and second graders. The cognitive competence domain contained a number of scholastic skills for first graders and rudimentary skills for kindergartners; the social competence subscale assessed the student's relationship with his or her peers; the physical competence subscale focused on competency in sports and outdoor games; and the maternal/child relationship competence domain consisted of particular maternal activities or behaviors that mothers engage in with 4- to 7-year-olds. Each of the 24 items was pictorially represented in a bound booklet of pictures. The child was read a brief statement about each child in the picture. He or she was first asked to pick the child who was most like him or her, and then to indicate, by pointing to the appropriate circle, whether that child was a lot like him or her (the big circle) or just a little like him or her (the smaller circle). Items were scored from 1 (low competence) to 4 (high competence).

RESULTS

Students' Language Competence

SOLOM Ratings. The Student Oral Language Observation Matrix (SOLOM) consisted of teachers' evaluations of students' oral language proficiency in Spanish in five domains. As expected, teachers evaluated the Spanish language ability of the Spanish-dominant children much higher than that of the English-dominant children. This was true in both grade levels. Interestingly, English-dominant children tended to have higher rankings in comprehension and pronunciation than in fluency, vocabulary, or grammar.

Idea Proficiency Test. The Idea Proficiency Test examined students' language proficiency in both English and Spanish. Scores from the IPT were also used to categorize students, in terms of their language proficiency in each language, into one of three groups (nonproficient, limited proficient, and fluent proficient). Thus each student was classified into one of three proficiency groups in both his or her dominant and nondominant languages.

It is not too surprising that students consistently had higher scores in their dominant language. Among the kindergarten students, for example, 73% of the English-dominant and 55% of the Spanish-dominant students were classified into the "fluent proficient" category (for their language of dominance). For the first graders, the corresponding percentages were 100% and 54% (see Lindholm, 1988).

Spanish-dominant students also tended to be more proficient in their second language than English-dominant students in theirs. In the kindergarten, 40% of the English-dominant students, compared with 31% of the Spanish-dominant students, were classified as "nonproficient" in their respective second language. For the first graders, 100% of the English-dominant students, compared with 49% of the Spanish-dominant students, were classified as "nonproficient" in their respective second language.

Academic Achievement in Spanish (La Prueba)

The results from *La Prueba Riverside de Realización en Español* clearly indicated that students performed at average or above average levels (all of the stanine scores were 5 or above, and the percentile ranks were 49 or above). Most noteworthy was the performance of the English-dominant first graders in math, where their score was equivalent to a percentile rank of 83.

In addition, each of the scales in *La Prueba* consisted of several subscales: reading (i.e., comprehension, vocabulary, and word study skills) and mathematics (i.e., computation and problem solving). In concert with the findings for the mean scores from *La Prueba*, students correctly answered over half of the items on each subscale of the test. This level of performance corresponded to an "average" performance on all subscales, according to conversion tables provided by the test developers (see Cole, Trent, & Wadell, 1984).

Analyses were conducted to examine differences between the language groups (Spanish versus English) on each of the three total scores. On each measure, and for both grade levels, there were no significant differences between the Spanish and English speakers at either the kindergarten or first-grade levels. (See Lindholm, 1988, for details.)

Language Proficiency and Academic Achievement Gains

In order to ascertain gains in language proficiency and academic achievement for the bilingual immersion students, pre- and posttests were obtained on the Bilingual Syntax Measure and the CTBS-Español. Also, comparison data were available on the CTBS-U from a control group of students who were not enrolled in the bilingual immersion program.

Bilingual Syntax Measure. The Bilingual Syntax Measure (BSM) assessed oral mastery in both Spanish and English. Although students showed increases from the pretest to the posttest in both English and Spanish, the only significant increases occurred for (a) Spanish-dominant kindergartners in Spanish proficiency, (2) Spanish-dominant kindergartners in English proficiency, and (3) Spanish-dominant first graders in English proficiency. Although Spanish-dominant and English-dominant children tended to have higher scores in their language of dominance, the largest gains in language proficiency occurred for English-dominant students in Spanish proficiency, and for Spanish-dominant students in English proficiency. In sum, none of the students experienced a loss in native language skills and most of the students experienced some gains in second-language skills.

CTBS-Español (First Graders). The CTBS-Español assessed academic achievement in a Spanish language instrument. Pre- and posttest data were collected for the first graders participating in the bilingual immersion program.

According to the percentile rankings at the pretest and the posttest, students made considerable gains in reading and mathematics. Among the English-dominant students, rankings in reading ranged from 24 to 71 at the pretest, but from 63 to 76 at the posttest. Thus the students were performing above average at the posttesting. In mathematics, their achievement gains were even more dramatic. Pretest rankings in mathematics ranged from 24 to 65, whereas posttest rankings ranged from 91 to 94. Grade equivalencies also demonstrated the fact that students began the program at or below grade level, but finished the program at or above grade level.

Among the Spanish-dominant students, equally impressive results were obtained in mathematics, although the reading percentile rank and stanine scores tended to decline from the pretest to the posttest. Grade equivalencies showed the students performed above grade level in both math and reading at the posttest.

These gains in terms of percentile rankings, stanines, and grade equivalencies were paralleled by gains in mean scores. Here, English-dominant and Spanish-dominant first graders scored significant achievement gains in every subscale of the CTBS-Español (Math Computations, Math Concepts, Math Total, Word Recognition I, Word Recognition II, Reading Comprehension, and Reading Total).

CTBS-U: Bilingual Immersion Versus
Non-Bilingual Immersion

Bilingual immersion students were compared with a sample of non-bilingual immersion students on the CTBS-U. For the kindergarten students, comparisons were made across three groups (English-dominant bilingual immersion, Spanish-dominant bilingual immersion, and non-bilingual immersion) for reading and math subscales of the CTBS-U. Findings from these comparisons are presented in Lindholm (1988).

The significant differences (all with $p < .05$) were as follows: (a) The mean visual recognition score for the non-bilingual immersion group (15.0) was higher than that for the Spanish-dominant bilingual immersion group (11.6) but not higher than the mean for the English-dominant bilingual immersion group (13.6); (b) the mean vocabulary score for the nonimmersion group (11.1) was higher than that for the Spanish bilingual immersion group (9.3) but not higher than the mean for the English bilingual immersion group (10.1); and (d) the mean math concepts score was higher for the English bilingual immersion group (9.8) than for the Spanish bilingual immersion group (7.0) but not higher than the math concepts score for the non-bilingual immersion group (8.8).

For the first-grade students, the same comparisons were made, as above, and for additional subscales in language expression, math computation, and a math total (see Lindholm, 1988, for details). Significant group differences emerged on the following subscales: (a) the English bilingual immersion mean (20.7) was significantly higher than the Spanish bilingual immersion mean (13.6) for reading vocabulary but not significantly higher than the non-bilingual immersion mean (14.9); (b) the language expression mean was higher for the English bilingual immersion group than the Spanish bilingual immersion group (10.6) but not significantly greater than the non-bilingual immersion mean (12.3); (c) the math concepts mean for the English bilingual immersion group (22.4) was significantly higher than the mean either for the Spanish bilingual immersion group (16.5) or the non-bilingual immersion group (17.5), although these latter two groups did not significantly differ; and (d) the math total mean for the English bilingual immersion group (20.3) was significantly higher than the non-bilingual immersion mean (15.4) but not significantly higher than the Spanish bilingual immersion mean (15.6).

Summary of Achievement Findings

In sum, the students performed at a satisfactory achievement level considering that the English speakers were instructed in a second language and received only 10% of their instructional day in English language arts, and the Spanish speakers were instructed almost totally in their first language with only 10% of the instructional day spent in language arts in their second language.

Spanish speakers performed average to above average on Spanish achievement tests. In addition, they made significant progress over the year as measured by the gains from the CTBS-Español pretest to the posttest. On English language achievement tests, the kindergartners scored below average as expected for their level of English instruction. However, by first grade, the students performed only slightly below average. In fact, they were functioning only slightly below grade level and did not differ significantly from the non-bilingual immersion students except on one subtest for the Spanish speakers. This was an impressive result considering the small amount of English instruction they had received.

The English-speaking students did very well on both English and Spanish achievement tests. On the Spanish tests, the kindergartners scored average in reading and on the composite, and slightly above average in math. The first graders scored slightly above average in reading and on the composite, but well above average in math. Also, the students scored significantly higher on the CTBS-Español posttest than on the pretest. In terms of English achievement, the kindergartners scored slightly below average on all subtests except sound recognition, but their scores did not differ significantly from those of the non-bilingual immersion students. Performance was even better at the first-grade level, where reading and language scores were average and math scores ranged from slightly above average to well above average. Furthermore, on every subtest, the bilingual immersion students scored higher than the non-bilingual immersion students, with significantly higher scores in math.

Perceived Competence

The mean score for the cognitive domain was 3.5 for kindergartners and 3.4 for first graders, which represents a high level (given a possible range of 1 to 4) of perceived competence related to academic functioning in the students. These mean scores are equivalent to mean scores obtained from another sample of kindergarten (3.6) and first-grade (3.4) students (Harter & Pike, 1984). In Harter and Pike's sample, the 56 kindergarten and 65 first-grade students were middle-class, largely (96%) non-Hispanic Whites.

Similar scores were obtained in the physical domain, where almost all of the children felt that they were competent with respect to their physical skills and abilities in outdoor games and activities (mean = 3.5). Again, these mean scores are almost identical to the mean scores obtained by Harter and Pike's sample of kindergarten and first graders (mean = 3.4).

A mean score of 3.2 and 3.1 was obtained for kindergarten and first-grade students, respectively, in the peer domain, also demonstrating that the students perceived themselves as having a fairly high level of competence in relating to their friends and classmates. Harter and Pike's sample of kindergarten and first-grade students obtained mean scores of 2.9 and 3.1, respectively.

Finally, the mean score obtained in the maternal domain was 3.3 for kindergartners and 2.9 for first graders. This was the only domain in which there was a statistically significant difference between students, with kindergartners scoring significantly higher than first graders. Comparing the mean scores with Harter and Pike's students yielded slightly higher mean scores for the Edison students over Harter and Pike's kindergarten (mean = 2.9) and first-grade (mean = 2.8) students.

In sum, the kindergarten and first-grade students consistently presented high levels of perceived competence in each of the domains assessed. In fact, their mean scores compared very favorably with the mean scores of children in a non-language minority sample.

DISCUSSION

This report presented the results of a study of Edison Elementary School after its first year of implementing its bilingual immersion program. The major research questions sought to determine (a) the levels of first- and second-language proficiency and whether there were gains in first- and second-language proficiency over the year; (b) the levels of math and reading achievement in Spanish and English and whether there were achievement differences related to the language background of the students; and (c) the levels of students' perceived academic, peer, physical, and maternal competencies.

In terms of the students' language development, all of the students made gains in both languages. Native language proficiency was high, with about two-thirds of the students rated at the fluent proficiency level and one-third at the limited proficiency level. Second-language proficiency varied considerably, with some students rated at the nonproficient level, others at the limited proficient level, and still others at the fluent proficient level. More Spanish-dominant students were fluent in the second language than were English-dominant students.

Both the Spanish-dominant and the English-dominant students scored at an average to above average level in achievement performance. The Spanish-dominant speakers scored in the average to above average range on Spanish achievement tests and made significant gains from the fall to the spring. Even the English-dominant students scored well on the Spanish achievement tests; the kindergartners scored average in reading and slightly above average in math, but the first graders scored above average in reading and well above average in math. In addition, the first graders made significant progress from the fall to the spring. On English achievement tests, the Spanish-dominant kindergartners scored below average but the first graders performed only slightly below average, and they did not differ significantly from the non-bilingual immersion students. The English-dominant kindergartners scored slightly below average, but the first graders performed average in reading and language and slightly above average to well above average in math. Furthermore, on every subtest, the English-dominant kindergartners scored higher than the non-bilingual immersion students, with significantly higher scores in math.

Teachers can benefit from knowledge of these results in at least two ways. First, it is important for teachers to recognize the differential manner in which language develops. Children learn functional language much earlier than they learn the more formal rules of vocabulary and grammar. Teachers of young children can capitalize on this feature of language acquisition by emphasizing, in the early years, language skills that are more tied to their functionality than their formal rules.

Second, this research clearly establishes that both Spanish-speaking monolinguals and English-speaking monolinguals can benefit from their mutual language interaction. Indeed, immersion in Spanish, for English monolinguals, greatly facilitates their second-language acquisition without retarding the development of their English language skills or their academic achievement. Similarly, children with limited English proficiency benefit most—in terms of language development and general academic achievement—by first developing their native language skills. Teachers can rely on these children's broader social-linguistic environments to provide the informal instruction in English language skills.

REFERENCES

Cole, N. S., Trent, R. E., & Wadell, D. C. (1984). *La Prueba Riverside de Realización en Español*. Chicago: Riverside.

Harter, S., & Pike, R. (1983). *Procedural manual to accompany the Pictorial Scale of Perceived Competence and Social Acceptance for young children.* Denver, CO: University of Denver.

Harter, S., & Pike, R. (1984). The inadequacy of English immersion as an educational approach for language minority students. In *Studies on immersion education: A collection for U.S. educators* (pp. 144–183). Sacramento: California State Department of Education.

Lindholm, K. J. (1987). *Directory of bilingual immersion programs* (Educational Report 9). Los Angeles: University of California, Center for Language Education and Research.

Lindholm, K. J. (1988). *Edison Elementary School's bilingual immersion program: Student progress after one year of implementation* (Technical Report No. 9). Los Angeles: University of California, Center for Language Education and Research.

PART IV

Theory into Practice:
Strategies for the Classroom

Part IV provides the real substance of the volume by focusing on specific guidelines for how teachers can accomplish many of the goals outlined earlier, with an emphasis on the teaching of content and language simultaneously. This integration is accomplished by purposely using the second language to teach the traditional academic content of math, social studies, science, and art and the humanities.

Donna Christian, George Spanos, JoAnn Crandall, Carmen Simich-Dudgeon, and Karen Willetts, in "Combining Language and Content for Second Language Students" (Chapter 9), provide the broad parameters of language-content integration. They provide specific examples of classrooms using integrative approaches, and show teachers how to develop content-language lesson plans and activities. Appendixes to the chapter provide sample lesson plans and suggestions for further reading.

George Spanos and JoAnn Crandall, in "Language and Problem Solving: Examples from Math and Science" (Chapter 10), question the unidimensional concept of language proficiency and emphasize the distinction between basic interpersonal communication skills and the language skills required of scholastic environments. They suggest that teachers must be cognizant of the difference between social language and the more cognitively demanding and "decontextualized" academic language necessary to perform school tasks. Spanos and Crandall also identify the special language "registers" of math and science, and present transcripts of samples of teacher-student dialogues. The primary implications for teachers are to design lesson plans that integrate language and content, provide a variety of activities, encourage peer-group cooperation, and use authentic text materials.

Marguerite Ann Snow and Donna M. Brinton, in "Innovative Second-Language Instruction at the University" (Chapter 11), provide a detailed description, with evaluative data, of a language/content integration model in a university setting. The UCLA Freshman Summer Program (FSP) is described with a focus on the program's strengths and limitations. Their evaluation indicated positive outcomes for the limited-English-proficient freshmen participating in the program.

Joy Kreeft Peyton provides two related chapters: "Dialogue Journal Writing: Effective Student-Teacher Communication" (Chapter 12) and "Beginning at the Beginning: First-Grade ESL Students" (Chapter 13). The first chapter provides a detailed description of a comparatively recent innovation in teacher-student communication: the dialogue journal. The dialogue journal is a written communication between teacher and student that allows the building of a meaningful interpersonal relationship. Although the dialogue journal model is intentionally nonevaluative, students acquire writing skills because of the activity's meaningful context and interaction with a positive adult writing model (i.e., the teacher). The second chapter elaborates on the dialogue journal approach and presents the findings from a case study using dialogue journals in an early elementary classroom. Taken together, Peyton's chapters provide teachers with sufficient details to implement a dialogue journal in their own classrooms.

Evelyn Jacob and Beverly Mattson, in "Cooperative Learning: Instructing Limited-English-Proficient Students" (Chapter 14), discuss the utility of cooperative learning strategies with diverse linguistic groups. The purposes of cooperative learning include language and content mastery as well as positive intercultural relations. They review varieties of cooperative learning techniques, describe learning outcomes, and suggest steps for classroom implementation.

Karen Willetts and Donna Christian, in "Material Needed for Bilingual Immersion Programs" (Chapter 15), offer guidelines for appropriate and effective materials and curricula. They note that these programs require a wide variety of materials that must provide instruction in two languages and must be suitable for at least two groups of students with very different language proficiencies. Moreover, Willetts and Christian strongly urge the adoption of bilingual materials for the teaching of the traditional academic content areas. They discuss the availability of materials, the preparation of lesson plans, and provide appendixes with clearinghouse addresses and a listing of sample materials.

Finally, Halford H. Fairchild and Amado M. Padilla, in "Innovations in Bilingual Education: Contributions from Foreign Language Education" (Chapter 16), provide a summary of the volume and integrate contributions from the closely allied field of foreign language education (see Padilla, Fairchild, & Valadez, 1990) in the context of the current volume. The chapter, and the volume, conclude with some speculations about the future of bilingual education in the United States.

REFERENCE

Padilla, A. M., Fairchild, H. H., & Valadez, C. M. (Eds.). (1990). *Foreign language education: Issues and strategies*. Newbury Park, CA: Sage.

9

Combining Language and Content for Second-Language Students

DONNA CHRISTIAN
GEORGE SPANOS
JOANN CRANDALL
CARMEN SIMICH-DUDGEON
KAREN WILLETTS

Many students are faced with the daily challenge of learning through a language other than their mother tongue, whether through English as a second language (ESL) or foreign language immersion settings. They need to develop the required language skills for participating in all aspects of schooling while they strive to keep pace with other students in content mastery as well. Many educators have found that combining language and content instruction can be an effective way of helping these students progress toward both goals.

In this chapter, we explore the integration of language and content and suggest some specific strategies for teachers to use in the classroom. Such integration may be twofold:

(1) *Content material is incorporated into language classes.* Material from academic content areas provides practice in using specific terminology, types of reading passages, required writing styles (e.g., science lab reports), and cognitive thinking skills. This type of instruction, referred to as content-based language instruction, prepares the students for the academic demands that subject area classes impose.

(2) *Accommodation is made for the students' limited language proficiency in content classes.* This occurs through the adaptation of language and materials and the presentation of information that is more comprehensible to these students. This type of instruction, referred to as language-sensitive, or "shel-

tered," content instruction, assists these students in their pursuit of academic success.

The following discussion illustrates both approaches and considers how they can be implemented in a variety of settings. We focus on the situation of language minority students learning English as a second language, but it will become clear that the same principles apply to English-speaking students learning other languages as well.

A LANGUAGE-SENSITIVE CONTENT CLASS

In an intermediate school located in the Chinatown of a major metropolitan city, ninth-grade students are seated in groups of four or five at round wooden tables, conversing in a mixture of Mandarin and Cantonese, with a sprinkling of English. The instructor enters and begins to distribute the contents of a large brown bag. The students continue to chatter in Chinese, their interest piqued by the paper towels, soup-sized plastic bowls, rolls of masking tape, and pennies that she lays out in the middle of the wooden tables.

Speaking in English, the instructor tells each group to choose a student as recorder. Once the students have done this, she asks the recorder to jot down the following instructions:

(1) Tape the penny to the middle of a plastic bowl.

(2) Fill another bowl with water.

(3) Place the bowl with the penny in the middle of the table.

(4) Look at the penny and move back until you can no longer see the penny. Stay still.

(5) Choose one student to fill the penny bowl with water from the other bowl.

(6) The rest of you stay where you are. Observe what happens. Discuss this with your group.

(7) Tell your recorder to write down what you have observed.

When the teacher says "Begin," the resulting scene is tumultuous, as students start to order one another to carry out the directions in a combination of English and Chinese. Naturally, there are a few hitches—for example, spilled water and students falling off their chairs as they attempt to position their bodies to make the pennies disappear. The teacher calmly moves from group to group to ask questions like "What step are you on?" or "What happens to the pennies when you put water in the bowl?"

Once all the groups have completed the seven steps, the instructor reconvenes the class. When she asks for volunteers to report on what happened, eager students vie with each other for the opportunity to speak. It is interesting to note that the students' conversations have now shifted to English and that the reports are surprisingly fluent.

With about 15 minutes left, the teacher asks the students to explain in writing why they think the pennies seemed to move as water was added to the bowls. Several students begin referring to their science textbooks, specifically to the section that deals with refraction, or the bending of light. At this point, it becomes clear that the goal of the lesson is to present a scientific principle, namely, that light bends when it moves from one medium to another medium at an angle; but the class has been conducted according to well-established language teaching principles as well. The result is that students were actively communicating in small groups using oral and listening skills to discover the scientific principles involved in the exercise.

A CONTENT-BASED ENGLISH AS A SECOND LANGUAGE CLASS

In our first example, a science teacher used language learning methods and techniques in what we call language-sensitive content instruction, enabling the instructor to facilitate both content learning and language acquisition for limited-English-proficient (LEP) students. Next, we have a chance to look in on a second-grade ESL classroom.

Large sheets of paper are taped around the room with the following headings: "My name is _____," "I live in _____," "I eat _____," "I wear _____," and "I am _____." Small groups of students are huddled around pictures and books about various animals—lions, panda bears, whales, jaguars, buffalo, kangaroos. Each group is engaged in research, finding the answers to the questions: "Where does a (lion) live?" "What kinds of food does a (panda bear) eat?" "What kind of covering does a (whale) have?" "What word best describes a (kangaroo)?"

One student in each group is leading the discussion; another is recording the group's decisions. In one group, a student suggests that the panda lives in the zoo. Another agrees, but wants to know in what country. They look through the books and magazines until they find a map that shows where the panda lives. The recorder writes "China" on their sheet. They come across a picture of a panda eating bamboo. They decide to write bamboo in the "I eat _____" column. A lively discussion begins when they try to find one word to describe the panda. They know pandas look "cuddly," but they also know that pandas can be "fierce." Another group chose the jaguar. They are filling in the chart on the bulletin board, listing the jaguar's home as "South America" and the animal's covering as "fur."

After the groups complete their work and present their findings to the class, the teacher asks them to talk about the similarities and differences among these animals. She poses questions such as "How are these animals the same?" Finally, she asks them: "How many pandas are living?" "How many jaguars?" The students conclude that these animals are all in danger of extinction.

It is easy to see how this content-enriched ESL class differs from the traditional ESL class. Although the students are learning English language skills—listening, speaking, reading, and writing—and getting practice in using particular grammatical patterns (*wh*-questions) and new vocabulary, the class also does much more: It builds on academic content (e.g., characteristics of animals) and develops academic language skills (such as classification and comparing/contrasting), which assist them to function more effectively in a mainstream academic classroom.

INTEGRATING LANGUAGE AND CONTENT INSTRUCTION

The focus of many language classrooms today is on the development of oral communication skills in order to help students talk about themselves, relate to their peers and teachers, and function appropriately in the language. This development of interpersonal communicative skills is important, but it is not enough. We also need to provide students with meaningful content-area instruction and contexts upon which to base their language skills.

Students who speak English as a second language need to master more than conversational skills in order to do academic work in English. They must also be able to use English to read science books, do math word problems, or reflect upon and evaluate history lessons. These latter skills, referred to as Cognitive Academic Language Proficiency (CALP) by Cummins (1981), take longer to develop (five to seven years) than interpersonal communicative skills (or BICS—Basic Interpersonal Communication Skills). Both facets of language proficiency can and should be developed together. By using academic content as a basis for language lessons, teachers can focus attention on higher-order thinking skills such as analyzing, synthesizing, or predicting, and can provide students with the appropriate language labels and conventions for participating in content classes.

As we have seen earlier, this approach is not limited to the language classroom. All teachers can make content instruction more meaningful by using hands-on approaches that relate math and science, for example, to real-life activities. Our first example presented a language-sensitive content classroom where a science teacher used language teaching methods and techniques to facilitate both content learning and language acquisition for LEP students. Students get needed support after transition if the mainstream or content teacher uses a language-sensitive approach in the classroom. Further, research suggests that second-language learning is facilitated when the learner is taught using meaningful input, when new information is presented and linked to already known information, and when the learning environment is relaxed and motivating (Krashen & Terrell, 1983).

Integrating Language and Content in Bilingual Education

Whereas the focus in the sections above has been on language minority students in ESL and English language content classes, content-based instruction is also a "natural" for bilingual education. In bilingual education programs, content-area instruction may be delivered in two languages. Theoretically, students are taught content in their first language while they develop skills in English. However, bilingual students need to study the same curriculum and acquire the same knowledge as their English-speaking counterparts. Using academic content as the basis for ESL instruction can help the students toward that goal. Although we may expect skills and knowledge to transfer from the native language to English, there are inevitably alternative vocabulary, structures, and conventions that the students need to learn to become "academically bilingual." Content-based ESL instruction can provide the context for such language development.

Foreign Language Programs

Students learning languages other than English, either in foreign language classrooms or in two-way bilingual programs, can also benefit from the combination of language and content instruction. In foreign language immersion classrooms, for example, two educational goals exist side by side: the learning of another language and the acquisition of content knowledge and basic skills. Students receive all instruction in a language that is not native to them. By integrating language and content, we can work toward both educational goals at the same time. In fact, it is important that this be done so that academic language skills are developed during the process. When a social studies unit in French is presented to native English speakers, relevant vocabulary, grammatical structures, and language functions can be systematically treated so that both the content and the language are taught.

We can use this approach in traditional foreign language classes as well. In a German class that meets twice a week, for example, lessons can revolve around topics taught in content classes. A unit from the music class on great composers could be adapted for the German class, or a geography class could be reviewed by focusing on the topography of Europe. New content can also be introduced, especially when relevant to the language and culture under study.

Two-Way Bilingual Programs

In two-way bilingual programs, where language minority students and English-speaking students come together for instruction in both languages, the needs of both groups are served by integrating language and content. In a program using Spanish and English as languages of instruction, for example, lessons that incorporate English and math instruction for the Spanish speaker, and science and Spanish for the English speaker, provide language and concept development for both groups.

HOW TO COMBINE LANGUAGE AND CONTENT

Language and content-area instruction can be integrated in one lesson or unit, or the approach can form the basis for an entire curriculum. Even though the extent of implementation may vary widely, the underlying principles and procedures remain the same. In fact, teachers may start with one lesson or unit and later pool resources with other teachers to develop a whole curriculum from this approach.

(1) *Develop one lesson.* To plan a single lesson, teachers can take an objective from a content-area curriculum, such as science, and think about what language students need in order to be able to accomplish that objective. The language development goals should include specific vocabulary items as well as grammatical structures and language functions (such as requesting information or defining) that are important for the lesson. Naturally, the level of proficiency of students will need to be considered. Once the content and

language objectives of the lesson have been identified, activities that will accomplish both can be planned. The sample lessons (in Appendix A) provide models for developing an integrated lesson. The plans include the following kinds of information, which should be taken into consideration when planning a lesson:

- grade level
- language level
- subject area
- topic
- key content competencies
- core vocabulary
- thinking skills
- language skills
- literacy skills
- study skills
- materials needed
- extension activities
- assessment

Close cooperation between language and content-area teachers is especially helpful in the planning stages, and ongoing collaboration is desirable.

(2) *Develop a unit in one academic area.* This level provides a more sustained effort than a single lesson, but the approach is the same. A unit in math, social studies, science, or any other content area can be adapted in this way. For example, a unit on word problems in math is ideal for integration with language objectives (think of the practice on English comparatives that could be incorporated, based on phrases like "greater than," "faster than," and so on). Again, content objectives need to be examined to determine what language structures and functions can be taught or reinforced at the same time.

The advantage of developing a series of lessons is that it then becomes possible to spiral the language being taught, building from one lesson to the next. In other words, a particular structure can be introduced in one lesson, then reinforced and expanded in later lessons in the unit.

(3) *Develop a content-based ESL or sheltered English curriculum.* This is, of course, the most ambitious project to undertake. In most school systems, teams of teachers regularly collaborate on curriculum development, either informally or at the request of the school district. Such teams could be made up of teachers who have tried combining language and content instruction in

their classes so that they can pool resources and experience. As mentioned above, the collaboration of content area and ESL teachers is particularly effective.

Naturally, a curriculum should reflect local needs. Requirements for content-area topics need to be considered, as well as the choice of a format best suited to the local population. A totally integrated curriculum for LEP students combines language instruction with all content areas. Alternatives include content-enriched English language instruction and language-sensitive content classes, such as sheltered English classes for LEP students. For example, an ESL curriculum might be developed in conjunction with the social studies strand or reflect selected topics across a number of content areas. In a bilingual program, the content-enriched ESL class might reinforce concepts taught in the native language. In an ESL pullout situation, the curriculum would reinforce concepts presented in English in a mainstream classroom, where LEP students might number only a few among a class of native speakers of English. In a self-contained classroom, the ESL curriculum could provide the entire social studies component for a group of LEP students.

Whether a single lesson or a whole curriculum, teachers can integrate language and content area instruction in ways that make learning each one more effective. Although some careful preparation is needed in advance to plan the lessons, it is well worth the effort. For further reading on combining language and content for second-language students, see Appendix B.

REFERENCES

Cummins, J. (1981). The role of primary language development in promoting educational success for language minority students. In *Schooling and language minority students: A theoretical framework*. Sacramento: California State Department of Education.

Krashen, S., & Terrell, T. (1983). *The natural approach*. San Francisco: Alemany.

APPENDIX A:
Strategies for Integrating Language and Content

I. SOCIAL STUDIES

(Developed by Melissa King, Stephen Matthiesen, and Joseph Bellino)

Purpose: This strategy introduces and reviews important events, people, dates, and concepts in the social studies content area using color-coded sentence strips. As constituents of sentences are manipulated, content information is presented and the following language foci are addressed:

- develop sentence structure and vocabulary
- review WH-questions
- promote oral language proficiency and the transition to reading/writing

Language Level: Beginning to Intermediate
Educational Level: Grade one or higher
Materials:

Strips of colored paper and colored cards

Colored markers

Pocket chart (optional) for visual display

Magnetic tape (optional) for display of cards/sentences on magnetic chalkboard or thumbtacks for display on bulletin board

The Basic Approach: This strategy involves the use of color-coded sentence strips to present content information and develop a variety of language skills.

Step 1. Prepare the following materials:

color-coded sentence strips with content information that is to be focus of lesson(s)

color-coded WH-question cards that correspond to specific sentence parts on the colored strips

color-coded word cards that contain key words/phrases from the target sentences

Example:

Cortez	went from Cuba	to Mexico	in 1519	to look for gold.
blue	red	green	purple	orange

Who	from Where	Where	When	Why
blue	red	green	purple	orange

Step 2. Introduce content information on "World Explorers" to students by

(a) breaking target sentences into constituent parts
  - build up sentence constituent by constituent
  - tape or tack strips to board as they are added
  - have students repeat or read constituents as they are added

(b) eliciting appropriate responses to WH-questions about the content
  - ask questions about each constituent as it is added, then
  - review by asking basic questions and alternate forms (such as "What country did he come from?") after complete sentence developed

(c) eliciting appropriate WH-questions to correspond with given content information
  - point to the answer and have students supply the question

(d) distributing question cards and word cards to students for physical response drills
  - have student with question card stand up and ask, then student with appropriate answer stand up and answer

(e) distributing word cards to students so they can reconstruct target sentences by standing up in correct order

Step 3. Encourage student-student interaction with color-coded cards and sentence strips. Have students pair up to practice with each other.

Step 4. Move from oral practice into writing activities:

(a) have students write appropriate content information or WH-question following an oral cue
(b) have students write target sentences when given a word or phrase as an oral stimulus
(c) have students create new sentences (following the structural pattern) when given additional content information

Extension: Model other similar sentences for an oral and/or written review, for example:

(1) Cabot went from England to America in 1497 to find a trade route.
(2) Cartier went from France to Canada in 1534 to find a trade route.

This strategy could easily be adapted to other social studies units as well as other content-area subjects.

II. USING PHYSICAL RESPONSE STRATEGIES: ART

(Developed by Carolyn Andrade, Carol Ann Pesola, and Donna Christian)

Purpose: A major difficulty in teaching language to beginners is how to get started and how to facilitate the early stages of language learning. The use of physical response strategies can be an effective way to approach this problem, particularly in immersion settings. In this technique, teachers use only the target language, and students are expected to respond physically but not verbally. In other words, students demonstrate understanding through means other than oral production. The approach shares its conceptual underpinnings with those of the "total physical response" (TPR) and "natural" approaches.

The physical response orientation has a number of advantages for early language learning. It involves processes that resemble natural language acquisition, by developing comprehension and involving action responses, and it reduces the level of anxiety in the new language situation. In the classroom, the approach further has the advantage of pairing mental processing with action, which may lead to greater retention, and all students are able to participate. For young children, this involvement orientation is especially important, as is the fact that no reading or writing skills are required (although they may be developed).

Integrating language and content instruction using physical response strategies can be particularly effective in art, music, and physical education classes. Concepts appropriate to the age levels of students can be taught, and the content lends itself well to physical rather than verbal responses from the students. The teacher's language can be geared, in variety and complexity, to the language level of the students, while still allowing the teacher to promote concept learning.

The following activities suggest ways in which physical response activities can facilitate the learning of language and basic concepts in art. The lessons are designed for beginning language learners (in a foreign language or ESL context) in various elementary grades.

The Basic Approach:

Step 1: Planning

- set language and content goals for the lesson
- determine the vocabulary needed for the lesson
- break down the lesson/task into steps
     teacher: language + gestures + context
     student: physical responses
- define sequence of activities
- identify and gather materials needed

Step 2. Conducting the lesson

- teach vocabulary using visuals, movement, and demonstration; use familiar commands (*put, take*, and so on) and allow for lots of manipulation of vocabulary through novel commands (new combinations of familiar command structures with new vocabulary)
- introduce and practice concepts through sequenced activities, with teacher using language, gesture, and demonstrations, and students responding with action, first as a group and then in smaller groups or individually
- combine and reinforce concepts, continue practice

Step 3. Ending the lesson

- end with a quiet activity to calm students down before the next class; because of the active nature of this approach, it is important to provide the students with a "cool-down" or quiet time before moving on to the next activity; a good example is a short story (told orally or read)

Sample Lesson

Objective: basic shapes and colors (making a mobile)
Language Level: Beginning (ESL or foreign language)
Educational Level: Elementary
Materials:

Colored paper in at least five colors
Objects to trace basic shapes (rectangle, square, circle, triangle)
Pencils
Scissors
String
Wooden sticks (approximately 18–24 inches long)

Activities:

(1) Setting the stage: demonstrate/teach vocabulary

    (a) action verbs: *put, take, cut, draw, make, find*

    (b) colors: *red, blue, yellow, green, black, white*

    (c) shapes: *square, rectangle, circle, triangle*

(2) Demonstrate tracing shapes and cutting them from paper of different colors. Have children cut out pieces of various shapes in various colors:

Find a circle; draw a circle on the red paper; cut out the circle.

Make a square on the blue paper; cut it out.

Put the box (rectangle) on the yellow paper; draw the rectangle; cut out the rectangle.

Make a green triangle.

Then let children cut out shapes and colors as they choose.

(3) Once children have a number of shapes cut out, practice sorting and naming the shapes and colors. Get children moving around as they sort.

Put all the triangles together. Who has a red triangle? If you have a red triangle, stand up. Put all the red triangles on the table and sit down.

Who has a black rectangle? Put the black rectangles by the window.

Put all the blue pieces together. Take the blue squares to the blackboard.

Continue sorting, then redistribute shapes so that each child has at least 2 of each shape in different colors.

(4) Demonstrate gluing strings of different lengths to shapes and tying them to the wooden sticks, more or less evenly spaced. Allow children time to design arrangements of shapes to their liking. With older children, two sticks may be crossed and nailed together to make a more complex mobile.

(5) Hang children's work around room and use at later times to practice shapes and colors in follow-up activities.

APPENDIX B:
Further Reading

The following articles and books provide additional information about integrating language and content instruction.

Cantoni-Harvey, G. (1987). *Content-area language instruction: Approaches and strategies.* Reading, MA: Addison-Wesley.

Chamot, A., & O'Malley, M. (1986). *A cognitive academic language learning approach: An ESL content-based curriculum.* Silver Spring, MD: National Clearinghouse for Bilingual Education.

Crandall, J. A. (Ed.). (1987). *ESL through content-area instruction.* Englewood Cliffs, NJ: Prentice-Hall Regents.

Crandall, J. A., Dale, T., Rhodes, N., & Spanos, G. (1989). *English skills for algebra.* Englewood Cliffs, NJ: Prentice-Hall Regents.

Crandall, J. A., Spanos, G., Christian, D., Simich-Dudgeon, C., & Willetts, K. (1988). *Combining language and content instruction for language minority students.* Silver Spring, MD: National Clearinghouse for Bilingual Education.

Cuevas, G. (1984). Mathematics learning in English as a second language. *Journal for Research in Mathematics Education, 15*, 134–144.

Curtain, H., & Pesola, C. (1988). *Languages and children: Making the match.* Reading, MA: Addison-Wesley.

Evans, R. (1986). *Learning English through subject areas: The topic approach to ESL.* Victoria, Australia: Ministry of Education, Curriculum Branch (Schools Division).

Krashen, S., & Terrell, T. (1983). *The natural approach.* San Francisco: Alemany.

Mohan, B. (1986). *Language and content.* Reading, MA: Addison-Wesley.

Northcutt, L., & Watson, D. (1986). *S.E.T.: Sheltered English teaching handbook.* Carlsbad, CA: Northcutt, Watson, Gonzales.

Penfield, J. (1987). ESL: The regular classroom teacher's perspective. *TESOL Quarterly, 21*(1), 21–39.

Short, D., Crandall, J., & Christian, D. (1989). *How to integrate language and content instruction: A training manual* (CLEAR Educational Report No. 15). Los Angeles: University of California, Center for Language Education and Research.

Snow, M. A., & Brinton, D. M. (1988). *The adjunct model of language instruction: Integrating language and content at the university* (CLEAR Technical Report No. 8). Los Angeles: University of California, Center for Language Education and Research.

Spanos, G., Rhodes, N., Dale, T., & Crandall, J. A. (1988). Linguistic features of mathematical problem-solving: Insights and applications. In R. Cocking & J. Mestre (Eds.), *Linguistic and cultural influences on learning mathematics* (pp. 221–240). Hillsdale, NJ: Lawrence Erlbaum.

Willetts, K. (Ed.). (1986). *Integrating language and content instruction* (CLEAR Educational Report #5). Los Angeles: University of California, Center for Language Education and Research.

Willetts, K., & Crandall, J. A. (1986). Content-based language instruction. *ERIC/CLL News Bulletin, 9*(2). (Washington, DC: Center for Applied Linguistics)

10

Language and Problem Solving

Some Examples from Math and Science

GEORGE SPANOS
JOANN CRANDALL

Although it was previously possible to think of language proficiency as a single construct and to evaluate users of a language with regard to their pronunciation, grammar, and vocabulary along a continuum from "beginning" to "advanced" proficiency, a number of factors have called this conclusion into question.

As early as 1966, sociolinguists and ethnographers of communication demonstrated that individuals have a large repertoire of language from which they choose and that different situations require different rules and expectations of appropriate language use (Hymes, 1964; Labov, 1966). An individual who might be proficient in using a language at home or at church might not be able to use that language as effectively in school or at work.

Students who are expected to receive their education in a second dialect or language may find that the differences between the language spoken at home and that expected at school may be overwhelming. While they may be able to quickly acquire the language needed for informal communication at school, they may find the more formal academic language much more of a challenge. Thus language minority students in the United States who are seemingly proficient in English when talking with their peers or teachers may not function equally well in using the language in their academic work when they are "mainstreamed" into all-English instruction. Over time, they may fall increasingly behind their English-speaking peers.

The research of Cummins (1981) and Snow (1984) provides insights into the source of the problem. Cummins, in his analysis of the situation faced by Canadian language minority children in English medium classrooms, suggested that language proficiency might be characterized broadly as consisting of "social" language and "academic" language. The social language proficiency, which Cummins originally referred to as *Basic Interpersonal Communication Skills*, is used in informal or casual situations, where much of the message is conveyed by the setting, the shared background of the speakers and a variety of other contextual cues. Academic language proficiency, referred to as *Cognitive Academic Language Proficiency*, is characteristic of that required in classrooms, where most of the message is conveyed by a language that is more formal, more abstract, and more cognitively demanding, where the contextual clues are greatly reduced. Academic language is the means by which students receive instruction, ask for clarification, and demonstrate that they have understood.

Many students can use English to talk with friends or the teacher, or to perform relatively simple tasks (e.g., participate in recess games, read lunch menus, write short notes to the teacher). However, the same students may not be able to use English in more demanding academic tasks where a variety of texts and displays of information (charts, graphs, maps) are used. Such tasks require application of thinking skills in contexts where language is the major carrier of information.

Both Cummins and Snow have suggested that degree of contextualization and cognitive complexity are major factors in the difficulty of academic tasks. According to Snow, school requires the effective use of decontextualized language—that is, the ability to understand and use language that is impersonal, complex, and remote, what Cummins might refer to as "cognitively demanding" uses of the language in "context-reduced" situations. Whereas a chat between friends is highly contextualized and cognitively simple, reading a history text or writing a lab report of a science experiment involves the use of relatively little context and rather demanding cognitive effort.

Although students may acquire social language skills in one to two years, it can take children from five to seven years to acquire the more cognitively demanding academic language to perform school tasks (Collier, 1987; Cummins, 1981). When language minority students initially make the transition to English instruction, the first course they study in English is often mathematics, a course in which the language requirements appear relatively undemanding. Actually, the language demands are sufficiently great to cause many language minority students to experience considerable difficulty in their classes. Their resulting underachievement in math slows their overall academic progress and prevents them from pursuing either scientific or technical fields. In previous work (Spanos, Rhodes, Dale, & Crandall, 1988), we described the difficulties that math language imposes upon students and identified some of the specific features that are most problematic. Students who have not acquired the features of this math language may not be able to participate effectively in their math classes. Even English-speaking students may have difficulty because they may not have fully acquired math language or academic language in general.

A number of studies have demonstrated a positive correlation between language proficiency and mathematics achievement. Aiken (1971) found that, for monolingual English speakers, English reading ability and mathematics achievement were highly correlated. Mestre (1981) found a similar high correlation between math achievement and English language proficiency among Hispanic college students. Cuevas (1984) showed that language contributes both to math learning and to assessment of math achievement. Halliday (1975) identified features of what he terms a "mathematics register," which is generally abstract, is conceptually dense, and has reduced redundancy.

INVESTIGATING THE MATHEMATICS REGISTER

Crandall, Dale, Rhodes, and Spanos (1984) undertook a two-year research project with mathematics educators at three postsecondary institutions. They used classroom observations, interviews with students and teachers, analysis of texts, and small group problem-solving sessions, where students talked aloud as they attempted to answer questions or to solve math problems.

This enabled them to identify some of the specific lexical, syntactic, semantic, and pragmatic features of the math register that make mathematics problem solving difficult for all students, especially those for whom English is a second language. Some of the syntactic features included

(1) the use of comparatives such as *greater than/less than, n times as much as, n as _____ as*; an example of an algebraic problem with this feature is

Wendy is as old as Jack.
Jack is three years older than Frank. Frank is 25.
How old is Wendy?

(2) the use of prepositions, especially in the difference between *divided into* and *divided by*, but also generally in the use of *by*; and

(3) reversal errors, in which students are misled by the surface structure of the expressions, for example, concluding that "the number *a* is five less than the number *b*" is expressed by a = 5 – b rather than a = b – 5.

The semantic difficulties are reflected in both lexical and referential categories. Students have problems with the following kinds of vocabulary:

(1) new technical vocabulary, such as *coefficient* or *monomial*;

(2) natural language vocabulary that has a different meaning in mathematics, such as *square* or *power*;

(3) complex strings of words or phrases, such as *the quantity, y + 3, squared*;

(4) the use of synonymous words or phrases for the same operation, such as *add, plus, and, combine, sum*, and *increased by* to signal addition;

(5) new symbols and mathematical notation, such as >, <, ≥, ≤; and

(6) differences between similar terms such as *less* and *less than*.

Reference is an equally difficult semantic problem. For example, students have difficulty identifying the referent for *the number* in: "five times a number is two more than four times the number," often asking if this is an "x problem" or an "x and y problem."

At the pragmatic level, students often have difficulty because of restricted knowledge or experience with the concepts central to the word problems, which can hinder comprehension. A student who has never been engaged in business may find terms such as *selling price, markup*, and *cost* confusing. Similarly, a student who has always paid 5% sales tax may force the answer to a sales tax problem to that same rate.

An example of the difficulty students have in word problems follows. This problem was one of several presented to groups of students in group problem-solving sessions that were audio-taped, transcribed, and then analyzed for syntactic, semantic, and pragmatic features. A small portion of the transcript is reproduced below:

Word Problem: *The sales tax is $15 on the purchase of a diamond ring for $500. What is the sales tax?*

    Student 1:   *Well, we know here in Miami it's 5%. So you have to divide by ... OK! 15 over 100, I mean 500. I don't know.*

    Student 2:   *Can I help? I suggest that you divide 500 by 15 and that will give you the rate.*

Student 1: *Right!*

Researcher: *Tell me again. You divide 500 by ...*

Student 1: *15*

Researcher: *Let's do it and see what we get.*
(Student 1 calculates the answer)

Student 1: *OK. It's 3%.*

In this session a student tries to make the solution to the problem correspond to the sales tax rate in Miami, which was 5% at the time this session was conducted. The student also makes a semantic error in translating the term *divide by* into mathematical notation, not knowing if 15 is the numerator or the denominator. A second student compounds the problem by suggesting that they divide 500 by 15, a syntactic reversal error. In spite of all of this, the students get the right answer!

INVESTIGATING THE LANGUAGE OF PHYSICAL SCIENCE AND BIOLOGY

Consideration of the role of language in math learning leads naturally to investigations of how language can both confound, and simplify, the learning of science. The group problem-solving approach used in identifying linguistic problems in mathematics was adapted for use with eighth-grade physical science students and tenth-grade biology students. In that research we identified a number of problems similar to those in the mathematics research. At the syntactic level, both passive voice and conditionals are difficult. They are also pervasive and often crucial. Consider the function of passives in describing processes and the function of conditionals in stating hypotheses and conclusions/generalizations. Many limited-English-proficient students have not fully acquired these by the time they are mainstreamed into science classes. This, coupled with related inexperience in the scientific method, may account for some of the difficulties students had with moving from results/conclusions to generalizations.

At the semantic level, both lexical and referential problems occur. For example, at the lexical level students need to learn (a) new technical vocabulary, such as *absolute zero, inertia, alveoli, hypothesis,* and all the Latin- and Greek-based terminology; (b) natural language vocabulary that has a different meaning in science, such as *force, pressure, class,* or *order*; and (c) new symbols and notational systems, such as H_2O, *NO*, *Fahrenheit*, *Celsius*, and abbreviations used in the metric system.

Problems at the pragmatic level may perhaps be best understood by looking at some of the transcripts of problem-solving sessions with physical science and biology students.

The eighth-grade physical science students were divided into groups of three or four and asked to read and answer questions based on the following passage adapted from Allen and Widdowson (1974, p. 1):

> The earth is surrounded by a layer of air. This is between 150 and 200 km thick and is called the atmosphere. Air is invisible and therefore it cannot be seen. But it occupies space and has weight in the same way visible substances do.

Among the questions the students were asked to answer were the following:

(1) Is air a substance? How do you know?
(2) What are some substances that are similar/different to air? How are they similar/different?

One group of students produced the following discussion:

Researcher: *What's a substance? What do you think? Can you figure it out from there?*

Student 1: *It's ... um ... (long pause)*

Researcher: *It's OK. What are some substances? Let's try that.*

Student 1: *Like chemical substances?*

Student 2: *Like the water.*

Researcher: *What do they all have in common that would make them a substance?*

Student 3: *They're the same color.*

Researcher: *Is water the same color as acid?*

Student 1: *No.*

Researcher: *Not always. Read that again and see if you can find out what a substance is.*

Student 1: *It's something that has weight and occupies space.*

Researcher: *OK, what are some other substances that are similar to air?*

Student 2:   *Water.*

Researcher: *Why is it similar?*

Student 2:   *Because the water is not invisible, but you cannot see like color.*

Another group produced this discussion:

Researcher: *Well, Terry, while Quoc (student 3) is thinking about [whether air is a substance], can you tell me why you think air is a substance?*

Student 1:   *Well, because I know it's invisible, but every time you have a hurricane, it [blows] and it makes the trees and houses move.*

Researcher: *OK, so what does air have?*

Students 1 & 2:   *Weight.*

Researcher: *It has weight and ...*

Student 1:   *Space.*

Researcher: *It occupies space. It's somewhere. You can't see it . . .*

Student 3:   *You can see it.*

Student 2:   *Like when ... with a balloon, and it makes the balloon bigger.*

In the first discussion, the researcher is attempting to get the students to answer question 1, a task that requires that they grasp a tacit definition of *substance*, that is, something that occupies space and has weight. The passage requires the students to locate this definition in the discussion of the relationship between invisible substances, such as air, and visible substances, which are left unspecified. After a long pause on the part of the first student, the researcher attempts to lead the students to the definition by getting them to consider the common properties of various substances. The third student wrongly states that chemical substances are the same color, a response that either indicates a lack of knowledge about or restricted experience with chemical substances. The first student, however, realizes that water and acid are not always the same color. After the researcher asks the students to read the passage again, that same student finds the relevant definition. However, when asked to name some substances that are similar to air (i.e., invisible components of the atmosphere like oxygen, hydrogen, and nitrogen), the second student surprisingly, although not incorrectly, names a visible substance, water. The reason given for this response is that water, while not invisible, does not display color, although the student uses inappropriate syntax to say so (e.g., "Because the water is not invisible but you cannot see like color" instead of "Even though water is visible, it is colorless like air"). He does seem to be on track in terms of his knowledge of the subject. This student's response manifests knowledge of information that is accurate, but unfortunately irrelevant to the researcher's question, which was intended to determine if the students could demonstrate their understanding of the definition by reference to invisible gases in the atmosphere, not a visible substance, like water.

The second discussion is interesting because of the personal experience that the students express. The first student, a Cambodian, uses the example of a hurricane to explain why she thinks that air is a substance, or something that occupies space and has weight. The third student, a Vietnamese student who had been unable to answer the researcher's question about air, contradicts the researcher's assertion that "You can't see [air]." This information is then supported by the second student who says that you can see air when you blow up a balloon and the balloon gets bigger.

These transcripts suggest that the physical science register is rich in terms of the pragmatic beliefs and experiences that students bring with them into problem-solving contexts. Because examples of concepts and principles are often closely tied to student experiences (e.g., the hurricane example above), students are able to inject a good deal of their knowledge into the discussion, allowing them to practice language in a focused manner. Discussion also allows the instructor to gain insight into what students know, as well as any misconceptions that they might have. Thus an argument can be made that students should be given greater opportunity to talk to each other and to interact with their teachers in their science classes in order to allow for the expression of prior knowledge, opinions, and beliefs.

The research with tenth-grade biology students also provides support for a more communicative approach in science classrooms, because extended conversation provides students with opportunities to express what they know (after having learned it in another language) and for the teacher to be able to identify what they don't know as well. Groups of three or four students were shown in Figure 10.1 They were then asked to do a number of things, including the following:

(1) Write the names of the animals.
(2) Group the animals according to size, the length of time they live (life span), and where they live (habitat).

Portions of the transcripts for two groups of students follow:

Figure 10.1   Animal Life Spans

SOURCE: From the book, *Life Science Activities for Grades 2–8*, by Marvin N. Tolman & James O. Morton (1986). Used by permission of the publisher, Parker Publishing Company, Inc., West Nyack, NY.

Transcript 1

3 students: Student 1 (Iranian), Student 2 (Hispanic), Student 3 (Hispanic)

Researcher: *OK. Now the butterfly and the frog have something in common. Can, can you think of what that is? (Pause) There's something about those two animals that makes them similar. (Pause) OK. Let* me give you a hint. Do you know? Before you have a butterfly, what do you have?

Student 2: *What do you mean?*

Researcher: *Well, before this becomes a butterfly, what is it? Anybody know?*

Student 3: *A kind of worm, or something like that?*

Researcher: *A worm. What's that worm called? (long pause) It's called a caterpillar.*

Student 1: *Caterpillar.*

Researcher: *Caterpillar. OK now. How about the frog? Before it's a frog, what is it?*

Student 1: *It's first an egg, then it changes to the (unclear), something like that ...*

Researcher: *Uh huh.*

Student 1: *But it exist in the water.*

Researcher: *Right. OK. So the frog, when it's a baby, is under water, right? What is it called when it's in the water? Did you study that yet?*

Student 3: *No, well, um ...*

Researcher: *You know what it is in your language, probably.*

Student 3: *Yeah, I don't.*

Researcher: *OK. Well, we call it a tadpole.*

Researcher: *OK. So now, can someone tell me what the frog and the butterfly have in common?*

Student 3: *Both of them started life in different ways. And, when they, they grow in their change their body and their way of life, also.*

Transcript 2

4 Hispanic Students

Researcher: *Which animals can live under water?*

Student 1: *The turtle and the frog.*

Student 2: *Half and half.*

Researcher: *Half and half. OK. What kind of animals are those? There's a name for those, isn't there, in biology?*

Student 1: *Aquarium ... How do you say ... Aquarium ...*

Student 3:   *I mean, there is, I don't know how you say it in English. Aquatee ...*

Student 4:   *In Spanish?*

Student 3:   *Don't speak Spanish.*

Researcher: *It's OK. You can speak Spanish. Give me the word in English.*

Student 1:   *I don't know. I know to say in Spanish.*

Researcher: *What is it in Spanish? The word for animals that can live in or out?*

Student 1:   *Aquarios.*

Student 2:   *Yes. They can live inside and outside the water. They can come out and things.*

Researcher: *Do you know the word "amphibian"?*

Student 1:   *Uh uh.*

Student 2:   *Amphibian?*

Researcher: *Amphibian. (writes word on board) Yes, I think so. Animals that can live in or out. Do you know what ... this part of the word? (point out—bian)*

Student 3:   *It's a hard word.*

Although the transcripts indicate student difficulties in the use of appropriate syntax (e.g., "But it exist in the water") and knowledge of relevant lexical items (e.g., *caterpillar*), the students are able to make sense of the question. Their difficulties relate primarily to their lack of facility with nontechnical English structures and vocabulary; that is, an inability to express in English the generalizations and relationships that they have acquired through schooling or personal experience.

For example, in Transcript 1, none of the students knows the terms *caterpillar* or *tadpole*, but they do know the relationship between butterflies and caterpillars ("a kind of worm"), and frogs and tadpoles ("It's first an egg, then it changes to the [unclear], something like that ... But it exist in the water"). When asked what the frog and the butterfly have in common, the third student clearly indicates an ability to generalize by stating "Both of them started life in different ways. And when they, they grow in their change their body and their way of life, also."

Transcript 2 indicates that the students know that there are animals that can live either in or out of water, that is, amphibians, but they lack the terminology in both English and their native language, Spanish, although they do produce the terms *aquarium* and *aquarios*, which relate generally to the habitat of frogs and tadpoles. Through this conversation the teacher/researcher can support student knowledge while making corrections in a non-threatening, communicative manner.

IMPLICATIONS FOR INSTRUCTIONAL PRACTICE

Because academic language—the language of mathematics, of science, or of any other discipline—is more abstract, cognitively demanding, and likely to provide barriers to learning for language minority students, it is important for both language and content teachers to provide opportunities for that language to be learned and for students to be able to learn the subject areas through the language. Both the language teacher and the content teacher can become responsible for ensuring that the transition to academic instruction in English is successful.

The content teacher can adapt instruction to reduce the academic language demands being made on the students and can provide increased contextualization, at least in early stages. Thus, when explaining concepts such as "force" and "pressure," demonstrations that convey the difference, and opportunities to test out one's understanding through carefully structured activities, will offer the needed transition to a more verbal approach.

Both the content and the language teacher can provide opportunities for students to become accustomed to using the academic language through such activities as group problem solving, writing essays in mathematics, or orally explaining what happened in a lab experiment before asking students to write a more formal lab report on that experiment.

The language teacher can gradually introduce authentic texts into the class, while carefully structuring the presentation to increase the contextualization and to reduce the distance and abstraction in that text. In the beginning, a topic can be drawn from the math or science classroom and objectives selected from that field to teach along with language and skill objectives. Thus a language teacher might teach the language needed for addition—*plus, sum, in addition to, increased by, combine, and*—while the math teacher is teaching the problem-solving skills needed to work through addition problems using these terms. In both classes, students might work in small groups creating addition problems and solving them by working together.

In science, the lesson might deal with language required for comparison and classification of species. Students should be encouraged to work together, to try to solve problems aloud together, to share information, to present the information they have collected using a variety of formats or language modes, and in other ways to become more familiar and comfortable with the academic language skills required for the content class. What is most important is increasing the potential for interaction using the science language that will be needed in the classroom.

To assist students in coping with the academic language demands of math and science, the following approaches can be effective:

(1) integrating language and content instruction;
(2) providing a variety of learning tasks and texts with different formats and registers;
(3) increasing peer interaction and cooperative learning;
(4) encouraging students to use language productively in oral tasks;
(5) relating new learning to students' prior experience; and
(6) gradually introducing authentic texts.

Specific attention to the languages of math and science can help students overcome those difficulties. Materials that promote peer interaction can be very helpful. For example, Crandall, Dale, Rhodes, and Spanos (1984) developed an interactive mathematics language approach and a set of materials to encourage peer tutoring—where students learn to use math language productively in their math and algebra problem solving. The approach is appropriate for language minority students at the middle school, high school, and college—even for training foreign teaching assistants—and is also effective with English-speaking college students in developmental mathematics programs. A comparable set of materials for biology and physical science addressing the language of science have also produced promising results. Of particular interest, this approach and these materials have helped science teachers to identify the gifted and talented among their limited-English-proficient students while providing opportunities for all students to acquire more difficult academic language.

REFERENCES

Aiken, L. R. (1971). Verbal factors and mathematics learning: A review of research. *Journal for Research in Mathematics Education, 2*(4), 304–312.

Allen, J. P. B., & Widdowson, H. G. (1974). *English in physical science.* Oxford: Oxford University Press.

Collier, V. P. (1987). Age and rate of acquisition of second language for academic purposes. *TESOL Quarterly, 21*(4), 617–641.

Crandall, J., Dale, T. C., Rhodes, N. C., & Spanos, G. (1984). *The language of mathematics: The English barrier* (Fund for the Improvement of Postsecondary Education, Grant No. G-00840473). Washington, DC: Center for Applied Linguistics.

Cuevas, G. (1984). Mathematical learning in English as a second language. *Journal for Research in Mathematics Education, 15*, 134–144.

Cummins, J. (1981). The role of primary language development in promoting educational success for language minority students. In California State Department of Education, Office of Bilingual Bicultural Education, *Schooling and language minority students* (pp. 3–50). Los Angeles: California State University, Evaluation, Dissemination and Assessment Center.

Halliday, M. A. K. (1975). Some aspects of sociolinguistics. In E. Jacobson (Ed.), *Interactions between linguistics and mathematics education: Final Report of the Symposium Sponsored by UNESCO, CEDO and ICMI* (Nairobi, Kenya, September 1–11, 1974; UNESCO Report No. ED-74/CONF. 808; pp. 64–73). Paris: UNESCO.

Hymes, D. (1964). Introduction: Toward ethnographics of communication. In J. J. Gumperz & D. Hymes (Eds.), The ethnography of communication. *American Anthropologist, 66*(6, Pt. 2), 1–34.

Labov, W. (1966). *The social stratification of English in New York City.* Washington, DC: Center for Applied Linguistics.

Mestre, J. P. (1981). Predicting academic achievement among bilingual Hispanic college technical students. *Educational and Psychological Measurement, 41*, 1255–1264.

Snow, C. E. (1984). Beyond conversation: Second language learners' acquisition of description and explanation. In J. Lantolf & R. DiPietio (Eds.), *Second language acquisition in the classroom setting.* Norwood, NJ: Ablex.

Spanos, G., Rhodes, N., Dale, T. C., & Crandall, J. (1988). Linguistic features of mathematical problem solving: Insights and applications. In R. R. Cocking & J. P. Mestre (Eds.), *Linguistic and cultural influences on learning mathematics* (pp. 221–240). Hillsdale, NJ: Lawrence Erlbaum.

11

Innovative Second-Language Instruction at the University

MARGUERITE ANN SNOW
DONNA M. BRINTON

The nation's colleges and universities are faced with the mounting question of how to educate the steady stream of underprepared students entering higher education. These students, from both language majority and language minority backgrounds, frequently enter the university lacking the essential skills required to succeed academically. For language majority students, the lack of skills required to synthesize lecture and text material, and to express this information in writing assignments and on examinations, hinders their progress at the university. For language minority students, these problems are even more pronounced. In addition to being inexperienced in certain academic skills, language minority students may be less proficient in English, therefore, further limiting their potential for university success.

This chapter describes the Freshman Summer Program (FSP), a seven-week intensive program established at UCLA to bridge the gap between high school and college. The primary academic goal of FSP is to introduce underprepared incoming freshmen to the academic rigors of the university. Equally important goals of FSP are to provide students with the social and recreational needs that are important during this transition period, to build positive self-images, and to ensure emotional stability throughout the program. The primary goal is achieved through FSP's academic component; the latter goals are accomplished through the program's on-campus residential program, academic and personal counseling services, forums and social programs, and tutorial services.

The chapter is divided into four sections. The first section presents a rationale for the adjunct model. The second section provides a detailed description of the instructional model employed in FSP and describes key features of the program, including the academic component, student population and placement, curriculum, methodology, instructor coordination, text selection and adaptation, and the role of the language instructors. The third section summarizes the results of three studies that were undertaken at CLEAR to examine the effectiveness of the adjunct model and to document whether students transferred the skills learned in FSP to courses they took during the regular school year. The final section of the chapter provides a critique of the adjunct model, pointing out its strengths and potential limitations. The applicability of this model to other instructional settings is also discussed.

RATIONALE FOR THE ADJUNCT MODEL

In the past few years, there has been growing interest in content-based approaches to the teaching of second and foreign languages at the elementary and secondary levels (Willetts, 1986). This report describes the adjunct model, an example of a content-based model implemented in the university context that capitalizes on the disciplinary links available in a university setting. In an adjunct program, students are concurrently enrolled in a language course and a content course. The two courses are linked by the shared content base, and instructors complement each other with mutually coordinated assignments. In this way, the reading, writing, and cognitive skills required of the content course become integrated into the language curriculum.

The rationale for the adjunct model used in FSP can be found in the theoretical underpinnings of at least three movements in language teaching. The first movement, "Language Across the Curriculum" (*A Language for Life,* 1975), originated in Britain for use with native English speakers. A basic tenet of this movement is that effective language teaching must cross over all subject matter domains. The perspective taken is that of a reciprocal relationship between language and content. Students must be given opportunities to "learn to write" and to "learn to read" but must also be allowed to "write to learn" and to "read to learn" in order to fully participate in the educational process.

A second rationale for the adjunct model used in FSP can be found in the English as a second language (ESL) literature, specifically in the English for Special Purposes (ESP) literature. Widdowson (1983, pp. 108–109) noted:

> In ESP we are dealing with students for whom the learning of English is auxiliary to some other professional or academic purpose. It is clearly a means for achieving something else and is not an end in itself. ... This being so, ESP is (or ought logically to be) integrally linked with areas of activity (academic, vocational, professional) which have already been defined and which represent the learners' aspirations.

Elsewhere, Widdowson (1978, p. 16) advocated integrating or linking language teaching in the schools with other subjects (e.g., physics, chemistry, biology, map drawing) "as this not only helps ensure the link with reality and the pupils' own experience, but also provides us with the most certain means of teaching language as communication, as use rather than simply as usage." Thus integrated or content-based instruction represents a curricular innovation in keeping with the current learning across the curriculum movement at the secondary level in American schools (see Anderson, Eisenberg, Holland, Wiener, & Rivera-Kron, 1983) and the extensive work in ESP.

The third rationale for the adjunct model comes from perhaps the most documented model of content-based language instruction—immersion education (also see Snow, 1990, "Language Immersion: An Overview and Comparison"). In immersion programs, monolingual English-speaking children at the elementary and secondary levels receive the majority of the standard school curriculum in the second language. Begun in Montreal in 1965, this model of foreign language teaching has since spread throughout Canada and the United States. The successes of immersion with language majority students have been replicated in a number of different target languages (e.g., French, Spanish, German, Cantonese) and in a variety of ethnolinguistic settings (Rhodes & Schreibstein, 1983).

While the three movements discussed above differ in their implementation of content-based curricula and in their target populations, they share the same basic pedagogical assumption: Successful language learning occurs when students are exposed to content material presented in meaningful, contextualized form, with the focus on acquiring information. Moreover, the approaches represent an effective method of integrating the language curriculum—whether for native, second-, or foreign-language speakers—with the academic or occupational interests of the students.

DESCRIPTION OF THE UCLA
FRESHMAN SUMMER PROGRAM

Academic Component

UCLA's FSP provides an excellent example of a content-based instructional program designed to meet the linguistic and academic needs of students who lack exposure to the types of tasks required for success at the university. The writing curriculum of FSP is based on the adjunct prototype at California State University, Dominguez Hills (Sutton, 1978), and on the research findings of Rose (1980), who examined the kinds of writing required of UCLA undergraduate students in a variety of subject matter disciplines. Rose's findings indicate that the most common written discourse mode required in both assignments and examinations is exposition; specifically, university students are asked to write essays of seriation, classification, summary-to-synthesis, comparison/contrast, and analysis.

The academic component of FSP consists of the various ESL/English composition courses and selected content courses. In the past, introductory-level courses such as in anthropology, computer science, geography, political science, psychology, and social science have been offered. These survey courses are typical of those that undergraduates take to fulfill their general educational requirements at the university. Students attend 12–14 hours of language classes weekly, while the combined lecture/discussion section format of the content course constitutes approximately eight contact hours per week. Course content in both the language and the subject matter classes parallels that of courses offered during the normal academic year, with minor modifications made to facilitate coordination between the two disciplines.

Student Population

Every summer, approximately 700 incoming freshman students are invited to attend FSP. The participants primarily consist of low-income, ethnic minority, or linguistic minority students who come from high schools in the greater Los Angeles metropolitan area. The majority of the students are regularly admitted students, that is, they meet the general University of California admission requirements. They are routed into FSP, typically, because they applied to UCLA as affirmative action students or received SAT verbal scores below 300.

All prospective FSP students who accept the invitation to participate in the program take the University of California Subject A Exam. This essay exam is evaluated to place all incoming students into courses that fulfill the composition requirements. Student essays that exhibit ESL "markers" (e.g., lack of articles, incorrect word forms) are flagged, and these students are required to take the UCLA English as a Second Language Placement Exam (ESLPE). Based on their Subject A placement score or their ESLPE results, students are tracked into the parallel sequences of native speaker or ESL courses.

ESL student population. Because the emphasis of the current study is on the ESL subpopulation of FSP, their characteristics are described in more detail. The bulk of the ESL students attending FSP are Asian immigrants who completed their secondary education in the United States. In a recent summer, students enrolled in the lower-proficiency-level ESL classes (ESL 33B) had an average SAT verbal score of 255, while their average mathematics score was 527. Clearly, the large discrepancy between the verbal and mathematics scores indicates gross underdevelopment in English language skills. The Sequential Test of Educational Progress (STEP) also provided evidence of the weak reading skills of the ESL students in FSP. Their average percentile ranking on the STEP was .1, thus ranking them lower than approximately 99.9% of entering college freshmen (Snow & Brinton, 1984).

Curriculum

In order to realize the goal of linking the language and content courses, extensive planning must take place prior to the summer term. During the curriculum development process of FSP, a needs assessment of the required skills of the content discipline is conducted to determine the instructional priorities of the language class. The needs assessment includes feedback from the instructors of the content courses, analyses of the content materials (e.g., textbooks, supplementary readings), review of the language syllabi and materials, and interviews with experienced instructional staff (both content and language instructors). The resulting language curriculum is a synthesis of the needs identified in this assessment process.

ESL curriculum. The ESL 33B curriculum is determined by taking into consideration two factors: (a) the standard ESL 33B curricular objectives, which are based on the academic language skills appropriate for students at that level of proficiency, and (b) the feasibility of integrating the language and content objectives of the two courses. During the curriculum planning stage, the content and language teams discuss the optimal sequence of topics and skills so that the objectives of the two courses overlap most effectively. For example, during weeks one and two, in which the Psychology 10 professor presents an overview of the field of psychology and introduces basic psychological principles, the language course reflects these emphases in its coverage of the definition mode and grammatical constructions needed to write sentence definitions (e.g., articles and relative clause constructions). Additionally, there is a strong focus on study skills in the language course during these first two weeks (especially reading and note-taking strategies) in order to assist students in processing the content course materials.

Similarly, in weeks four and five, during which the content course treats developmental psychology and personality, the language course concentrates on the classification mode. For instance, students receive practice in this mode using exercises adapted from the content material (e.g., dictations and dictocomps, or delayed dictations, concerning the various stages of cognitive development). Next, students summarize portions of their content course text and lecture notes as a prewriting activity for their extended essay assignment on Piaget's stages of cognitive development. Finally, conditional structures are practiced via the topic of personality. Exercises during this week require students to take key terms and concepts from the content material, such as *introversion* and *aggression*, and to create sentences using the conditional structures. Thus students produce conditional sentences such as "If a person is introverted, he/she often feels uncomfortable in large groups," or "Unless shy people learn to be more assertive, they feel that others take advantage of them."

Coordination

Clearly, the adjunct model requires close coordination between the entire staff of the linked courses (e.g., administrative staff, instructors, tutors, and counselors) in order to achieve its goals. All instructors attend a series of meetings before the term begins to determine the shape and specifics of the program. In these meetings, discussion usually focuses on how best to merge the English/ESL syllabus with that of the content course, and decisions are made on what discourse mode to focus on each week (e.g., definition, seriation, comparison/contrast). Of particular importance to the English/ESL staff are the criteria by which the content course staff will grade written work, with emphasis on how to evaluate structural and stylistic problems (especially for the ESL students). Finally, both groups discuss complementary assignments and the coordination of efforts to help improve students' study skills.

To ensure continued cooperation between the two teams throughout the instructional period itself, weekly meetings are scheduled. These provide a forum for discussion of the week's evaluation activity (examination or paper assignment) in the content course and of individual student progress and/or problems. When necessary, decisions are made to refer students to tutorial and counseling services. Finally, these meetings allow for continued coordination to reinforce program objectives for every instructor.

Text Selection and Adaptation

Given the highly specific nature of the two courses, issues of text selection and materials preparation are very important. One very legitimate question concerns the choice of an appropriate content course text: If students have low-level language skills, can they read and comprehend college-level academic texts? Experience has confirmed the view that using simplified texts does the students a disservice; and, selecting a convoluted, poorly written text does them an equal disservice, because they will be frustrated in their attempts to apply their developing reading strategies. The program's goals are to use *authentic* content material and to assist the students in their attempts to grapple with the text by providing access to improved reading and study skill strategies. In theory, the answer lies in choosing a challenging, well-written content text with adequate visuals, study guides, glossary, and other ancillary materials.

A second question that arises is whether commercial ESL materials are usable in adjunct ESL instruction, and, if so, to what extent they need to be adapted. Our experience argues for the use of ESL texts as a reference on which both teachers and students can depend. For example, commercial ESL texts are useful for treatment of the English article system or transitional expressions of comparison/contrast. However, it is imperative to supplement commercial texts with teacher-developed materials that relate directly to the content course materials, and much instructor time is devoted to such tasks as preparing reading guides, writing sentence-combining exercises based on the content area material, devising sample essay questions, and providing model answers.

The Role of the ESL Instructors

The underlying philosophy of the adjunct model requires that language instructors assume a dual responsibility. Their primary purpose is to provide instruction that will promote English language development. Because this is done through the medium of the content material, the language instructor must also be familiar with this material. Thus, for the English/ESL instructor to be maximally effective, a substantial amount of time must be devoted to:

(1) learning the material of the content course,

(2) developing language teaching materials based on the content, and

(3) providing feedback both on the linguistic aspects of the students' work and (to a lesser degree) on the quality of the content.

Even with the emphasis placed on the content course material, the English/ESL instructor still has to face the responsibility of meeting the specified objectives of the language course. Instructors in an adjunct program, therefore, may have to juggle the demands of the standard language syllabus with the constraints placed on it by the adjunct relationship and attempt to resolve possible disparities between these to the best of their abilities. Clearly, there are limitations to the dual responsibilities of the language teacher. Because the FSP instructional model requires collaboration between the English staff and the teaching staff of the content courses, close coordination of effort is required to maintain a balance of responsibilities.

PROGRAM EVALUATION

It is clear from the preceding sections that there has been extensive work in the design and implementation of the adjunct model in the UCLA Freshman Summer Program (a more detailed discussion of FSP can be found in Brinton, Snow, & Wesche, 1989). However, little formal research has documented the effectiveness of the model. The previously collected data consisted mainly of some student background information, student program evaluations, and individual course/teacher evaluations. As such, a research plan was designed to build on the existing data base and to attempt a more comprehensive examination of the ESL component of FSP. The results are summarized in this section for the three studies that developed out of the research plan. (A detailed presentation of the studies is available in Snow & Brinton, 1988a, 1988b.)

The first study sought to provide a profile of the ESL students enrolled in FSP and to have the former students retrospectively evaluate FSP. The majority of the 224 former students located for the study were Asian immigrants who had chosen science majors at UCLA. In general, all former participants rated FSP very highly. The majority of the students believed that they were better writers as a result of FSP and that the FSP language adjunct class had helped them to read their content course texts more effectively. In addition, the former students gave high ratings to "other" benefits of FSP such as adjusting to university life, increased self-confidence, and gaining familiarity with UCLA facilities.

In the second study, FSP students in the lower-proficiency courses were surveyed to obtain information regarding their home language backgrounds, their prior exposure to academic skills in high school, and their self-assessment of improvement in these skill areas during the summer term. The most interesting finding of the home language survey was that 46% of the students enrolled in the composition course designed for native English speakers reported native languages other than English. Students reported having experience with a variety of writing activities in high school, but, upon closer inspection, it was revealed that few had been exposed to the types of writing (e.g., argument, classification, process) that are typically required in college. Results of the self-assessment scale indicated that the current students generally felt that they had improved their academic skills during FSP. Students reported the most improvement on the various activities associated with writing, for example, getting started on writing assignments, revising written work, and organizing ideas for an essay exam.

The third study provided a comparison of two ESL groups: students who had completed FSP the previous summer and students enrolled in a standard (non-FSP) ESL class. The purpose of the third study was to assess the extent to which the FSP students had been prepared for the academic demands of the university. Students from the two groups were administered a simulated midterm exam that required them to listen to an audio-taped university lecture and read an excerpt from an introductory college text. The students were then asked to answer a series of objective questions, provide short-answer definitions, and write an essay that synthesized the lecture and reading material. The results revealed that, despite having significantly lower English placement scores, the FSP students performed as well as the comparison group on the simulated exam. Thus the former FSP students demonstrated the ability to handle academic tasks that tested listening and reading comprehension and required the higher-order thinking and writing skills of synthesis and evaluation.

STRENGTHS AND LIMITATIONS OF
THE ADJUNCT MODEL

The adjunct model of language instruction provides a sound pedagogical framework for introducing underprepared students to the academic demands of the university. With the focus in the ESL class on essential modes of academic writing, academic reading, study skill development, and the treatment of persistent structural errors, students are trained to cope with assignments in the content course; and, more importantly, they are prepared for courses during the regular school year. Indeed, the adjunct model, as exemplified by the UCLA Freshman Summer Program, constitutes an ideal framework for integrating language and content teaching in the university context and for preparing students to write effectively across the curriculum.

The activities of the content-based language course are geared to stimulate students to think and learn in the target language by requiring them to synthesize information from the content-area lectures and readings. Because these materials provide authentic content for students to discuss and write about, the adjunct model provides a context for integrating the four traditional language skills. Furthermore, the pedagogical organization of the model offers ESL students a critical, but often neglected, option. It gives them access to native-speaker interaction and the authentic, unsimplified language of academic texts and lectures in the content course while at the same time providing sheltered ESL instruction in the language class where their particular linguistic needs can be met.

An underlying assumption of this pedagogical framework is that student motivation in the language class increases in direct proportion to the relevance of its activities, and, in turn, student success in the content course reflects the carefully coordinated efforts of this team approach. The program evaluation findings and student self-reports appear to validate this assumption: Former students reported that they felt they were better readers and writers as a result of FSP. Moreover, results from the comparison study indicated that the FSP students were able to perform on par with their non-FSP peers despite lower English language placement scores. In sum, the results of this series of studies provide evidence of the effectiveness of FSP in preparing underprepared ESL students for the demands of university study.

From an instructor's point of view, the adjunct model offers multiple strengths. The most immediately evident of these is the efficacy of its pedagogical framework in an academic setting. In addition to this, there are a number of other attractive features of the model. Among these is the student population itself, which is more homogeneous (in skill level) and more uniformly motivated than the traditional ESL class. In addition, by expanding the dynamics of teaching to include general academic preparation as well as language instruction, the model offers ESL teachers a more broadly defined domain of teaching and the opportunity to be truly involved in preparing students for actual university study. Thus the essence of the adjunct model's appeal to instructors involves the following: the rewards of working within a sound pedagogical framework, the challenge of materials development and coordination responsibilities, the insights gained by direct involvement with the academic demands placed on students, and the opportunity to share in the students' content course successes and failures.

Clearly, the adjunct model offers multiple pedagogical strengths; however, there are a number of factors limiting its applicability. For instance, because the model depends on the availability of content course offerings, a full-blown adjunct model is probably not feasible at an intensive language institute. Further, as we have described it, adjunct instruction assumes that students can cope (with assistance from the language and content staff) with the authentic readings and lectures in the content course. Thus the model is not applicable to beginning proficiency levels. Next, the model requires an administration willing to fund the large network of instructors and staff that the program necessitates; it also requires a strong commitment of time and energy on the part of the language and content teachers to integrate the content materials with the language teaching aims. This team teaching effort may not be possible in all settings. Finally, more than anything else, the adjunct model rests on the strength of its central administration and the effectiveness of the various coordination meetings held before and during the term. In cases where these conditions cannot be met, the implementation of the model will be severely hampered.

In sum, there are many practical issues involved in the design and implementation of content-based programs in any setting. Staff development is a key factor in the success of content-based programs. Second, there must be flexibility in the design of the program to allow for the practical realities of each instructional setting. Continuity of the administrative and instructional staff is another important issue. The curriculum and materials development demands of content-based programs require sustained commitment and effort. Finally, issues in program evaluation and student assessment must be considered very carefully as they strongly affect the successful development of content-based programs. We believe the adjunct model can be adapted to fit other institutional settings and populations. As evidence of this, similar adjunct programs exist both here and abroad: with undergraduate international students studying human geography at Macalester College in St. Paul, Minnesota (Peterson, 1985); undergraduate immigrant students at San Diego

State University (Johns, 1988); graduate students in pharmacy (Seal, 1985) and business law (Snow & Brinton, 1984) at the University of Southern California; foreign students studying the philosophy of science (Jonas & Li, 1983), American history, and economics (Spencer, 1986) in the People's Republic of China; and francophone and anglophone students at the bilingual University of Ottawa, who are learning English and French through such subject matter courses as psychology and history (Wesche, 1985).

Overall, we believe that the adjunct model offers a pedagogical approach that has far-reaching implications for educational planning and policy. First, the current movement in second-language education at all levels of instruction (elementary through higher education) is toward content-based approaches. The studies summarized in this chapter document the effectiveness of one type of content-based approach, the adjunct model. A second major policy implication concerns the multicultural reality of contemporary education in the United States, particularly in large urban areas with burgeoning populations of limited-English-proficient students. The adjunct model holds great promise as a viable approach for assisting students who speak English as a second language to succeed at the university.

REFERENCES

Anderson, J., Eisenberg, N., Holland, J., Wiener, H., with Rivera-Kron, C. (1983). *Integrated skills reinforcement: Reading, writing, speaking, and listening across the curriculum*. New York: Longman.

Brinton, D. M., Snow, M. A., & Wesche, M. B. (1989). *Content-based second language*. New York: Newbury House.

Johns, A. M. (1988). *Models of EAP at the university: Issues in implementation*. Paper presented at TESOL, Chicago.

Jonas, D., & Li, X. L. (1983). *The revised adjunct concept in China*. Paper presented at TESOL, Toronto.

A language for life. (1975). London: HMSO.

Peterson, P. W. (1985). The bridge course: Listening comprehension in authentic settings. *TESOL Newsletter, 19*(6), 19.

Rhodes, N. C., & Schreibstein, A. R. (1983). *Foreign language in the elementary school: A practical guide*. Washington, DC: Center for Applied Linguistics.

Rose, M. (1980). Teaching university discourse. In *Teaching/writing/learning* (monograph). Toronto: Canadian Council of Teachers of English.

Seal, B. D. (1985). *Some observations on adjunct courses*. Paper presented at CATESOL, San Diego, CA.

Snow, M. A. (1990). Language immersion: An overview and comparison. In A. M. Padilla, H. H. Fairchild, & C. M. Valadez (Eds.), *Foreign language education: Issues and strategies*. Newbury Park, CA: Sage.

Snow, M. A., & Brinton, D. (1984). *Linking ESL courses with university content courses: The adjunct model.* (ERIC Document Reproduction Service No. D 244 515)

Snow, M. A., & Brinton, D. (1988a). *The adjunct model at the university: Integrating language and content at the university* (Technical Report No. 8). Los Angeles: University of California, Center for Language Education and Research.

Snow, M. A., & Brinton, D. (1988b). Content-based language instruction: Investigating the effectiveness of the adjunct model. *TESOL Quarterly,* 22 (4) pp. 553–574.

Spencer, L. (1986). *An adjunct model ESP program: Balancing content and skills.* Paper presented at TESOL, Anaheim, CA.

Sutton, M. (1978). The writing adjunct program at the Small College of California State College, Dominguez Hills. In J. P. Neal (Ed.), *Options for the teaching of English: Freshman composition* (pp. 104–109). New York: Modern Language Association.

Wesche, M. B. (1985). Immersion and the universities. *Canadian Modern Language Review,* 41(5), 931–940.

Widdowson, H. (1978). *Teaching language as communication.* Oxford: Oxford University Press.

Widdowson, H. (1983). *Learning purpose and language use.* New York: Oxford University Press.

Willetts, K. (1986). *Integrating language and content* (Educational Report No. 5). Los Angeles: University of California, Center for Language Education and Research.

12

Dialogue Journal Writing
Effective Student-Teacher Communication

JOY KREEFT PEYTON

All teachers would like to have more time to communicate with their students—to learn about their backgrounds and interests, to find out what they are learning and would like to learn, and to reflect with them about personal and academic issues. When students are learning English as a second language, the need to communicate with them is intensified. At a minimum, they bring to school different language and cultural backgrounds. They may also be nonliterate in their native languages, may have had little or no schooling in their own countries, and might well have suffered considerable trauma as they left their countries to come to the United States. If they are new arrivals to the United States, they are adjusting to a new way of life at the same time that they are learning a new language. It is with these students that communication, on a one-to-one basis, is crucial—not only to help them adjust but also to help the teacher understand them and address their special needs.

Many teachers of limited-English-proficient students, in bilingual, ESL, and mainstream classrooms, have found *dialogue journals*—interactive writing on an individual basis—to be a crucial part of their teaching. Dialogue journals allow for individualization of student-teacher communication that may not have been previously possible, while they also provide a context for language and writing development. Students have the opportunity to use English in a nonthreatening atmosphere with a proficient English speaker. Because the interaction is written, it allows students to use reading and writing in purposeful ways and provides a natural, comfortable bridge to other kinds of writing that are done in school (also see Peyton, 1986, in this connection).

WHAT IS A DIALOGUE JOURNAL?

A dialogue journal is a written conversation in which two people communicate regularly over an extended period of time. In its traditional form (described by Staton, 1980), students write to their teacher, as much as they choose, about topics of their choice. The teacher regularly writes back to each student, often responding to the student's topics, but also introducing new topics; making comments, offering observations and opinions; requesting and giving clarification; or asking and answering questions. The teacher's role is as a participant with the student in an ongoing, written conversation, rather than as an evaluator who corrects or comments on the writing. Although several variations on this basic format have been developed (student-student journals, writing on computers, and variations in content), this chapter describes the basic dialogue journal concept: writing between a teacher and students, in a bound notebook, about student-chosen topics. Adaptations of this basic theme can easily be made. Peyton (Chapter 13, this volume) provides a detailed case description of the use of dialogue journals in one classroom.

The following examples, excerpted from the dialogue journals of two sixth graders learning English as a second language (from El Salvador and the Philippines, respectively), illustrate the nature of the writing:

Claudia: *The new teacher or helper in our class is very good. I like her, don't you like her? Today she helped me and us a lot. But Tony didn't want help. Why doesn't Tony want us to help him?*

I will try & bring my lunch every day from now on because the turkey stew & other lunches put me sick. I hate them. When I am very hungry I have to eat them but when I get to my house my stomach hurts & I am sick for 3 days. Can't the teachers protest or say something about the food that they give here?

What do you feed chickens here? We have a hen that layd an egg.

Teacher: *The lunches are not that bad! I've eaten them sometimes. You are wise to bring your own lunch. That is usually what I do, too. You have such good food at home that nothing served here could taste so good!*

Tony is embarrassed. He wants help, but he does not want anyone to know that he needs it. Offer to help him and if he says "no" then leave him alone.

Chickens will eat scraps of bread, wheat, seeds, water and some insects.

Claudia: *but the hen has wat it looks like worms, do you know how to get the hen of her stomach sickness or is it usual for her to be like that because she is laying eggs and she could even lay 30 eggs so I do not know if it is usual or if it is a sickness of her.*

oh poor hen she cooks & cooks when I say pretty hen in a low low voice & she looks like she is used to children because she is cook & cooking when I say pretty things, oh she's so nice.

Teacher: *I've never heard of a hen having worms—but it is possible. Go to a pet shop or to a veterinarian and ask them. Who gave you the hen? Maybe they will know.*

We say that a hen clucks. It is a pleasant little sound as though they are happy. They cackle when they lay an egg! That is usually loud! Does your hen cackle?

I think hens like having people or other hens around, don't you?

* * *

Ben: *I got a chance to look at all those weird bones. They're weird because I usually see them with their skin, bones, and hair and with their eyes or eyeballs. Where did you get all of those bones? Did you got them from the desserts? I feel sorry for the turtles or the animals that lived in the deserts and got run over by those cruel men and women ... I like and loved tamed animals.*

Teacher: *Yes, I've collected the bones, and my children, as they've grown up, have found and brought me bones because they know I like to use them in teaching. Have you looked at the teeth? Some come to a sharp point and some are very flat with ridges on the top. All animals die—and if their bones are uneaten, the sun and wind and rain clean and dry them out. So many of those animals may have died a natural death.*

Students write about topics that are important to them. They are not constrained by established topics or by a preset schedule of topics and genres that must be covered in sequence. Sometimes their concerns and interests are personal, as in Claudia's complaint about the food at school. Likewise, journal entries may relate to academic material covered in school, as in Ben's entry. At other times, activities and interests at home generate the opportunity for learning in the journal, as occurred in the discussion of Claudia's hen. Students may write descriptions, explanations, narratives, complaints, or arguments with supporting details, as the topic and communicative purpose dictate. Entries may be as brief as a few sentences, or they may extend for several pages. Topics may be introduced briefly and dropped, or discussed and elaborated on by teacher and student together for several days.

Because teachers want to communicate with their students, their writing can be roughly tuned to individual students' language proficiency levels. Just as they learn to adjust to each student's level of understanding in speech, teachers can easily become competent at varying their language in a dialogue journal with individual students to ensure comprehension (Kreeft, Shuy, Staton, Reed, & Morroy, 1984). For example, in the exchange below, from the dialogue journal of a student in the early stages of learning English, the teacher uses relatively simple syntax and words that the student knows or has used in her entry. In contrast, the same teacher's entry to Ben, above, is linguistically much more complex, as is his writing.

> Laura: *Today I am so happy because yesterday my father sad he was going to by a new washengmashin [washing machine] then yesterday he came with a new car a beg new car is a Honda and she has the radio. Leticia like to talk abowt me yesterday she sad every thing abowt my diat to the boy I danth like that.*
>
> Teacher: *How nice! A new car! What color is it? Did you take a ride in the new car?*
>
> *I'm sure Leticia did not think when she told the boys about your diet! She is so thin she does not need to think about a diet so she does not understand how you feel. Tell her!*

An essential characteristic of dialogue journal writing is the lack of overt error correction. Teachers usually have sufficient opportunities to correct errors on other pieces that students write or, if more direct instruction related to language used in the journals is desired, the teacher can take note of common error patterns and use them as the basis for later lessons in class. The journal interaction itself should be one place where students may write freely, without focusing on language form and structure. The teacher's response in the journal serves as a model of correct English usage in the context of the dialogue. In the dialogue journal interaction below, the teacher's entry models several different structures that the student has attempted to use. (These structures are in bold type here for easy identification; the teacher did not draw attention to them by underlining them.)

Michael: *today morning you said this is **my lovely friends** right? She told me about book story name is "the lady first in the air." She tell me **this lady** was first in the air, and she is flying in Pacific ocean, and she lose it **everybody find her but they can't find it. They looked in the ocean still not here.** Did she know everything of book?*

Teacher: ***My lovely friend** Mrs. P reads a lot. She has read the book about **Amelia Earhart**. It is a good story and it is a true story. **They looked and looked but they never found her airplane or her**.*

This example clearly demonstrates teacher modeling. In many cases, however, modeling of particular structures and vocabulary is neither possible nor desirable, for it would make the journal interaction stilted and unnatural. More often, modeling takes the form of correct English usage by the teacher, roughly at the student's level of ability, and related to something the student has written about, such as in the interchanges with Ben, Claudia, and Laura, shown above.

BENEFITS OF DIALOGUE JOURNAL WRITING

Many teachers, from early elementary grades through adult education, cite as benefits of dialogue journal writing the extended contact with their students and the increased opportunities to get to know them more intimately. In the journals, the student's native culture, problems in adjusting to the new culture and school, and personal and academic interests may be discussed. This not only builds strong personal ties but also gives students individualized access to a competent, adult member of the new language and culture. Through this relationship, the student may reflect on new experiences and emerging knowledge and think together with an adult about ideas, problems, and important choices (Staton, 1984b). The written record gives the teacher important information about the student's language and cognitive development.

There are also benefits related to managing a classroom of students with varying language and ability levels. All students, no matter what their language proficiency level, can participate in the activity to some extent. In classes composed of students with a range of ability levels, or with newly arrived immigrants, dialogue journals afford the opportunity for participation in an important class activity. Because students' entries give continual feedback about what they understand in class as well as about their language progress, the teacher receives information that can lead to individualized instruction.

Another benefit relates to language acquisition and writing development. Dialogue journal interactions can provide positive conditions for written language acquisition (Kreeft, 1984a, 1984b; Staton, 1984a). They focus on meaning rather than on form and on real topics and issues of interest to the learner. The teacher's written language can serve as input, modified to just slightly beyond the learner's proficiency level; thus the teacher's entries can provide reading texts that may be even more complex and advanced than the student's assigned texts, but that are comprehensible because they relate to what the student has written (Staton, 1986). Beyond the modeling of language form and structure, the teacher's writing also provides continual exposure to the thought, style, and manner of expression of a proficient English writer.

Studies have shown that many students spend very little time writing anything that is not teacher-assigned and evaluated (Applebee, 1984). Dialogue journals provide frequent opportunities for students to write on their own topics in a nonthreatening, nonevaluative context.

As they continue to write and to read the teacher's responses, students develop confidence in their ability to express themselves in writing (Hayes & Bahruth, 1985). Teachers using dialogue journals report that their students' writing becomes more fluent, interesting, and correct over time, and that writing ability developed in dialogue journals transfers to other in-class writing as well (Hayes & Bahruth, 1985; Hayes, Bahruth, & Kessler, 1986).

Finally, dialogue journals are adaptable for use with a wide variety of student populations. They were first used successfully with sixth-grade students, both native and nonnative English speakers (Kreeft, Shuy, Staton, Reed, & Morroy, 1984; Staton, 1980; Staton, Shuy, Peyton, & Reed, 1988). They are now being used with limited-English-proficient students, from early elementary grades (Peyton, this volume) through university classes (Gutstein, 1987; Steffensen, 1988); adults learning ESL who are non- or semiliterate in their native languages (Hester, 1986); migrant children and youth (Davis, 1983; Hayes & Bahruth, 1985; Hayes, Bahruth, & Kessler, 1986); deaf children (Bailes, Searls, Slobodzian, & Staton, 1986) and adults (Walworth, 1985); mentally handicapped and gifted teenagers and adults (Farley, 1986; Farley & Farley, 1987; Peyton & Steinberg, 1985); and in teacher training courses (Brinton & Holten, 1988; Roderick, 1986; Roderick & Berman, 1984). Recently, the use of dialogue journals has extended beyond the United States to overseas settings (Hall & Duffy, 1987; Kitagawa & Kitagawa, 1987; Lindfors, 1988a, 1988b, 1988c; also see *Dialogue*, April 1988).

If students are beginning writers—young children or nonliterate adults—there need be no initial pressure to write. They can begin by drawing pictures, with the teacher drawing pictures in reply and perhaps writing a few words underneath or labeling the pictures (see detailed description of this process in Peyton, Chapter 13, this volume). The move to writing letters and words can be made when students feel ready. At beginning levels, where students' ability to write is limited, the interaction may be more valuable as a reading event, with more emphasis placed on reading the teacher's entry than on writing one. In classes where native language literacy is the focus, it is possible to conduct the dialogue journal interaction in the student's native language. The move to English can occur in line with course objectives or student readiness.

Dialogue journals need not be limited to language arts or ESL classes. In content courses—science, social studies, literature, and even math—they can encourage reflection on and processing of concepts presented in class and in readings (Atwell, 1984; Steffensen, 1988). They can also be a way to promote abilities needed for composition (Kreeft, 1984b; Peyton, Staton, Richardson, & Wolfram, (in press); Shuy, 1987).

GETTING STARTED

The following guidelines should help interested teachers start and maintain a successful dialogue journal program.

- Each student should have a bound, easily portable notebook, used only for this purpose. Paperbound composition books, that are large enough to allow sufficient writing and small enough for the teacher to carry home after class, are the best. A student may fill several notebooks during a term. If it is more convenient, computer diskettes can be used instead of notebooks. The important thing is that the dialogue journal be kept separate from other schoolwork.
- The writing of both student and teacher must be done regularly, but the frequency can be flexible, depending on the number of students in a class, the length of the class, the teacher's schedule, and the needs of the teacher and students.
- Most teachers prefer to give their students time to write during the class session. This time can be scheduled at the beginning of the class as a warm-up, at the end as a wind-down, or before or after a break as a transition time. Likewise, the teacher may allow the students to choose their own time for writing. Ten or fifteen minutes is usually adequate to read the teacher's entry and to write a new one. Teachers usually respond outside class time.
- Early in the use of dialogue journals, it may be desirable to set a minimum amount that students must write each time (such as three sentences), but the

amount of writing beyond that should be up to each student. Students should understand, however, that long, polished pieces are not required.

- When introducing the idea of dialogue journals, the teacher should inform students that they will be participating in a continuing, private, written conversation; that they may write about any topic that they choose; and that the teacher will write back each time they write, without correcting errors. The mechanics of when they will write, when the journals will be turned in, when they will be returned, and so on should be explained. When students are unable to think of something to write, the teacher might suggest one or two possible topics. The important thing is that everyone have something to write and that they feel comfortable with it.

- Some teachers in content courses prefer that the dialogue journal focus on course content. This has worked successfully when students are given considerable flexibility within the overall topic parameters. When too much restriction on topic is imposed, the dialogue begins to look like an assigned piece of writing.

- It is important that the teacher enter into the journal interaction as a good conversationalist and an interesting writer, and expect students to do the same. The goal is to be responsive to student topics and ask questions about them at times, but also to introduce topics and write about oneself and one's own interests and concerns (Peyton & Seyoum, 1989). Teacher entries that simply echo what the student wrote or that ask a lot of questions (typical "teacher talk") can stifle rather than promote interaction (Hall & Duffy, 1987).

- Finally, the teacher should relax and enjoy the writing! At first, the interaction might seem somewhat strained, as student and teacher find topics of mutual interest (see Lindfors, 1988b; Peyton, 1988, for discussion). But when the point of having mutual topics is reached, the dialogue flows easily. For many teachers, reading and writing in dialogue journals is the best part of the day—a wonderful time to find out about the people with whom they are spending the semester or year, to reflect on the past day's work, and to think about where their work together is taking them.

A NOTE OF CAUTION

Although dialogue journal writing was a teacher-initiated practice rather than an outgrowth of educational theory or research, it is compatible with current theories and research about effective environments for promoting language acquisition and writing development (Kreeft, Shuy, Staton, Reed, & Morroy, 1984; Peyton, this volume), and these benefits of dialogue journal writing have been cited throughout this chapter and the following chapter. However, a note of caution is in order. The primary purpose of dialogue journal writing and the key to its success was initially, and must remain, communication, with language and writing development as secondary benefits. When Leslee Reed, an elementary school teacher in Los Angeles and the first "dialogue journal teacher," began using them 20 years ago, it was for a very practical purpose—to communicate effectively with her students. Her primary goal was not to improve their English or their writing, and it was only upon later examination of this written communication that it became clear that this was happening as well. If priorities were reversed, and language and writing development became the primary goals of dialogue journal writing, it is likely that they would quickly become indistinguishable from other kinds of teacher-assigned exercises and lose their value as a place where limited-English-proficient students can freely and openly express themselves.

REFERENCES

Applebee, A. N. (1984). *Contexts for learning to write.* Norwood, NJ: Ablex.

Atwell, N. (1984). Writing and reading literature from the inside out. *Language Arts, 61*(3), 240–252.

Bailes, C., Searls, S., Slobodzian, J., & Staton, J. (1986). *It's your turn now: A handbook for teachers of deaf students.* Washington, DC: Gallaudet University.

Brinton, C., & Holten, C. (1988, March). *Perceptions of novice teachers: Insights gained through dialogue journals.* Paper presented at the 22nd Annual TESOL Convention, Chicago.

Davis, F. (1983). Why you call me emigrant? Dialogue journal writing with migrant youth. *Childhood Education, 60*(2), 110–116.

Farley, J. W. (1986). An analysis of written dialogue of educable mentally retarded writers. *Education and Training of the Mentally Retarded, 21*(3), 181–191.

Farley, J. W., & Farley, S. L. (1987). Interactive writing and gifted children: Communication through literacy. *Journal for the Education of the Gifted, 10*(2), 99–106.

Gutstein, S. (1987). *Toward the assessment of communicative competence in writing: An analysis of the dialogue journal writing of Japanese adult ESL students.* Unpublished doctoral dissertation, Georgetown University, Washington, DC.

Hall, N., & Duffy, R. (1987). Every child has a story to tell. *Language Arts, 64*(5), 523–529.

Hayes, C. W., & Bahruth, R. (1985). Querer es poder. In J. Hansen, T. Newkirk, & D. Graves (Eds.), *Breaking ground: Teachers relate reading and writing in the elementary school* (pp. 97–108). Portsmouth, NH: Heinemann.

Hayes, C. W., Bahruth, R., & Kessler, C. (1986, September). The dialogue journal and migrant education. *Dialogue,* pp. 3–5.

Hester, J. (1986, September). Features of semi-literate writing: One student's development. *Dialogue,* pp. 5–7.

Kitagawa, M. M., & Kitagawa, C. (1987). Journal writing. In M. M. Kitagawa & C. Kitagawa (Eds.), *Making connections with writing: An expressive model in Japanese schools* (pp. 58–66). Portsmouth, NH: Heinemann.

Kreeft, J. (1984a). *Dialogue journals and the acquisition of grammatical morphology in English as a second language.* Unpublished doctoral dissertation, Georgetown University, Washington, DC.

Kreeft, J. (1984b). Dialogue writing: Bridge from talk to essay writing. *Language Arts, 61*(2), 141–150.

Kreeft, J., Shuy, R. W., Staton, J., Reed, L., & Morroy, R. (1984). *Dialogue writing: Analysis of student-teacher interactive writing in the learning of English as a second language* (National Institute of Education Grant No. NIE-G-83–0030). Washington, DC: Center for Applied Linguistics. (ERIC Document Reproduction Service No. ED 252 097)

Lindfors, J. W. (1988a). From helping hand to reciprocity to mutuality: Dialogue journal writing with Zulu students. *Journal of Learning, 1*(1), 63–85.

Lindfors, J. W. (1988b). From "talking together" to "being together in talk." *Language Arts, 65*(2), 135–141.

Lindfors, J. W. (1988c). Zulu students' questioning in dialogue journals. *Questioning Exchange, 2*(3), 289–304.

Peyton, J. K. (1986). Literacy through written interaction. *Passage: A Journal for Refugee Education, 2*(1), 24–29.

Peyton, J. K. (1988). Mutual conversations: Written dialogue as a basis for building student-teacher rapport. In J. Staton, R. W. Shuy, J. K. Peyton, & L. Reed (Coauthors), *Dialogue journal communication: Classroom, linguistic, social and cognitive views* (pp. 183–201). Norwood, NJ: Ablex.

Peyton, J. K., & Seyoum, M. (1989). The effect of teacher strategies on students' interactive writing. *Research in the Teaching of English, 23*(3), 310–334.

Peyton, J. K., Staton, J., Richardson, G., & Wolfram, W. (In press). The influence of writing task on ESL student's written production. *Research in the Teaching of English.*

Peyton, J. K., & Steinberg, R. (1985, May). "I *can* write!" Written interaction of mentally handicapped students. *Dialogue,* pp. 3–5.

Roderick, J. (1986). Dialogue writing: Context for reflecting on self as teacher and researcher. *Journal of Curriculum and Supervision, 1*(4), 305–315.

Roderick, J., & Berman, L. (1984). Dialoguing about dialogue journals: Teachers as learners. *Language Arts, 61*(7), 686–692.

Shuy, R. W. (1987). The oral language basis of dialogue journal writing. In J. Staton, R. W. Shuy, J. K. Peyton, & L. Reed (Coauthors), *Dialogue journal communication: Classroom, linguistic, social and cognitive views* (pp. 73–87). Norwood, NJ: Ablex.

Staton, J. (1980). Writing and counseling: Using a dialogue journal. *Language Arts, 57*(5), 514–518.

Staton, J. (1984a). Dialogue journals as a means of enabling written language acquisition. In J. Kreeft, R. W. Shuy, J. Staton, L. Reed, & R. Morroy. *Dialogue writing: Analysis of student-teacher interactive writing in the learning of English as a second language* (National Institute of Education Grant No. NIE-G-83–0030). Washington, DC: Center for Applied Linguistics. (ERIC Document Reproduction Service No. ED 252 097)

Staton, J. (1984b). Thinking together: Interaction in children's reasoning. In C. Thaiss & C. Suhor (Eds.), *Speaking and writing, K-12.* Champaign, IL: National Council of Teachers of English.

Staton, J. (1986). The teacher's writing as a reading text. *Greater Washington Reading Council Journal, 11*, 3–4.

Staton, J., Peyton, J. K., & Gutstein, S. (Eds.). (1988, April). Dialogue journals in international settings [Theme issue]. *Dialogue*.

Staton, J., Shuy, R. W., Peyton, J. K., & Reed, L. (1988). *Dialogue journal communication: Classroom, linguistic, social and cognitive views.* Norwood, NJ: Ablex.

Steffensen, M. (1988, March). *Semantic/rhetorical patterns and two types of dialogue journals.* Paper presented at the 22nd Annual TESOL Convention, Chicago.

Walworth, M. (1985). Dialogue journals in the teaching of reading. *Teaching English to the Deaf and Second Language Students, 3*(1), 21–25.

13

Beginning at the Beginning
First-Grade ESL Students Learn to Write

JOY KREEFT PEYTON

From recent research with children learning to write in English as a second language, we have learned a great deal about the contexts that support their writing development (see Peyton, Chapter 12, this volume, for a description of one effective context). This chapter examines two major findings that derive from this research, with reference to a number of observational studies and reviews of the research by Hudelson (1984, 1986). The chapter then describes the onset and growth of writing ability among students in a first-grade classroom, many of whom were initially nonliterate in their native language and in English. In this classroom, the children were encouraged to read and write, and they blossomed as readers and writers of English.

WHAT WE KNOW ABOUT ESL CHILDREN'S WRITING

When working with students whose English proficiency is limited, it is tempting to concentrate on developing their mastery of basic English skills before giving them opportunities to read and write extended, open-ended

---

AUTHOR'S NOTE: I am grateful to Donna Christian, Sarah Hudelson, Judith Lindfors, and Dick Tucker for very helpful comments on earlier versions of this chapter.

texts. Franklin (1986), for example, described two teachers of limited-English-proficient students who believed that writing was too difficult for these students. Before the teachers allowed or encouraged their students to write, they spent long periods of time teaching basic vocabulary and metalinguistic information about sounds, letters, and words. Not only did the students have great difficulty with this basic language drill work, they spent so much time with it that by the end of the school year they had done very little actual reading or writing. While the native English speakers in one of the classes wrote extended and creative texts on a daily basis, the native Spanish-speaking children wrote only in response to highly structured assignments. Franklin hypothesized that this cautious approach to developing the writing proficiency of limited-English-proficient children actually retarded their literacy learning.

Recent research supports this hypothesis, showing that basic skill approaches do not promote writing development and may even inhibit it. Edelsky (1986) and Hudelson (1989) found that students' development as writers depended a great deal on their teachers' expectations of what they could do. Children whose teachers focused on phonics and spelling and correct writing conventions produced neat and correctly spelled papers that completely lacked life and originality and resembled workbook exercises. Children whose teachers believed that quantity of writing was a mark of writing development produced long pieces, with large open spaces between words and multiple repetitions of words, phrases, and longer chunks of text. Children whose teachers believed they were capable of expressing their thoughts and opinions effectively in a variety of types of extended writing wrote stories, poems, jokes, and thoughtful pieces about personal experiences.

Edelsky and Jilbert (1985) found that instruction focusing on basic skills and correct form could also have a negative effect on previously developed writing abilities and perceptions about writing. When children who had been producing a variety of thoughtful and creative pieces moved into a higher grade, in which they did exercises in writing rather than writing to communicate, the growth they had experienced stopped.

Similarly, Harste, Woodward, and Burke (1984) cited examples of native English-speaking children who came to school with a strong sense of reading and writing as vehicles for conveying meaning, but lost this sense in school, as they learned to focus on basic metalinguistic skills instead of overall meaning and text creation (discussed in Franklin, 1986).

One important generalization that can be derived from research is that *children learning ESL can and should begin writing long before they have complete control of oral English and have mastered its written systems.* Whether they are learning to write in their native language or another language, all children learn to write much as they learn to speak—through continually observing and participating in interactions, receiving informal feedback as they do so. As they observe how written language is used, they make and test hypotheses about how it works and make use of what they *do* know (which initially might be to draw pictures, make writing-like scribbles, or write a couple of words) to produce messages. At the same time, they use the resources around them to learn more.

Studies of literacy development before schooling have shown that most children have some knowledge of print before they come to school. Even students from non-English-speaking homes come to school with the ability to read some of the English print in their environment—on advertising billboards, cereal boxes, popular products, restaurant menus, and so on (Ferreiro & Teberosky, 1982; Goodman, Goodman & Flores, 1979). Placed in a context in which meaningful writing is encouraged, these children make use of this print knowledge, as well as various sources of print within the classroom, as resources for their writing. As they continue to interact with print by reading books and their own and their peers' writing, they begin to use knowledge gleaned from these texts for their own writing purposes (Martin, 1987).

Children learning English as a second language can begin writing very early in the process of learning English. Studies of young limited-English-proficient children just beginning to write have found that they use a number of approaches for getting started. They draw, copy words and phrases from print in their environment and reading texts, and invent spellings by sounding words out (Bartelo, 1984; Edelsky, 1986; Ewoldt, 1985; Flores & García, 1984; Hudelson, 1989). Some children write extended texts in English before they do much speaking (Edelsky, 1986; Kreeft, Shuy, Staton, Reed, & Morroy, 1984). The writing of these children reflects their developing English competence and provides important information for the teacher about their progress in learning English.

A second major finding is that *the contexts that promote writing are those in which children have frequent opportunities to meaningfully communicate in writing.* The contexts that best promote writing development are the following:

- Writing activities are integrated with reading, listening, and speaking within a meaningful social context.
- Writing activities build cooperation and self-esteem and encourage experimentation and risk taking.
- Children have frequent opportunities and long blocks of time to write extended texts.

- Writing is treated as an act of communication rather than as an opportunity to practice or drill language form.
- Children write for their own purposes, about topics that are of personal interest to them, and the teacher shows genuine interest in the ideas expressed.
- Children talk about and reflect on their writing.
- Children receive extensive language input, through reading and being read to, as well as through oral and written interactions with the teacher or their peers.
- Children receive feedback about their writing through oral or written interaction with the teacher or their peers. This feedback focuses first and primarily on content and secondarily on writing conventions and language form.

In sufficiently supportive classroom environments, students develop self-confidence and the motivation to continue to read and write. Hayes and Bahruth's (1985) sample of Spanish-speaking migrant youth, for example, initially showed extremely negative attitudes toward school and reading and writing activities. Once these barriers were eliminated in a supportive environment, they began to ask for books to take home, and by the end of the year they had published a number of books of their writings within the classroom.

In a supportive context for writing, children begin to take risks with written language. For example, in classes with young deaf children in which experimentation was encouraged and meaning was emphasized over form, the children "appeared not to feel shackled by the constraints of writing conventions," but began inventing their own spelling and language forms (Ewoldt, 1985, p. 119). Gradually, they incorporated standard writing conventions into their written work.

Children also learn how to look critically at and improve their writing. Studies by Urzúa (1986, 1987) have shown that limited-English-proficient children not only are able to react critically to other students' writing but are also able to make conscious decisions about ways to improve their texts in response to such feedback.

Ammon (1985, p. 82), after studying two third-grade ESL classrooms in which students had made writing gains superior to the other classes in the study, concluded that

> success in helping children learn to write in English as a second language hinges primarily on the use of instructional activities that are rich in opportunities for exposure to, production of, and reflection on English discourse … such activities must include frequent writing, with guidance and feedback, on topics of personal interest.

It is interesting that these are the same conditions and activities advocated by proponents of whole language approaches to literacy among native English-speaking children (Bissex, 1980; Calkins, 1983, 1986; Graves, 1983; Milz, 1985; and others). When these conditions exist, children learning English as a second language blossom as writers and show patterns of development that are similar in many ways to those of native English speakers.

THE ONSET AND DEVELOPMENT OF WRITING IN ONE ESL CLASSROOM: A CASE STUDY

During the 1986–1987 school year, Ruth Sedei—a teacher of a combined first- and second-grade class in Northern Virginia—and I studied the onset and development of writing in the beginning writers in her class of 20 students. The class consisted of 16 first and 4 second graders; the average age at the beginning of the school year was 6. Approximately half of the students were native Spanish speakers; the other half were native speakers of Vietnamese, Chinese, Farsi, or Turkish. Almost all of the first graders had very limited proficiency with spoken English at the beginning of the year and had no previous experience with reading and writing, either in their native language or in English. Either they had not attended kindergarten or they had done no writing in kindergarten (but those who had attended kindergarten had done a lot of drawing). Most told me in interviews at the beginning of the year that they did not have books or read at home.

Mrs. Sedei and I decided to focus our attention primarily on the students' dialogue journal writing. A dialogue journal is a written, ongoing interaction between individual students and their teacher in a bound notebook (see Peyton, this volume, for a detailed description). Dialogue journals have been used effectively with both native and nonnative English-speaking children (Kreeft, Shuy, Staton, Reed, & Morroy, 1984; Staton, Shuy, Peyton, & Reed, 1988) at upper elementary levels, and Mrs. Sedei had used them with lower elementary ESL students, but never with students with such limited previous schooling or at such early stages of learning to read and write. She planned to use dialogue journal writing as a starting point and then move to other kinds of writing. We hoped to understand how the journals could be used most effectively with these children, how they would handle the activity, and how they would develop as writers.

I spent one morning a week in the classroom, observing and taking field notes on activities, working with the students during their individual reading and writing times, interviewing them, and analyzing their dialogue journals and other writing.

At the end of the year, we believed that the dialogue journals had been a success—more successful than either of us had imagined possible, given the level of students we were working with. In the process, we learned a great deal about early writing in general—the contexts that seemed to promote it and patterns of writing development in a literacy-rich environment. What we learned fell under five broad themes, which confirmed the general research findings presented previously.

The Classroom Environment and Activities Provided a Rich Context for the Literacy Development of These Students

This could be called a "whole language" classroom, a classroom in which the children and the teacher used oral and written language functionally and purposefully for genuine communication, to meet personal and social needs (Goodman, 1986). The language the children were exposed to and used primarily was English, because the class was not part of a bilingual program. Their first language was respected, and they often used it with each other and were encouraged to use it when helping new students. They could use their first language in their writing, and, if they wrote in their dialogue journals in Spanish, the teacher responded in Spanish. Other than that, English was used.

Even before they began to read and write, the children had multiple exposures to print used for communication. They were read to every day from commercial books, introduced to a new nursery rhyme each week, which they learned to recite and "read" together, and about halfway through the year they read books on their own and wrote comments and reactions in a "reading journal." The room was filled with print media—books, dictionaries, posters, and bulletin boards.

After she had been reading to the children for about a month, Mrs. Sedei began to discuss various stylistic and mechanical features of the texts with them—the use of rhyming, dialogue and direct quotation, repetition, exaggeration, humor; the sounds that began and ended words and the letters that formed them; words that rhymed; and the stylistic use of punctuation, such as question, exclamation, and quotation marks.

We were surprised by the sophistication of the comments that the children began to make about the style and level of interest of their readings, and their ability to sound out words in new texts. Even though most of the first graders did not yet read or write themselves, they came to an early understanding that written text was a natural and important way to communicate a message.

After an Introductory Period, the Children Were
Able to "Start Right Off" Writing

Mrs. Sedei spent the first month introducing the children to school routines and behaviors, exposing them to written text and having them draw pictures in response to it, and letting their oral language facility develop before they actually began writing. Their first writing experience was with a dialogue journal. For about a week, Mrs. Sedei modeled the writing of a dialogue journal entry by writing an entry of her own on a large sheet of paper and talking through her process of thinking about what to write, deciding on a topic, and writing. The next week, the children drew and wrote (if they could) each day on large sheets of paper. For some of them, this was their first experience with putting something on paper; it was the first time a few of them had held a pencil. The following week, each child was given a bound notebook with primary-spaced lines and told that they would write and draw in it each day, and that the teacher would respond in writing. In the beginning most drew, but they were encouraged to write something as well, even if it was only their name, the date (copied from the board), or a few original words. Naveed's early entries, one of which is shown in Figure 13.1, are typical of those of most of the children. He has drawn a musical instrument with two fingers snapping (he explained to me), copied the date and "Monday" from the board, written some letters and "Monday music" (Monday we had music). The teacher's response is at the bottom of the page. (She responded to each entry written by the children.)

The children were given a considerable amount of time each day to write in their journals, and at first it took some of them a long time to produce an entry. As the year progressed, they had about 15 minutes at the beginning of each day and as much time as they needed later, during free reading and writing time, when they did a wide variety of writing—responses to stories read in class, group-written original stories, reactions to books they had read, daily observations of a plant's growth in science journals, and an occasional worksheet.

The purpose of their journal creations was to communicate a message to another person. In the beginning, Mrs. Sedei called each child during the free reading/writing time and asked them what they had "told" her in their journals. They explained or read their message, she wrote a reply and read it to them, and they read it aloud together. As soon as individual children seemed ready to read her replies with little help, they were no longer called to read with her, but received the journal with her reply the next morning.

October 4

TﬔE 2255 MondAY

MondAyMSEQ

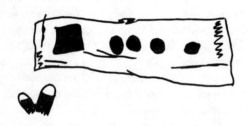

I _love_ music. I like

pianos. What instrument

do you like best?

FIGURE 13.1

Our first discovery during the starting-up process amazed us. We had expected that the children would have little trouble drawing in their journals, but we actually wondered what and how they would "write," because some of them did not even know the letters of the alphabet. They were permitted to ask for the spelling of one word a day, which they listed in a self-made, alphabetized book, but were on their own to write what they wanted to say.

What we discovered was that they did not seem to question, as we did, their ability to start writing. They simply started (an observation made also by Giacobbe, 1981, about native English speaking; and Flores & Hernandez, 1988, about nonnative English-speaking first graders). They *found* the resources they needed to create their written messages in the print that surrounded them. The room became a buzz of activity during dialogue journal time as they thought about what they wanted to write and gathered the resources for writing it. Everything in print—writing on the walls and blackboard, books, dictionaries, the names of other students printed in bold letters on each desk, previous journal entries, even the words *boys* and *girls* on the bathroom passes—became resources for their writing.

The first word that Gabriela wrote, after about three weeks of drawing pictures of people with no words on the page, was the name of one of the other students (above a picture), copied from the student's desk. She later added more student names to her pictures, along with the word *clock,* copied from the sign below the classroom clock directly above her desk. When Jeffrey decided he wanted to write about Christmas, he copied the first part of another student's (Christian's) name from his desk (Figure 13.2).

At times, the children planned their entries ahead and brought pieces of paper to school with the words and sentences they would need. When Marilyn brought a part of a shopping bag that had *K-Mart* written on it, she told us that she had gone to K-Mart the day before and wanted to write about it in her journal.

The books they were reading provided another resource for their writing. One day, Xin was writing about a game he had played. He wanted to say that his brother had won, and he remembered that he had read a story about someone who had won a race and shouted, "I win! I win!" So he found the book and looked up the word (Figure 13.3). Xin's reading provided not only words but also inspiration for his journal writing. One day he had a book he was reading open on his desk to a page that said, "Soon he came to a small house. It was the kind of house that witches live in. But he did not know that. 'I see you,' said a voice." That day Xin wrote, "My friend heard a voice when he talked to somebody. That was my voice" (Figure 13.4).

Prepackaged chunks of writing often served as triggers to get the children started. Each day the date was written on the board, and the date was the first

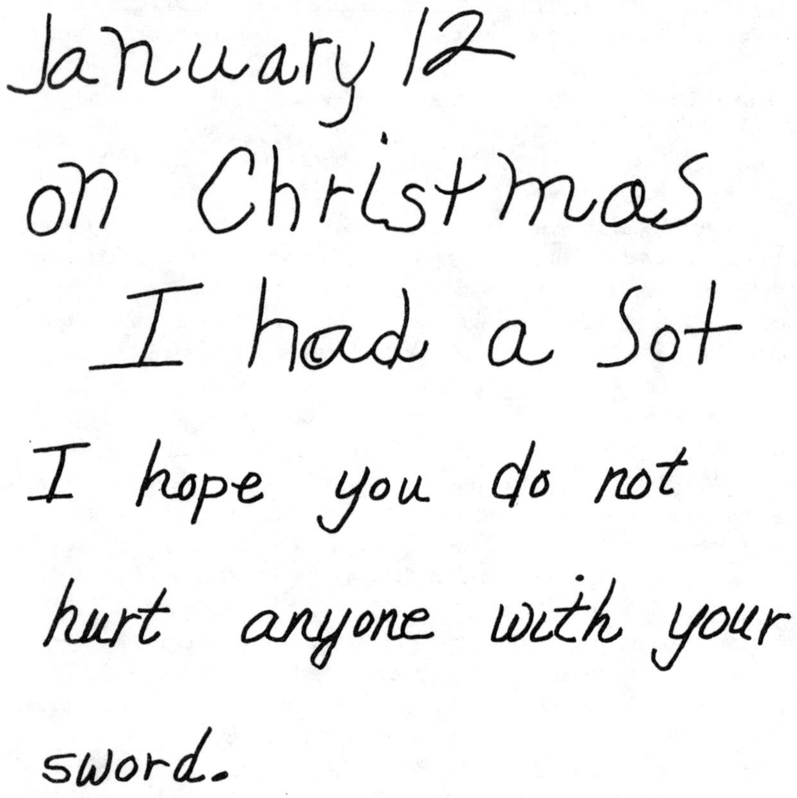

January 12

on Christmas

I had a Sot

I hope you do not

hurt anyone with your

sword.

FIGURE 13.2

thing every child wrote. Danny usually wrote the date and "I," and then stopped to think. I asked Gabriela once what she was going to write about that day, and she said, "First I write the date; then I think about what I'm going to write."

Their own and the teacher's previous writing in the journal were also resources that were constantly growing in size and complexity. It was common to see someone rifling through their journal, looking for a word or phrase they *knew* was in there. Once, when I took a student's completed journal home to photocopy, she asked me to be sure I brought it back the next week, as she would need it to look up words.

Mach 9

I play at my House I play bengo my littl brolvre win

Did you play number Bingo or word Bingo? I guess your little brother was happy when he won.

FIGURE 13.3

The point is that, even though these children had no formal training in the mechanics of producing written text, they didn't seem to have any feeling at all that they couldn't do it. They simply started, using the resources they had immediately available to them and gradually building on those, including the growing body of their own and the teacher's writing. After some time, they no longer relied as heavily on copying print resources in their immediate environment but used invented spelling to write original messages not tied to their immediate context.

December 10

moy farn herr a

voice wen He Tooc

to som bode va+ wos

moy voice

FIGURE 13.4

***Freedom to Write Combined with Talk About Writing
Were Essential Components of the Learning Process***

A crucial element of the children's literacy development was the freedom
they had to produce their texts. They were given long periods of time in
which to read and write at their own pace. They used that time not only to
read and write, but also to walk around the room looking at dictionaries,
writing needed words in their self-made word lists, and talking to each other
about their work. Given this freedom to read, write, talk, and to develop
more or less at their own pace, these children gradually learned *how* to read
and write.

However, they were not simply left alone to write without guidance. We know from studies of oral language development (Cazden, 1983; McNamee, 1979; Wells, 1986) the important role of adult guidance and assistance, just slightly beyond the learner's current level of production. Edelsky and Jilbert (1985, p. 65) found that when children had "no guidance in learning to increase [their] purposes for writing ... and no instruction in expanding the repertoires of options for accomplishing [their] own intents, [their] growth as writers plateaued." With the children in Mrs. Sedei's class, discussions and oral and written feedback were as important to their writing development as the freedom to experiment.

Early in the year, Mrs. Sedei held whole class discussions of what kinds of things might be interesting to write about. When many children seemed fixed on a single style, such as writing "I like _____" every day, the class gathered again to discuss possibilities for more variety and interest in their entries. The children suggested that they might write about what they had done, planned to do, thought about, or wished for. These group discussions were crucial for helping them move into new stages in their writing.

However, guiding and advancing writing is ultimately a very individual matter. The children not only were developing in very different ways but were at different stages in their development. Most of the interactions about writing were done individually, during conversations as the children wrote, in discussions with the teacher after she had written her response, and in the teacher's journal writing itself. Therefore, comments and questions were closely tied to what the children were writing or had written.

One area in which we pushed the children was to provide elaboration in their writing. About midyear, most of them had reached the point where they had no trouble writing a single proposition, and that is what their journals contained—precisely one proposition, as if they believed they were supposed to write that much. But as we made comments and asked questions, we found that they were usually eager and able to revise their writing to accommodate the need to expand on a topic. One day, for example, Jeffrey simply wrote, "It was boring yesterday." I stopped by his desk before he turned in his journal and asked him why yesterday was boring. Later, when I read his journal, I discovered he had added, "My friend didn't came out siede" (come outside). This was the first time that he had written more than one proposition in his journal.

Gabriela, who began the year with no knowledge of English, learned how to write "My school is fun," and wrote that as her journal entry almost daily. When asked one day *why* she thought school was fun, she added "because the people is fun," which provided the impetus for adding another point, "I think sanh (some) people is not fun." In several of her following entries, she elaborated on her original thought with "because _____," until she learned other ways of elaborating on topics.

Students were also asked in the journal to provide more details in their writing. Deny, for example, was one of the most capable first graders in the class, able to write at the beginning of the year. Mrs. Sedei pressed him for detail both in discussions and in their journal, as in the interaction in Figures 13.5 and 13.6.

Not all of the assistance that occurred was content-related or occurred on the level of discourse. Some focused on the writing and reading of individual words and on writing conventions. In the following discussion of the journal interaction shown in Figure 13.7, Mrs. Sedei concentrated on Christian's recognition of a single word, *bike*.

Mrs. Sedei: *OK, see if you can read what I wrote to you.*

Christian: *I have a [pause]*

Mrs. Sedei: *What are we talking about? What did you tell me that you have?*

Christian: *bike*

Mrs. Sedei: *bike. OK, let's read again … [They read her entry together] All right, where is the word "bike"?*

Christian: *Here.*

Mrs. Sedei: *OK, you wrote it there. Where did I write the word "bike"?*

Christian: *Here.*

Mrs. Sedei: *OK, how many times did I write the word "bike"?*

Christian: *Two.*

Mrs. Sedei: *Show me where I wrote the word "bike."*

Christian: *[Points]*

Mrs. Sedei: *Very nice. I'm proud of you and what you're writing in your journal. It's very nice.*

In the exchange in Figures 13.8 and 13.9, Naveed picks up on the teacher's spelling of *field trip* in his next journal entry. (On February 3, Naveed wrote "Today I forgot to bring my field trip slip." On February 9, he wrote "When we went on the field trip and when we went to the maze I tried to get lost, but I couldn't get lost"—Figure 13.9.)

November 20

yesterday I went to
Komac and doa I
bought mae a Toy
three Tay
   Please tell me tomorrow
about the toys you
bought

FIGURE 13.5

November 26

I bought a super man

I Mock a hunter

house werf My Little

brothers and my big

brothers

Did you make a Haunted

House inside or outside?

FIGURE 13.6

Assistance of this kind, from content and discourse features to matters of form, *must* occur if children's writing is to develop. But rather than deciding ahead of time what they need to learn and teaching it to the entire class, this assistance involves working with young writers at *their* stage of development, as manifested in their writing (at their "zone of proximal develop-

January 12

MY baec is black
MY baec is gray

I have a red bike.
I like to ride my bike.

FIGURE 13.7

ment," in Vygotsky's, 1978, terms). A student who writes "I like _____"
every day needs to be asked to write about something else—"things you like
to do, think about, or wish for." For another student, writing "I like _____"
may be a new and important stage of development. Some students may need
to learn to find and copy words they need. Others, who have been busy
gathering and using these "sight words," may need to become more independent and less bound to environmental print, to sound words out, and to take
risks with spelling. Those who write one or two brief sentences and decide
that their journal entry is finished may need to be encouraged to elaborate on
those beginning ideas so that their writing is more interesting and under-
standable. Others, who write long journal entries, may need to be assured
that length is not really important and encouraged to stop, think about, and
plan what they want to say. With one student, having written anything at all
may be a victory. Another may need to pay more attention to what his or her
audience might be interested in or need to know. As children write, read what
the teacher has written specifically for them, and talk about their writing,
they develop in their writing and reading in a way that should be both comfortable and challenging for them.

February 3

Today I frgod
To dreg My

7ueSiepSleP
Please try to remember
your field trip slip
tomorrow.   We're going
on a great field trip.

FIGURE 13.8

Fedruary 9

when we po to

the field triP ANd

when we went
to the maze I
Sroi to pod Lost
dot I Kdat gadt
Lost

FIGURE 13.9

The Children Began to Act and Talk Like Writers

Over time, we watched these children progress as writers. They went through the standard stages of writing that we had expected, based on earlier studies of young children's writing development: moving from drawing to writing; moving from reliance on copied sight words to sounding out words and using invented spelling, which gradually approximated conventional spelling; demonstrating knowledge of written conventions (spaces between words, punctuation, capitalization); elaborating on topics; and showing an awareness of audience.

Of special interest was their developing *behavior* as writers and the important functions that writing began to have for them. As Graves (1983) found with native English-speaking children who wrote daily, these children came to think of themselves as authors who thought independently about writing and initiated their own topics and activities. Writing became a natural and essential means of communicating. For example, after some particularly raucous behavior on a field trip to the planetarium, the children were asked to sit quietly at their desks and think about what had happened during this time. One wrote Mrs. Sedei a note saying "I am soer at the planetarium I was rode I am very soer" (I am sorry. At the planetarium I was rude. I am very sorry.) One day another student asked Mrs. Sedei if she could have a piece of paper, and she vented her frustrations with her brother (Figure 13.10).

Some students began, unbidden, to write stories at home and bring them in to share with the class. As they shared these stories, others were inspired to write stories as well, and one of the classroom activities became the printing, illustrating, and binding of their stories in book form so that they were available for other children to read.

The children began to associate thinking with writing. While at the beginning of the year they were simply trying to get something on paper, at the end of the year they started talking about the need to think. They were learning that their thoughts rather than their circumstances could determine what they would write about.

They also began to plan their writing ahead of time. The papers they brought in with words and sentences that they intended to use in their writing showed that they had been planning. Students would often come into class in the morning or after music, P.E., or lunch and tell us about something they intended to write about or try out a sentence or idea on us. One student told me, "Yesterday I decided I would write this today." When I asked another student how she decided what she was going to write about in her journal, she said, "I decide because when I take my bus, when I'm waiting on my bus

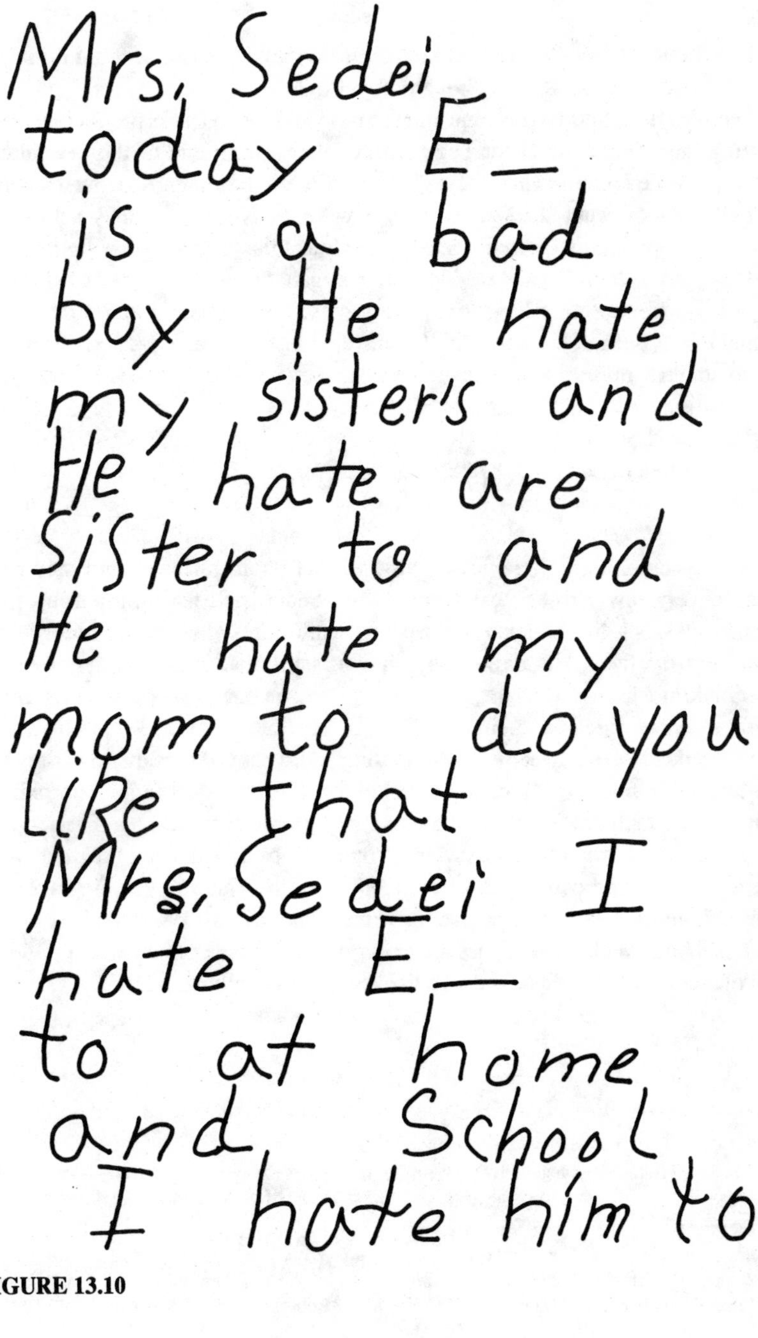

Mrs. Sedei
today E—
is a bad
box He hate,
my sister's and
He hate are
Sister to and
He hate my
mom to do you
like that
Mrs. Sedei I
hate E—
to at home,
and School,
I hate him to

FIGURE 13.10

stop, I think. Then when I go in the school, I can write fast without thinking about it because I've already thought about it."

Finally, the children became much more independent in producing their writing than they were at the beginning of the year. In end-of-the-year interviews, I asked them what they did when they didn't know how to spell something they wanted to write. Very few students said that they asked the teacher. Instead, they offered strategies such as this: "I just spell it by myself; I think and I do it." One student, who began the year unwilling to write anything without first asking for spelling help, said, "I sound it. Sound it like I think. . . . [Before] I asked Mrs. Grant [the classroom aide]. Then one day I try to spell by myself and I did."

CONCLUSION: LESSONS FROM THE CASE STUDY

These beginning writers never had a formal phonics lesson, and they performed very few writing "exercises." Mrs. Sedei tried teaching a couple of spelling lessons but stopped when she wasn't sure what the children were learning from them. Her philosophy, in contrast to that of the teachers studied by Franklin (discussed at the beginning of the chapter), was that they *could* learn to write, even as their oral English proficiency was developing, and they would do so by reading and writing. And they did learn to write: by reading, watching writing being modeled for them, and writing regularly in a context in which writing was functional, communicative, and nonthreatening. They had the freedom to pursue their own topics and develop at their own pace, and they received constant feedback on what they were writing. Throughout the year, they increasingly acted and talked like—they became— writers. And we learned to trust the process of development that previous researchers had described, because these children demonstrated it.

REFERENCES

Ammon, P. (1985). Helping children learn to write in ESL: Some observations and some hypotheses. In S. W. Freedman (Ed.), *The acquisition of written language: Response and revision* (pp. 65–84). Norwood, NJ: Ablex.

Bartelo, D. M. (1984). *Getting the picture of reading and writing: A look at the drawings, composing, and language of limited English proficiency children.* Alexandria, VA: United States Department of Education. (ERIC Document Reproduction Service No. ED 245 533)

Bissex, G. (1980). *GYNS AT WRK*. Cambridge, MA: Harvard University Press.

Calkins, L. M. (1983). *Lessons from a child*. Portsmouth, NH: Heinemann.

Calkins, L. M. (1986). *The art of teaching writing*. Portsmouth, NH: Heinemann.

Cazden, C. (1983). Adult assistance to language development: Scaffolds, models, and direct instruction. In R. Parker & F. Davis (Eds.), *Developing literacy: Young children's use of language*. Newark, DE: International Reading Association.

Edelsky, C. (1986). *Writing in a bilingual program: Había una vez*. Norwood, NJ: Ablex.

Edelsky, C., & Jilbert, K. (1985). Bilingual children and writing: Lessons for all of us. *Volta Review, 87*(5), 57–72.

Ewoldt, C. (1985). A descriptive study of the developing literacy of young hearing-impaired children. *Volta Review, 87*(5), 109–126.

Ferreiro, E., & Teberosky, A. (1982). *Literacy before schooling*. Portsmouth, NH: Heinemann.

Flores, B. M., & García, E. H. (1984). A collaborative learning and teaching experience using journal writing. *NABE Journal, 8*(2), 67–83.

Flores, B. M., & Hernandez, E. (1988). A bilingual kindergartner's sociopsychogenesis of literacy and biliteracy. *Dialogue, 5*(3), 6–7.

Franklin, E. A. (1986). Literacy instruction for ESL children. *Language Arts, 63*(1), 51–60.

Giacobbe, M. E. (1981). Who says that children can't write the first week? In R. D. Walshe (Ed.), *Donald Graves in Australia: Children want to write …* (pp. 99–103). Exeter, NH: Heinemann.

Goodman, K. (1986). *What's whole in whole language?* Portsmouth, NH: Heinemann.

Goodman, K., Goodman, Y., & Flores, B. (1979). *Reading in the bilingual classroom: Literacy and biliteracy*. Rosslyn, VA: National Clearinghouse for Bilingual Education.

Graves, D. (1983). *Writing: Teachers and children at work*. Portsmouth, NH: Heinemann.

Harste, J., Woodward, V., & Burke, C. (1984). *Language stories and literacy lessons*. Portsmouth, NH: Heinemann.

Hayes, C. W., & Bahruth, R. (1985). Querer es poder. In J. Hansen, T. Newkirk, & D. Graves (Eds.), *Breaking ground: Teachers relate reading and writing in the elementary school* (pp. 97–108). Portsmouth, NH: Heinemann.

Hudelson, S. (1984). Kan you ret an rayt en ingles: Children become literate in English as a second language. *TESOL Quarterly, 18*(2), 221–238.

Hudelson, S. (1986). ESL children's writing: What we've learned, what we're learning. In P. Rigg & D. S. Enright (Eds.), *Children and ESL: Integrating perspectives* (pp. 25–54). Washington, DC: Teachers of English to Speakers of Other Languages.

Hudelson, S. (1989). A tale of two children: Individual differences in ESL children's writing. In D. M. Johnson & D. H. Roen (Eds.). *Richness in writing: Empowering ESL students* (pp. 84–89). New York: Longman.

Kreeft, J., Shuy, R. W., Staton, J., Reed, L., & Morroy, R. (1984). *Dialogue writing: Analysis of student-teacher interactive writing in the learning of English as a second language* (National Institute of Education Grant No. NIE-G-83–0030). Washington, DC: Center for Applied Linguistics. (ERIC Document Reproduction Service No. ED 252 097)

Martin, N. (1987). What writers! What readers! What thinkers! *Language Arts, 63*(2), 170–176.

McNamee, G. D. (1979). The social interaction origins of narrative skills. *Quarterly Newsletter of the Laboratory of Comparative Human Cognition, 1*(4). (University of California at San Diego)

Milz, V. (1985). First graders' uses for writing. In A. Jagger & M. T. Smith-Burke (Eds.), *Observing the language learner* (pp. 173–189). Newark, DE: International Reading Association.

Staton, J., Shuy, R. W., Peyton, J. K., & Reed, L. (1988). *Dialogue journal communication: Classroom, linguistic, social and cognitive views.* Norwood, NJ: Ablex.

Urzúa, C. (1986, April). *I grow for a living.* Paper presented at the International TESOL Convention, Anaheim, CA.

Urzúa, C. (1987). You stopped too soon: Second language children composing and revising. *TESOL Quarterly, 21*(2), 279–304.

Vygotsky, L. (1978). *Mind in society: The development of higher psychological processes* (M. Cole, V. John-Steiner, S. Scribner, & E. Louberman, Eds. & Trans.). Cambridge, MA: Harvard University Press.

Wells, G. (1986). *The meaning makers: Children learning language and using language to learn.* Portsmouth, NH: Heinemann.

14

Cooperative Learning

Instructing Limited-English-Proficient Students in Heterogenous Classes

EVELYN JACOB
BEVERLY MATTSON

A major educational challenge is to help students with limited English proficiency to achieve academically and to develop the language skills necessary to successfully function in classrooms. Schools face a special challenge when students comprise diverse language groups at varying levels of English proficiency. How can these diverse needs be met?

In this chapter we discuss cooperative learning methods as a solution to the dilemma faced by teachers with heterogeneous classrooms that include limited-English-proficient (LEP) students. These heterogeneous classes may include students at different grade levels, from different language backgrounds, or with different levels of English language proficiency. We draw on theory, research, and interviews we conducted with teachers across the country.

WHAT IS COOPERATIVE LEARNING?

In cooperative learning students work together in small groups—two to six members—that are positively interdependent (Kagan, 1986). Positive interdependence means that the achievement of any team member contributes to the rewards of all.

Cooperative learning involves two primary features: cooperative task structures and cooperative reward structures. Cooperative task structures are those in which two or more individuals "are allowed, encouraged, or required to work together on some task" (Slavin, 1983, p. 5). This contrasts with independent task structures, where mutual assistance is impossible or forbidden. Cooperative reward structures are those in which two or more individuals are "in a situation where the task related efforts of any individual helps others to be rewarded" (Slavin, 1983, p. 4). This contrasts with competitive or individualistic reward structures. In competitive reward structures, one person's success is another's failure, while in individualistic reward structures, one person's performance has no influence on another's reward.

Cooperative learning methods contrast with both whole class methods and with small group methods. Whole class teaching methods usually involve neither cooperative task structure nor cooperative reward structure. Instead, students usually are required to work alone with either a competitive or an individualistic reward system. Learning in small groups is not necessarily cooperative. Although small group methods may employ a cooperative task structure in which students work together on some task or project, the reward structure may be competitive or individualistic.

TYPES OF COOPERATIVE LEARNING

While all cooperative learning methods share cooperative task and reward structures, there are various types of cooperative learning methods. Kagan (1985a) divides cooperative learning methods between those that apply across various subject areas and grade levels and those that apply only to specific subject matter and grade levels. Cooperative learning methods that can be applied across subject areas and grade levels include the following (see Kagan, 1985a, 1985b, 1986).

Peer Practice

In this approach, group members drill and assist one another in learning predetermined content (for example, vocabulary words or math facts) with the aim of bringing each to his or her highest level. In some instances, the group members cooperate to compete against other groups. Examples of peer practice methods are Student Teams Achievement Divisions (STAD) and Teams-Games-Tournaments (TGT) (Slavin, 1986).

Jigsaw

In this approach, all groups are given the same task—for example, mastering a learning unit or document. Within a "home" group each member is given primary responsibility for a unique part of the unit or document. Each student works with members from other home groups who have responsibility for the same content. After working in these "expert" groups, the students return to their home groups to teach them the material in which they are expert. Students are then evaluated on their mastery of the entire unit. Examples are original Jigsaw and Jigsaw II (Aronson, Blaney, Stephan, Sikes, & Snapp, 1978; Slavin, 1986).

Cooperative Projects

In the Cooperative Projects approach, students work to produce a group project that they may have selected from several options. Usually, individuals within each group make a unique contribution to the group's efforts. In addition, groups frequently make unique contributions to the class as a whole without overt between-group competition. Examples of cooperative project methods are Group Investigation (Sharan & Hertz-Lazarowitz, 1979) and Co-op Co-op (Kagan, 1985a, 1985b).

Learning Together

Learning Together is a framework for applying cooperative learning principles (Johnson & Johnson, 1975; Johnson, Johnson, Holubec, & Roy, 1984). It does not have a specific method of organization but outlines decisions teachers need to make to apply cooperative learning. It emphasizes positive interdependence among students, individual accountability, and students' use of collaborative skills.

There also are several curriculum-specific approaches that vary widely in their organization. *Finding Out/Descubrimiento* is a science and math curriculum for Spanish-English bilingual students in grades two and three (De-Avila, Duncan, & Navarrete, 1987). Team Assisted Individualization (TAI) is a math program for grades two through seven (Slavin, 1985). Rotation Science Centers (RSC) is a science curriculum for grade three and upward (Kagan, 1985a). Cooperative Integrated Reading and Composition (CIRC) is a reading and writing program for grades three and four (Slavin, 1986). While TAI, RSC, and CIRC can be used with LEP students, these materials are only available in English.

COOPERATIVE LEARNING AND LEP STUDENTS

To learn more about how cooperative learning methods are used with LEP students, we interviewed 17 teachers and 12 school administrators across the United States. These persons self-identified or were identified by others in response to announcements in newsletters indicating our interest in interviewing individuals who were experienced in using cooperative learning methods with LEP students. We conducted open-ended telephone interviews, asking teachers about their use of cooperative learning methods and asking administrators about the implementation of cooperative learning in their districts or schools.

We found that only recently have cooperative learning methods been explicitly used with LEP students. Moreover, while the approach has been implemented by districts for LEP students in a few states (California and Oregon), in the rest of the country the approach has been implemented primarily by individual teachers.

Individual teachers used cooperative learning most often where English was the language of instruction and the language of communication among the students. The classes frequently were ESL or sheltered English classes with LEP students representing a variety of language backgrounds, or they were self-contained regular curriculum classes with both native English speakers and LEP students.

All classes were characterized by considerable student heterogeneity. The number of different ethnolinguistic groups per teacher ranged from 2 to 13, with an average of 6 groups. Moreover, teachers typically had more than one grade level in their classes and a wide range of levels of English proficiency. In some classes there were native English speakers as well as LEP students.

Cooperative learning methods were used in all grade levels, from prekindergarten through adult education. While English and language arts were the most frequent subjects in which cooperative learning methods were used, they were also used in other academic and nonacademic subjects.

EFFECTS OF COOPERATIVE LEARNING METHODS

Teachers were enthusiastic in their support of cooperative learning methods. Almost all of the teachers we interviewed reported increases in their students' English language proficiency. Most reported improvement in academic achievement or student learning and in social relations among students. Several teachers also mentioned psychological benefits for individual students.

English Proficiency

Teachers reported that students increased their English vocabulary and usage, and that students "blossomed out" and were more confident in English. In addition, teachers felt that cooperative learning promoted spontaneous conversations among students and provided students more learning opportunities in English. These positive evaluations are exemplified through one teacher's written evaluation of one of her lessons that used a peer practice approach: "I was astonished by the amount of dedication to task, the ease of instruction on the part of the [tutors] and the concentration and total attention of the [tutees]. ... I could not believe the amount of English paraphrasing I heard."

Some teachers also mentioned that students' contributions to discussions in classes had increased. For example, one teacher said that students talked more, expressed more ideas in class, and generally contributed more to discussions.

The teachers' reports are consistent with current theory and research. Cooperative learning provides opportunities for face-to-face interaction among students around school tasks, which theory suggests is important for second-language acquisition (Krashen, 1981). Research indicates that cooperative learning methods resulted in greater improvement in English proficiency than traditional whole class methods (Bejarano, 1987; DeAvila & Duncan, 1977, as reported in Cohen, 1986; Sharan et al., 1985).

Academic Achievement

Three-fourths of the teachers reported that cooperative learning had a positive effect on students' academic achievement. Generally, teachers felt that students were performing better on class work and on quizzes. In particular, they stated that they had observed a higher quality of student learning, that students had greater retention and consolidation of material, and that students learned more from each other.

The teachers' reports are substantiated by research. There is strong and consistent evidence that cooperative learning raises the academic achievement of students in general (Slavin, 1983). Moreover, there is strong evidence, although from a limited number of studies, that cooperative learning raises the academic achievement of ethnic minority students (Lucker, Rosenfield, Sikes, & Aronson, 1976; Slavin, 1977; Slavin & Oickle, 1981).

Social Relations

In reporting better social relationships among students, teachers noted more praise and supportive comments among students (rather than put-downs or sharp criticisms), closer group feelings, and less competition. Teachers also commented on the benefits of cooperative learning for relationships between native English-speaking students and LEP students. They reported changes in attitudes toward minority students and cultural awareness as well as increases in cross-cultural help and cooperation.

Again the literature supports the teachers' reports. Cooperation promotes greater interpersonal attraction among heterogeneous individuals than do interpersonal competition and individualistic efforts (Johnson, Johnson, & Maruyama, 1983).

Psychological Adjustment

Several teachers mentioned affective benefits for individual students, such as improved motivation, positive attitudes toward classes and school, and increased self-esteem and self-confidence. Teachers also reported less absenteeism and fewer discipline problems.

Although this topic has been less thoroughly researched than the previous ones, the literature lends support to the teachers' comments. Johnson, Johnson, and Maruyama (1983) conclude that cooperative learning situations seem to promote higher levels of self-esteem than do competitive and individualistic situations.

DIFFICULTIES IN USING COOPERATIVE LEARNING

Some teachers we interviewed commented about the difficulties they experienced in implementing cooperative learning methods. The changes in the teacher's role and the social structure of the class required by cooperative learning methods involved some readjustment for many teachers. They also felt that cooperative learning methods require more teacher time in planning, preparation, and implementation in the initial stages. Some teachers reported difficulties in trying to use cooperative learning methods within the confines of class and school schedules without commercially available materials.

Several teachers also commented on problems in forming and maintaining the groups. They said that organizing heterogeneous groups by gender, ethnic group, achievement level, and level of English language proficiency can be complicated. Maintaining groups often requires much effort by teachers because of clashes in students' personalities within groups or because of the need to integrate students who are "loners" or non-English speakers.

TRAINING AND SUPPORT NEEDED

Teachers made suggestions concerning the training and information needed to implement cooperative learning methods with LEP students. They said that training should be longer than the typical one to three days of workshops, and that the instructors should use cooperative learning methods to present the workshops. The teachers wanted explicit help in integrating cooperative learning methods with language acquisition theory and research. They wanted to know how to implement cooperative learning methods in a way that follows principles of effective instruction for LEP students. The teachers also suggested that presentations of cooperative learning methods should include specific examples of lessons under each approach and explanations of similarities and differences among the approaches. Further, they wanted to know how to adapt cooperative learning methods for students of different cultural backgrounds and different levels of English proficiency, for different kinds of content or activities, and for different kinds of class schedules. Finally, they were interested in learning about commercially available materials and about ways to teach group process skills to their students.

Teachers felt that successful implementation of cooperative learning requires ongoing training and support after they begin implementing the methods. This could include coaching, support group meetings, and networking with others using the methods. They felt it was important to realize that successful implementation takes a commitment of time and resources, especially at the beginning, to develop activities.

Support from building- and district-level administrators is also crucial (Ellis, 1987). An innovation such as cooperative learning is most likely to work when administrators provide support such as released time, encouragement, and validation (Ellis, 1987). Moreover, administrators need to understand cooperative learning methods in order to provide helpful and valid evaluations. These suggestions are consistent with the general literature on training (Joyce & Showers, 1982).

DECIDING WHICH COOPERATIVE
LEARNING METHOD TO USE

Cooperative learning methods can be used in any type of program and with a wide variety of academic and nonacademic subjects. Teachers need not select just *one* method. Many teachers use more than one approach with their students. The specific methods selected will depend on a teacher's instructional goals—both for subject matter and for communication experiences in English. Teachers may also take into account their objectives for the development of students' collaborative skills; the ages, ethnicity, and levels of English proficiency of their students; the time allotted to a unit; and the daily schedule for an activity.

Subject Matter Instructional Goals

Peer practice methods appear best suited for learning basic skills and information. Jigsaw methods are useful for mastering text, while cooperative project approaches are useful for analytic and creative thinking. Learning Together emphasizes the development of interpersonal and group skills (see Kagan, 1985a).

Communication Goals

In peer practice approaches, students assume roles of tutor and tutee, with much of the interaction focused around drill and practice. In Jigsaw approaches, students may assume the additional roles of expert consultant or team leader. Interactions in Jigsaw may include expert presentations, discussion and analysis among experts, and tutoring. In cooperative project approaches, students' roles are expanded further to include investigator and resource gatherer. Interactions may become more complex and may include planning, decision making, critical analysis and synthesis, and creativity (see Kagan, 1985b).

IMPLEMENTING COOPERATIVE LEARNING

After selecting an appropriate method, teachers need to prepare the necessary materials and arrange the room to facilitate cooperative group work. This might involve developing study sheets and quiz sheets for peer practice approaches, or dividing up a text assignment into parts for a Jigsaw approach. Rearranging the furniture may include placing tables and chairs in circles, clusters, or pairs in discrete areas around the room. There should also be areas in which students can store their in-process projects.

Teachers need to divide the class into groups of two to six members, depending on the cooperative learning method chosen. Teachers generally use one of two methods: teacher-selected assignments or random assignments. With teacher-selected assignments, most approaches suggest that groups be heterogeneous with regard to factors such as ability, gender, native language, and English language proficiency.

Initially, teachers should establish guidelines on how groups will function. For example, students might be told that each group member should assist other members of the group with understanding the material or completing the project.

After explaining the task and desired behaviors, teachers need to monitor and intervene in groups, both for the accomplishment of academic tasks and for desired collaborative behavior. In some instances, teachers may need to assist students in resolving group difficulties.

After the groups have finished their work, they can be evaluated on task performance and on the way the groups functioned. Some teachers lead discussions about students' perceptions of the groups' processes and functioning.

CONCLUSION

The practical experience of teachers and administrators suggests that cooperative learning methods are an important approach in heterogeneous classes of LEP students. For successful implementation and long-term use, training teachers to use cooperative learning methods needs to be carried out over a long period of time, with intervening help and support from colleagues and administrators.

REFERENCES

Aronson, E., Blaney, N., Stephan, C., Sikes, J., & Snapp, M. (1978). *The Jigsaw classroom.* Beverly Hills, CA: Sage.

Bejarano, Y. (1987). A cooperative small-group methodology in the language classroom. *TESOL Quarterly, 21,* 483–504.

Cohen, E. G. (1986). *Designing groupwork: Strategies for the heterogeneous classroom.* New York: Teachers College Press.

DeAvila, E. A., Duncan, S. E., & Navarrete, C. J. (1987). *Finding Out/Descubrimiento: Teacher's resource guide.* Northvale, NJ: Santillana.

Ellis, S. (1987). *Introducing cooperative learning groups: A district-wide effort.* Paper presented at the annual meeting of the American Educational Research Association, Washington, DC.

Johnson, D. W., & Johnson, R. (1975). *Learning together and alone: Cooperation, competition, and individualization.* Englewood Cliffs, NJ: Prentice-Hall.

Johnson, D. W., Johnson, R., Holubec, E. J., & Roy, P. (1984). *Circles of learning: Cooperation in the classroom.* Alexandria, VA: Association for Supervision and Curriculum Development.

Johnson, D. W., Johnson, R. T., & Maruyama, G. (1983). Interdependence and interpersonal attraction among heterogeneous and homogeneous individuals: A theoretical formulation and a meta-analysis of research. *Review of Educational Research, 53,* 5–54.

Joyce, B., & Showers, B. (1982). The coaching of teaching. *Educational Leadership, 40*(1), 4–10.

Kagan, S. (1985a). *Cooperative learning resources for teachers.* Riverside: University of California, Printing and Reprographics.

Kagan, S. (1985b). Dimensions of cooperative classroom structures. In R. Slavin et al. (Eds.), *Learning to cooperate, cooperating to learn* (pp. 67–96). New York: Plenum.

Kagan, S. (1986). Cooperative learning and sociocultural factors in schooling. In Bilingual Education Office, California State Department of Education, *Beyond language: Social and cultural factors in schooling language minority students* (pp. 231–298). Los Angeles: California State University, Evaluation, Dissemination and Assessment Center.

Krashen, S. (1981). *Second language acquisition and second language learning.* Oxford: Pergamon.

Lucker, G., Rosenfield, D., Sikes, J., & Aronson, E. (1976). Performance in the interdependent classroom: A field study. *American Educational Research Journal, 13,* 115–123.

Sharan, S., & Hertz-Lazarowitz, R. (1979). A group-investigation method of cooperative learning in the classroom. In S. Sharan, P. Hare, C. D. Webb, & R. Hertz-Lazarowitz (Eds.), *Cooperation in education* (pp. 14–46). Provo, UT: Brigham Young University Press.

Sharan, S., Kussell, P., Hertz-Lazarowitz, R., Bejarano, Y., Raviv, S., & Sharan, Y. (1985). Cooperative learning effects on ethnic relations and achievement in Israeli junior high school classrooms. In R. Slavin et al. (Eds.), *Learning to cooperate, cooperating to learn* (pp. 313–344). New York: Plenum.

Slavin, R. (1977). *Student learning team techniques: Narrowing the achievement gap between the races* (Report No. 228). Baltimore, MD: Johns Hopkins University, Center for Social Organization of the Schools.

Slavin, R. (1983). *Cooperative learning.* New York: Longman.

Slavin, R. (1985). Team-assisted individualization: Combining cooperative learning and individualized instruction in mathematics. In R. Slavin et al. (Eds.), *Learning to cooperate, cooperating to learn* (pp. 177–209). New York: Plenum.

Slavin, R. (1986). *Using student team learning: The Johns Hopkins team learning project.* Baltimore, MD: Johns Hopkins University, Center for Research on Elementary and Middle Schools.

Slavin, R., & Oickle, E. (1981). Effects of cooperative learning teams on student achievement and race relations: Treatment by race interactions. *Sociology of Education, 54,* 174–180.

15

Material Needed for Bilingual Immersion Programs

KAREN WILLETTS
DONNA CHRISTIAN

Earlier chapters of this volume have presented a number of models of innovative language education programs. An important ingredient in the successful implementation of an innovative program is access to appropriate and effective materials and curricula. Very often, new programs must depend on their own locally developed materials for one of two reasons. In some cases, the program is truly unique, and no appropriate resources are available to be adopted or adapted. In other cases, however, implementors of innovative programs are not aware of available materials that could be used or modified. Often, such materials have been prepared for one school or for district-level use and are not easily shared. As a result, a perceived or real lack of accessible materials can prove to be a barrier in the establishment of promising new programs.

In this chapter, we consider the materials requirements of innovative language education programs, characterized in earlier chapters as the "two-way" or "bilingual immersion" model. Although the specific features of these programs may vary, they share some basic properties:

(a) The program essentially involves some form of dual language instruction, where the non-English language is used for a significant portion of the students' instructional day; (b) the program involves periods of instruction during which only one language is used; (c) both native English speakers and nonnative English speakers (preferably in balanced numbers) are participants; and (d) the students are integrated for most content instruction. (Lindholm, Chapter 6, this volume)

Although there is some variation, all of these programs have similar materials needs.

CATEGORIES OF MATERIALS

An important step in planning for innovative educational programs is a careful analysis of the resources needed to make them operational. For bilingual immersion programs (also called "two-way bilingual education") instructional materials appropriate for both language minority and majority students are needed. In a Spanish-English bilingual immersion program, for example, four categories of materials are required: instructional materials for native English speakers, for English as a second language speakers, for native Spanish speakers, and for speakers of Spanish as a second language. The required materials are not only for language arts (first and second languages) but also for various content areas (such as math, health/science, social studies/history, music, art, and physical education) because content instruction occurs in both languages. Language-sensitive content-based materials are a necessity for bilingual immersion programs (Crandall, Spanos, Christian, Simich-Dudgeon, & Willetts, 1987). The array of material types is summarized in Table 15.1.

Table 15.1 Categories of Materials Needed in Bilingual Immersion Programs

English	*Second Language*
Language arts for native speakers	Language arts for native speakers
English as a second language for nonnative speakers	Second language for nonnative speakers
Content areas selected for instruction in English, such as	Content areas selected for instruction in second language, such as
science social studies/history mathematics health art music	science social studies/history mathematics health art music

Curriculum planning must also take into account the categories reflected in Table 15.1. Because all students are learning another language, one strand of the curriculum must provide support for second-language development. In Spanish-English two-way programs, for example, time is typically set aside for specific instruction in English as a second language (ESL) and Spanish as a second language (SSL). If this instruction is content-based (see Chapter 9, this volume, on integrating language and content instruction), it can reinforce and expand on learning during other parts of the school day. This special language characteristic of the program means, however, that the language curricula need to be developed to establish the goals and objectives of the second-language component of the instructional program.

Another important component of two-way programs is mother tongue language arts for both groups of students. As long as the students' skills in the two languages are substantially different, they may need language arts instruction in their native language that differs from that which they receive in the second language. The school will also need to decide how initial reading and writing instruction is to proceed. As a result, the language arts strand of the curriculum may need to be adapted. For the English-speaking students, the curriculum plans may be identical to the larger district guidelines. However, for the students who are native speakers of the non-English language, a language arts curriculum (for their mother tongue) will be needed.

Finally, sheltered content programs must be included to provide instruction in the content areas to native and nonnative speakers. When content instruction is "sheltered," or language-sensitive, teachers adapt materials and teaching strategies to accommodate the lower language proficiency of nonnative speakers. The content is not diminished, but the language may be simplified and more attention is given to providing contextual support and multiple cues to meaning. In most cases, instructional curricula for bilingual immersion programs should be equivalent to those for students at the same grade level in regular district programs. However, those content areas that are taught in the non-English language require curricula in that language, and an exact translation from the English version may not be appropriate.

Thus two-way bilingual programs ideally have a number of curricular strands—involving language, language arts, and content-area instruction—interwoven into a coherent educational plan for the students. Schedules need to be carefully structured for teaching all required academic subjects using methods appropriate for the students' grade levels and for enabling both native English-speaking students and native speakers of the non-English language to acquire content, thinking/study skills, and language skills in both languages.

AVAILABILITY OF MATERIALS AND CURRICULA

According to the recent *Directory of Bilingual Immersion Programs* (Lindholm, 1987), one of the most common complaints in a new program is that few materials are readily available and curricula are not sufficiently adapted. Most of the 30 programs surveyed indicated that their teaching plans are based on districtwide curricula designed for the English mainstream classroom (Lindholm, 1987). Therefore, teachers need to fill in the gaps and adjust the curricula on a regular basis in order to allow for teaching in a non-English language (and the possible absence of student materials in that language) and for the special needs of students learning in a second language. A number of the programs listed in the *Directory* stated that they used teacher-made or adapted materials. Several were in the process of developing some of their own materials and curricula (see materials mentioned below). The hardest task for any program, it seems, is to find integrated language and content materials and curricula appropriate for both groups of students, that coincide with locally adopted texts and district requirements.

Naturally, materials for native English speakers in both language arts and content areas are the easiest to find, because a full range of curricula are already in place in most districts. Materials for ESL students are currently widely obtainable for language arts but are less available for various content areas. A number of commercially published text series are available for ESL at both elementary and secondary levels, and most districts with significant numbers of ESL students have developed curriculum guidelines.

Both texts and curricula for ESL tend to emphasize language development and language arts. However, with the increase in sheltered English programs and content-based pullout classes, more school districts are developing ESL content curricula that can also meet the needs of bilingual immersion programs. For example, at the elementary level, School District U-46 in Chicago is developing *Content Assistance Packets* (*CAPS*) in science and social studies for grades one through six. Although they are referenced to current district-adopted texts, they can supplement any text and are appropriate for both ESL and other students.

As far as non-English language materials are concerned, school districts with foreign language immersion programs have developed curricula and materials for the teaching of Spanish, French, German, and other languages as a second language, including various content area materials as well. For the most part, these programs are found in the elementary schools. There are several text series available from commercial publishers as well, particularly for teaching Spanish as a second language, because that has the largest market at the current time. At the secondary level, a number of texts are published commercially for language instruction, but these tend *not* to be aimed at developing communication abilities or integrating language with content.

As a result of curriculum development to meet the needs of their Spanish immersion programs, for example, the Cincinnati Public Schools offer a complete elementary series of *Spanish Bilingual Program Curriculum Guides* (Levels I-V) focusing on oral skills, content instruction, and reading/language arts. Separate Spanish language science and math curricula, and Spanish language worksheets to accompany the social studies curriculum, are also available. Because topics in the materials, such as the solar system, climate, plants, animals, government, and geography, are common to most school curricula, these materials could lend themselves to use in other districts for nonnative Spanish-speaking students.

Materials in Spanish for native Spanish speakers, once hard to find, are becoming more available as programs for them are increasing. However, the vast majority of these materials focus on language arts, whereas content-based materials are more difficult to locate. Many school districts with "regular" bilingual programs (those designed specifically for language minority students) have developed materials appropriate for the native Spanish speaker that parallel their English language curriculum. Several publishers also distribute texts and supplementary materials prepared for Spanish-dominant students in those programs. Both Spanish and English language versions of some text series in math, science, and social studies are available.

Among local school districts, San Diego has had both a "regular" bilingual program and a (two-way) bilingual immersion program for a number of years. There, staff have developed materials for K-6 music and art instruction (*El mundo de música y arte*) and a handbook for bilingual preschool teachers (*El mundo de los pequeños: Programa bilingüe preescolar*) among others. They have also produced three language programs: Spanish language arts for native-Spanish speakers, Spanish for native speakers of English, and English for native speakers of non-English languages (Torrance, 1982).

As mentioned above, language development and language arts dominate both ESL and other language instructional materials. An overview of resources available for bilingual immersion programs can be obtained from a recent analysis of the materials annotated in the CLEAR data base on materials, curricula and program descriptions in second-language education (Willetts, 1988). The resources listed in the data base represent samples submitted by publishers, distributors, and school districts, with an emphasis on the latter. (In the case of locally produced materials, they were included only if they were available for distribution—from the school district itself, an information clearinghouse such as ERIC, or another distributor.) A recent review of the data base contents revealed that over half of the entries are in the language arts category. More entries are found in social studies/history and health/science than in the other content areas (culture, math, music/art/physical education, and vocational). Of the materials listed, over half at the elementary level, one-fourth are at the secondary level, and the remaining one-fourth are teacher resources. The majority of the materials and curricula are for ESL and Spanish, with French coming in third. These proportions give an idea of the task facing the teacher of an elementary Spanish/English bilingual immersion program who is searching for appropriate materials and curricula.

PREPARING MATERIALS AND
CURRICULA AT THE LOCAL LEVEL

For teachers who still need to adapt or develop their own materials when suitable ones cannot be found elsewhere, several points should be noted. Naturally, the curriculum should reflect local needs. Requirements for content-area topics need to be considered as well as the choice of the format best suited to the local population. A totally integrated curriculum would combine language instruction with all content areas for both language minority and language majority students (Crandall, Spanos, Christian, Simich-Dudgeon, & Willetts, 1987). Care should be taken not to "water down" the academic content of the courses when making them appropriate for various language ability levels.

In addition, academic curricula should be integrated with language arts (Lindholm, 1987). There should be considerable articulation between the content that is taught and the language skills necessary to succeed in the content areas. Also, integration across content areas is particularly useful for bilingual immersion programs. An *integrated content curriculum* is one in which curriculum needs are determined, and a program of articulation across content areas is developed, based on thematic concepts. For example, thematic concepts such as seasons, animals, and countries can be discussed in all content areas: math, science, social studies, music, and so on. More specific suggestions for ways of combining language and content can be found in Chapter 9 of this volume and in Padilla, Fairchild, and Valadez (1990, chap. 13).

The New York City Schools curricula, *Learning in a Multicultural World*, for kindergarten through second grade (bilingual, ESL, or Spanish editions) provide a concrete example of an integrated content curriculum based on various themes. In the first grade, the themes deal with our school, our community, and animal and plant needs. In the second grade, they treat the supermarket, the library, and the environment. Objectives and skills in communication arts, science, math, and social studies are woven into the curriculum. A focus on themes that reach across the curriculum allows locally developed resources to be used or easily adapted by other districts. As more schools move toward producing such materials, the availability of adequate materials for bilingual immersion programs will greatly increase.

Until recently, materials used in two-way programs were largely from bilingual programs where an English basal series (in reading, science, or social studies) had been translated into Spanish (or vice versa) by a publisher. The accompanying supplementary worksheets and activities were designed to adapt the series to local programs. However, many educators are finding it preferable to use authentic language materials, rather than translated or adapted ones, whenever possible. As a result, new materials are needed to fill the gap. In one bilingual immersion program in California, they state that they use separate content area texts in Spanish and English; neither bilingual texts nor translations of the same text are used (Lindholm, 1987). This "nonbasal and supplement only" approach requires a wide selection of materials in both languages.

As mentioned earlier, the low availability of materials is complicated by the fact that those that have been prepared, particularly by schools, are not widely known. The networking of school districts having innovative language programs and materials is thus necessary for information to be shared. Some resources for information about language materials include CLEAR, the National Dissemination Center, the ERIC Clearinghouse on Languages and Linguistics, and the National Clearinghouse for Bilingual Education (addresses are provided in Appendix A). Materials developed by teachers in numerous school districts are accessible through these centers and the ERIC system.

In Appendix B, a partial, selected list of materials that may be appropriate for bilingual immersion programs is presented (where the two languages are Spanish and English). These represent materials in language arts and various content areas that schools have submitted to the CLEAR survey/data base. Although the list does not contain "recommended" materials as such, it may be useful as a source of information about school districts that have developed materials in areas suitable for bilingual immersion.

CONCLUSION

The materials requirements for bilingual immersion programs are complex and, as we have seen, they are being met largely at the local level through locally prepared or adapted curricula and materials. As the number of programs of this type grows, it should be possible for new programs to adapt or build on the efforts of others and to profit from the information accumulated about available resources, both commercial and noncommercial. The key to maximizing the limited resources lies in active networking among programs and the continued activity of clearinghouses such as those listed in Appendix A.

APPENDIX A:
Information Resource Centers

ERIC Clearinghouse on Languages and Linguistics. ERIC/CLL distributes the following materials on various language and education topics: ready-made data base searches, ERIC Digests, Q & A's (question and answer information sheets), and Mini-bibs (short annotated bibliographies). A book series produced by ERIC/CLL, *Language in Education: Theory and Practice*, is distributed by Prentice-Hall Regents, Inc.

> 1118 22nd Street NW
> Washington, DC 20037
> (202) 429–9292

National Clearinghouse for Bilingual Education (NCBE). NCBE's Electronic Information System contains several data bases, including curricula and materials, publishers and distributors of minority language materials, computer courseware materials, and listings of resource organizations and centers. Data-base searches, including full bibliographic citations on frequently requested topics, and a variety of publications are available.

> 8737 Colesville Rd.
> Suite 900
> Silver Spring, MD 20910
> (800) 321-NCBE
> (202) 467-0867

National Dissemination Center (formerly EDAC/Lesley College) (NDC), in cooperation with Fall River Public Schools. NDC distributes core curricula and supplementary materials in language arts and content areas (social studies, math, science) for several uncommonly taught languages, including Chi-

nese, Greek, Haitian Creole, Korean, Portuguese, and Vietnamese. Professional resources and handbooks are available.

417 Rock Street
Fall River, MA 02720
(617) 678–5696

APPENDIX B:
Selected List of Materials for Spanish-English Bilingual Immersion Programs

ESL LANGUAGE DEVELOPMENT
LANGUAGE ARTS MATERIALS

Alberta Education Committee Members. (1987). *ESL instruction in the elementary school: Curriculum guidelines and suggestions*. Publisher: Alberta Education Language Services Branch, Devonian Building, 11160 Jasper Avenue, Edmonton, Alberta, T5K 0L2, Canada. (ERIC: ED 293 376)

Cambridge Public Schools. (1988). *Amigos* [Curriculum handbooks in English or Spanish for two-way language immersion program for kindergarten]. Publisher: Cambridge Public School Department, Bilingual Program, 159 Thorndike Street, Cambridge, MA 02141.

Division of Curriculum and Instruction. (1985). *Look, listen, do! Read and write, too! A manual of ESL activities for beginner level*. Publisher: New York City Board of Education, Office of Bilingual Education, Dissemination Services Unit, Room 515, 131 Livingston Street, Brooklyn, NY 11201. (ERIC: ED 284 431)

ESL and Special Education Teachers. (1986). *Zoo animals* [For grades K-3]. Publisher: Fairfax County Public Schools, 3705 Crest Drive, Annandale, VA 22003.

SPANISH LANGUAGE DEVELOPMENT
LANGUAGE ARTS MATERIALS

Bilingual Department and Instructional TV Center. (1988). *Saludos: Beginning Spanish* [36 videotape lessons with 7 audiotapes]. Publisher: Broward County Public Schools, 6650 Griffin Road, Davie, FL 33314.

Note: The complete address is only listed the first time a publisher is mentioned.

Elementary Foreign Language Program. (1986). *Spanish curricula for kindergarten through fourth grade*. Publisher: Ferndale Public Schools, Ferndale High School, 881 Pinecrest, Ferndale, MI 48220.

ESOL/HILT Department. (1988). *Cuaderno de trabajo para estudiantes del program de immersion parcial*. Publisher: Arlington County Public Schools, ESOL/HILT Department, 1426 N. Quincy Street, Arlington, VA 22207.

Gullickson et al. (1983). *Spanish language arts—spelling* [3 spelling workbooks]. Publisher: Milwaukee Public Schools, PO Drawer 10K, Milwaukee, WI 53201–8210.

Multi-Language School Immersion Programs. (n.d.). *Mi diccionario de …* [Accompanies Mc-Graw-Hill Spanish Key Basal Reading Series]. Publisher: Milwaukee Public Schools.

Wraith, J. (1981). *Spanish language arts for the English speaker* [Subtitled: Teacher's workbook and vocabulary picture book, level B]. Publisher: San Diego City Schools. (ERIC: ED 234 646)

Zimmerman, L. (1982). *Spanish readiness activities* [For grade 1]. Publisher: Milwaukee Public Schools.

SHELTERED ENGLISH CONTENT-AREA MATERIALS

Coughran, C., & Merino, B. (Coordinators). (1986). *Project BICOMP—Bilingual integrated curriculum project* [For LEPs in grades 3–6, with computer-assisted lessons in science and activities in art, literature, and math]. Publisher: Washington Unified School District, 930 West Acres Road, West Sacramento, CA 95691.

ESL and Special Education Teachers. (1986). *Teaching directions: Using a controlled prepositional vocabulary* [For grades K-3; activities for math, art, and physical education]. Publisher: Fairfax County Public Schools.

ESL Unit. (1985). *Teaching English as a second language: Grades 3–8* [Lesson plans in math, science, and social studies]. Publisher: New York City Board of Education.

Johnson, G. (Ed.), Project Rainbow. (1983). *Content assistance packets (CAPs): Science, grade 5*. Publisher: School District U-46, 355 East Chicago Street, Elgin, IL 60120.

Office of Bilingual Education. (n.d.). *Learning in a multicultural world: First grade Spanish/ESL* (experimental ed.) [Spanish and ESL components with activities in language arts, science, math, and social studies]. Publisher: New York City Board of Education.

Office of Bilingual Education. (n.d.). *Learning in a multicultural world: Second grade ESL* (experimental ed.) [Integrates language arts, math, social studies, science, art, and music]. Publisher: New York City Board of Education.

Project Rainbow. (1985). *Content assistance packets (CAPs): Social studies, grade 2*. Publisher: School District U-46.

University of Southern California, Institute for Marine and Coastal Studies Sea Grant Program. (1983). *Wet and wild: Units I-VI* [Bilingual English and Spanish ed. for grades K-6; activities for language arts and various content areas]. Publisher: Evaluation, Dissemination and Assessment Center, California State University, LA, 5151 State University Drive, Los Angeles, CA 90032. (Unit I, ERIC: ED 261 889; Unit II, ERIC: ED 261 890; Unit III, ERIC: ED 261 891)

SPANISH CONTENT-AREA MATERIALS

Cruz, M. et al. (1986). *Primary approach to language* [Lessons in social studies, culture, math, and science for grades 1–3 immersion]. Publisher: Foreign Language Department, Rochester City School District, 131 W. Broad Street, Rochester, NY 14614.

Denise, M. et al. (Coordinators). (1983). *Spanish science program, teacher's edition, grade 1* [Adapted from Spanish version of Silver Burdett's *Science, understanding your environment*]. Publisher: San Diego City Schools.

Diaz, R. E. (1986). *Spanish bilingual program, curriculum de ciencias, primer grado.* Publisher: Cincinnati Public Schools, 203 E. 9th Street, Cincinnati, OH 45202.

Fairbanks, E. (1984). *Suggested math curriculum for Spanish immersion* [K level]. Publisher: Cincinnati Public Schools.

Gerstman, L. (1987a). *La gente necisita abrigo: Nivel I* [Social studies unit on housing]. Publisher: Montgomery County Public Schools, 850 Hungerford Drive, Rockville, MD 20850.

Gerstman, L. (1987b). *La gente necisita comida: Nivel II* [Social studies unit on food and nutrition]. Publisher: Montgomery County Public Schools.

Gerstman, L. (1987c). *La gente necisita ropa: Nivel I* [Social studies unit on clothing]. Publisher: Montgomery County Public Schools.

Kearney, N. Q. (1982). *Spanish worksheets to accompany grade 5 social studies curriculum* [U.S. history, government, leaders, and geography]. Publisher: Cincinnati Public Schools.

Met, M. et al. (1978). *Spanish bilingual program curriculum guides: Levels I-V* (2nd rev.) [Includes oral skills, content instruction, and reading/language arts]. Publisher: Cincinnati Public Schools.

Minneapolis Public Schools. (1988). *Science lessons K-6* [Translated district science curricula]. Publisher: Minneapolis Public Schools, 807 N.E. Broadway, Minneapolis, MN 55413–2398.

Montgomery County Public Schools. (1987). *La materia: Nivel II* [Based on district science curriculum]. Publisher: Montgomery County Public Schools.

Montgomery County Public Schools. (1987). *Seres vivos: Nivel I* [Based on district science curriculum]. Publisher: Montgomery County Public Schools.

Office of Bilingual Education. (n.d.). *El aprendizaje en un ambiente multicultural: Segundo grado, Spanish* [Units on the supermarket, library, and environment provide language and content activities]. Publisher: New York City Board of Education.

Runyon, K. S. (1984). *Spanish worksheets to accompany grade 4 social studies curriculum* [Geography, map reading, and area studies of Ohio, Japan, and Ghana]. Publisher: Cincinnati Public Schools.

Watkins, F., & Santos, J. (n.d.). *La caculadora: Hojas de ejercicios.* Publisher: Milwaukee Public Schools.

Wilbur Wright Middle School Immersion Program. (1987). *Math Skill Sharpeners* [For grades 6–8]. Publisher: Milwaukee Public Schools.

Wiley, P. D. (1987). *Morgan County Spanish curriculum guides for the elementary school* [5-language-level interdisciplinary guide integrates Spanish into various content areas]. Publisher: University of Tennessee, Knoxville, Department of Curriculum and Instruction, Foreign Language Education, CEB 218-D, Knoxville, TN 37996–3400.

REFERENCES

Crandall, J., Spanos, G., Christian, D., Simich-Dudgeon, C., & Willetts, K. (1987). *Integrating language and content instruction for language minority students*. Wheaton, MD: National Clearinghouse for Bilingual Education.

Lindholm, K. J. (1987). *Directory of bilingual immersion programs: Two-way bilingual education for language minority and language majority students* (Educational Report No. 8). Los Angeles: University of California, Los Angeles, Center for Language Education and Research. (ERIC: ED 291 241)

Padilla, A. M., Fairchild, H. H., & Valadez, C. M. (Eds.). (1990). *Foreign language education: Issues and strategies*. Newbury Park, CA: Sage.

Torrance, D. W. (Ed.). (1982). *An exemplary approach to bilingual education: A comprehensive handbook for implementing an elementary-level Spanish-English language immersion program* (Publication #I-B-82–58). San Diego: San Diego Unified School District.

Willetts, K. (1988). *Report on the survey of materials and curricula in second language education*. Unpublished manuscript, Center for Language Education and Research, Washington, DC.

16

Innovations in Bilingual Education
Contributions from Foreign Language Education

HALFORD H. FAIRCHILD
AMADO M. PADILLA

This volume presents a number of challenging perspectives for American education. The growing sensitivity to individual differences, and individual needs, has motivated a wide range of curricular innovations. Nowhere are these innovations more dramatic than in the field of bilingual education.

Unfortunately, our sensitivity to the need for curricular innovations has preceded the theoretical and empirical work that is needed to develop such innovations. As a result, many of the programmatic thrusts in bilingual education have been of a "trial and error" nature.

The early attempts to tailor education to the needs of non-English-speaking populations focused primarily on replacing those populations' native languages with English (see Snow, Chapter 4, this volume). It is only now that we realize the tremendous importance of first firmly establishing children's native language proficiency before attempting a transition to English. More important, the bulk of this work firmly identifies the cognitive advantages that accrue to individuals and the broader society from the maintenance of bilingual proficiency. Thus the developments in bilingual education dovetail nicely with work in foreign language education, where an emphasis has also emerged on communicative proficiency and the development and maintenance of language competence in more than one language.

Given this bridge of interest between bilingual education and foreign language education, we present chapter summaries of the companion volume to this one, which focuses on foreign language education (Padilla, Fairchild, & Valadez, 1990). That volume is organized into four parts: (a) perspectives, issues, and history; (b) research contributions and perspectives; (c) immersion education; and (d) content-based instruction.

CONTRIBUTIONS FROM FOREIGN LANGUAGE EDUCATION

Political and Historical Perspectives

Foreign language education has undergone a number of dramatic changes in the United States. Its history, and concomitant political agendas, are reviewed in Part I, "Political and Historical Perspectives," of the companion volume.

G. Richard Tucker (1990), in "Second Language Education: Issues and Perspectives," notes a critical shortage of "language-competent" residents in the United States. An exceedingly small number of Americans engage in any meaningful foreign language education, and fewer still demonstrate oral or aural proficiency. Associated with this foreign language incompetence, schools and universities are left without adequate materials, curricula, or instructional staff.

Using an international perspective, Tucker notes that bilingualism and multilingualism are worldwide norms. Indeed, so-called less developed countries are far advanced with respect to foreign language instruction and the development of bilingual proficiency. As a result, Tucker identifies a number of policy needs that underscore the positive benefits of foreign language education, including cognitive and intellectual benefits as well as benefits in the international trade arena. In this respect, Tucker's analysis complements Padilla's (this volume), and together Tucker and Padilla identify the personal, cognitive, and social benefits of bilingualism.

Tucker also notes the projections for a changing American demography that indicate an increasing linguistic diversity within the continental United States. In sum, Tucker suggests that the native English majority in the United States must redress five concerns: (a) the lack of foreign language education programs, particularly those that are geared to produce true communicative proficiency; (b) the lack of collaboration in different foreign language programs (e.g., from elementary through college); (c) the failure to fully develop teaching methods and curricula that produce foreign language competence; (d) the confusion resulting from mistaking language as an educational "end," versus a *means* to an end; and (e) the failure to accept language minority students as role models of the target foreign language.

Lynn Thompson, Donna Christian, Charles W. Stansfield, and Nancy Rhodes (1990), in "Foreign Language Instruction in the United States," suggest that foreign language education programming reflected, and was affected by, broader social and political events in the society and the world at large. They identify the changing foreign language needs as a result of European immigration during the nineteenth and early twentieth centuries, and point to the important changes mandated by the world wars. The authors also trace how foreign language teaching methodologies evolved to the current emphasis on communicative competence and proficiency in reading, writing, speaking, and listening. These changes, then, were reflected in the changing guidelines by the ACTFL (the American Council for the Teaching of Foreign Languages) for evaluating foreign language competence (also see Stansfield & Kenyon, 1990, in this connection). Thompson, Christian, Stansfield, and Rhodes (1990) conclude with a future-oriented perspective that sees an increasing emphasis on communicative proficiency, practical applicability, immersion models, and content/language integration. They note, however, a need to increase the priority given to foreign language education by the American public, educators, and policymakers.

Research Perspectives

Part II, "Research Perspectives in Immersion and Foreign Language Education," provides an overview of a number of research approaches and contributions in language education. Topics include language and cognition, second-language learning strategies, assessment, and the development of proficiency guidelines, particularly for the "less commonly taught languages."

Amado M. Padilla and Hyekyung Sung (1990), in "Information Processing Models and Foreign Language Learning," provide a nontechnical review of the way in which cognitive psychology and information processing can be applied to second/foreign language acquisition and instruction. Key terms and concepts from cognitive psychology, such as sensory memory, short-term memory, and long-term memory, are defined and discussed. The relevance of these concepts for foreign language acquisition is highlighted by numerous examples designed to show why and under what circumstances difficulties are encountered by students learning another language.

Padilla and Sung also discuss bilingual information processing and concepts of separate and shared memory. The chapter concludes with recommendations for language educators based on principles taken from information processing but applicable to foreign language instruction. The implication is that sound foreign language pedagogy can be informed by research whose primary intent has been to test various cognitive models of language and memory in monolinguals. The recommendations, although not unfamiliar to language educators, are shown to be based on empirically sound evidence rather than on common sense or folklore about how to best learn a second/foreign language.

Mary McGroarty and Rebecca Oxford (1990), in "Language Learning Strategies: An Introduction and Related Studies," provide an assessment of research on the relationship between foreign language learning strategies and foreign language acquisition. Three emphases emerge: (a) The strategies that students employ in learning a foreign language are vitally important; (b) different learning strategies have differential effectiveness; and (c) the efficacious strategies can and should be integrated into classroom activities.

McGroarty and Oxford then review the findings from two studies that examined the cognitive learning strategies employed by university students learning a foreign language (either beginning Japanese or beginning Spanish). The strategies most related to effective foreign language acquisition were guessing meaning from context, active questioning, selective attention, using media, risk taking, and practicing language output. The ineffective strategies were making inappropriate guesses, pretending to understand, interrupting oneself, and memorizing or cramming. McGroarty and Oxford also note important attitudinal influences in foreign language acquisition and conclude with suggestions to teachers.

Nancy Rhodes and Lynn Thompson (1990), in "An Oral Assessment Instrument for Immersion Students: COPE," review the research findings on immersion education and note the lack of a standardized instrument to assess language proficiency of immersion students. The available instruments are not typically suitable for elementary school children, and most foreign language tests are more oriented to the formal aspects of language rather than communicative proficiency.

The CLEAR Oral Proficiency Exam (COPE) addresses both students' academic language (their ability to effectively discuss subject matter) and students' social language (the ability to discuss their family, recreational activities, and social life). The instrument is targeted to fifth- and sixth-grade total or partial immersion programs. The authors review the development of the instrument and describe its contents and administration. They note that an important contribution of the COPE is the ability to identify students' strengths and weaknesses in separate language skill domains instead of only assessing overall proficiency.

Charles W. Stansfield and Dorry Mann Kenyon (1990), in "Extension of ACTFL Guidelines for Less Commonly Taught Languages," note the origins of foreign language proficiency guidelines with the Foreign Service Institute's Oral Proficiency Interview. With increasing interest in this area by academicians, the development of proficiency guidelines is beginning to include "less commonly taught foreign languages" (i.e., languages other than Spanish, French, and German).

Stansfield and Kenyon review the development of proficiency guidelines for Arabic, Indonesian, Hindi, and the African Language Group. Each language raises important issues that Stansfield and Kenyon argue are recurrent in the development of proficiency guidelines for the less commonly taught languages. For Arabic, the problem deals with the numerous Arabic dialects and their appropriateness in different locales or contexts. For Hindi, the issue has to do with code-switching between Hindi and English, and how that code-switching is interpreted differently in social versus formal situations. For Indonesian, the issue concerns a number of sociolinguistic factors and how Indonesian phrases carry information pertinent to social relationships. Finally, for the African languages, the issue has to do with limited resources for an extremely linguistically diverse continent. In sum, Stansfield and Kenyon emphasize the fact that proficiency guidelines must reflect the cultural milieu of the language under consideration and that these guidelines continue to evolve.

Immersion Education:
Design, Implementation, and Evaluation

Part III, "Immersion Education: Design, Implementation, and Evaluation," describes the state of the art concerning contemporary models of language education. These chapters cover the range of issues from program design to program evaluation.

Marguerite Ann Snow (1990a), in "Language Immersion: An Overview and Comparison," notes the historical origins of immersion education in the United States as deriving from the importation of Canadian French immersion models. She notes the four key features of immersion programs: (a) the delivery of subject matter (e.g., math, social studies) in the foreign language; (b) the separation of second-language students from native language speakers; (c) the promotion of additive bilingualism; and (d) the changing sequence and intensity of foreign language instruction as children move through the grade levels. Snow also notes the importance of participating in the immersion program for at least four to six years, of strictly separating the languages of instruction into different time periods, and of the critical role of home-school collaboration. Snow's overview chapter also identifies the goals of immersion education, including language proficiency, content mastery, and positive self- and cross-cultural attitudes and behaviors.

Snow reviews the literature on program effectiveness and on the variations in the immersion model. Her chapter concludes with a detailed description of three Spanish immersion programs that varied according to a number of features of program implementation. She reports that the best program was one that emphasized content instruction, was intense, involved the entire school, used separate English-speaking and Spanish-speaking instructors, and was associated with positive community integration in the program.

Nancy Rhodes, JoAnn Crandall, and Donna Christian (1990), in *"'Key Amigos': A Partial Immersion Program,"* trace the development of a partial immersion program at Key Elementary School in Arlington, Virginia. Their chapter includes a detailed program description, particularly with respect to the division of language instruction during the course of the program and the role of peer models. Their evaluation demonstrated high satisfaction on the part of students, teachers, and parents as well as significant achievement gains.

Kathryn J. Lindholm and Amado M. Padilla (1990), in "A High School Bilingual Partial Immersion Program," underscore the value of two-way immersion programs for both native English speakers and nonnative English speakers. The immersion program goals are to develop oral and academic Spanish proficiency, to increase school retention, to generate normal or above average academic achievement in the traditional (English language) content areas, and to develop positive interpersonal and intergroup attitudes and behaviors. The underlying assumptions include the idea that bilingualism is a cognitive advantage, that content mastery transfers between languages, that purposeful instruction maximizes second-language learning, and that classroom heterogeneity and cooperative learning enhance teaching outcomes.

Lindholm and Padilla describe a high school partial immersion program and compare that program with programs geared toward Spanish for native Spanish speakers and with a traditional Spanish instruction program that focuses on grammar and literature. In an analytical comparison, Lindholm and Padilla report a number of consistent differences among the three programs. Of course, native Spanish speakers obtained the highest proficiency scores, but, more important, the partial immersion students consistently outperformed the traditional Spanish track students and reported much greater exposure to Spanish in the broader linguistic environment (particularly in the use of Spanish language media). They conclude that bilingual immersion programs can be tailored to meet the individual learning needs of students.

Marguerite Ann Snow (1990b), in "Instructional Methodology in Immersion Foreign Language Education," is concerned with the teaching methods used in immersion foreign language education. She describes the strategies and techniques used by experienced immersion teachers, and draws on insights from similar programs that are beneficial for the immersion model.

Snow's focus on instructional methodology includes discussions on vocabulary development, the role of culture, personal attributes of teachers, and cooperative learning. She highlights the multiple skills required of immersion teachers and summarizes the features of immersion classrooms that enhance learning. Snow concludes with an itemization of the important issues that educators and administrators must address in implementing an immersion foreign language program.

Snow (1990c), in "Spanish Language Attrition of Immersion Graduates," concludes this part of the volume with the description of a pilot assessment of foreign language attrition (i.e., loss of skills) on the part of immersion graduates who completed an elementary school immersion program. She notes that the type and intensity of continuing exposure to the foreign language was most important in predicting language retention and maintenance.

Content-Based Instruction

In Part IV, "Content-Based Instruction and Foreign Language Education," JoAnn Crandall and G. Richard Tucker (1990), in "Content-Based Instruction in Second and Foreign Languages," define content-based instruction and describe techniques, strategies, and suggestions for program implementation. In addition, they cover areas of needed research and development.

Crandall and Tucker identify the benefits of content-based instruction for both language minority and language majority students. In exploring a variety of models of content-based instruction, they provide specific suggestions for developing instructional objectives, content-compatible language, curricular materials, and hands-on learning experiences. They conclude with a call for future work in teacher education, student assessment, program evaluation, materials development, and research into the process of content-based instruction.

Helena A. Curtain and Linda S. Martínez (1990), in "Elementary School Content-Based Foreign Language Instruction," review the background and rationales for content-based instruction and note that students both gain a general education and acquire a foreign language. Curtain and Martínez note that using the foreign language to teach traditional content areas makes the learning of the language *purposeful*, thereby enhancing acquisition.

Curtain and Martínez provide a number of specific guidelines for integrating language and content, including suggestions for planning the curriculum, instructional coordination among language teachers and content teachers, identifying materials, planning lessons, and evaluation. They note that instructors must be wary of providing a "watered down" curriculum and emphasize that the simplification of language should not connote the simplification of concepts. An appendix provides six sample lesson plans drawn from math, science, and social studies. A second appendix provides further readings.

Sheila M. Shannon (1990), in "Spanish for Spanish Speakers: A Translation Skills Curriculum," examines the unique foreign language learning needs of native speakers of the target language. These students, when mainstreamed with native English speakers, often meander in classes geared to develop only a minimal language proficiency. Shannon, therefore, describes a unique program of teaching Spanish to native Spanish speakers. The program involves using the students as translators and interpreters, thus contextualizing their language learning in a real-world application.

Shannon's description of the program is as one that "empowers" students (see Cummins, 1986). She reports the compromises made between the intended curriculum, the operationalized curriculum, and the experienced curriculum, and notes that students and teachers had to overcome some initial resistance to their empowerment.

Halford H. Fairchild and Amado M. Padilla (1990), in "Innovations in Foreign Language Education: Contributions from Bilingual Education," provide a synthesis to the volume. They note, as below, the varying strands of potential collaboration between foreign language educators and bilingual educators.

SYNTHESIS AND CONCLUSION

Bilingual education, foreign language education, and language education more generally are each concerned with a fundamental issue: the acknowledgment that language competence is a key to the successful personal and social adjustments necessary in modern society. In addition to the demographic projections for increasing ethnic and linguistic diversity within the

United States, modern society is characterized by increasing intercultural and cross-language interaction in the worldwide systems of business, commerce, and politics.

Bilingual educators and foreign language educators both recognize that bilingual proficiency confers a certain number of personal and societal advantages. At the personal level, bilingual proficiency appears to develop greater cognitive flexibility in abstract thinking (Hakuta, this volume; Padilla & Sung, 1990). In addition, a great deal of research has accumulated that demonstrates the enhancement of interpersonal and transcultural relationships.

Most important, the theme that recurs in this work is the concept of the *relevance* of education. The learning of languages is not an end but a means to an end. That end should not be limited to the acquisition of traditional academic content but should challenge students and teachers to develop critical thinking and communication skills about the very real problems that confront them, us, and the world in which we live.

In this regard, a very hopeful approach has been developed by Joy Kreeft Peyton, as reviewed in this volume. Her method of using "dialogue journals" is an ideal vehicle for establishing meaningful teacher-student communication and for enhancing teacher-student rapport. Most important, the dialogue journal procedure encourages students to bring *their* issues and concerns to the classroom, where meaningful discoveries may be made.

Other potential lies in the development of educational television programming that presents images of cooperative intercultural relationships, the nonviolent resolution of conflict, and the modeling of multilingual interactions. In this regard, Fairchild (1984, 1988) reports on the creation, production, and evaluation of an educational television program that presents ethnically diverse models cooperating in the pursuit of common goals. In a "re-creation" of his *Star Crusaders,* Fairchild (1988) explicitly calls for the portrayal of varying national groups, and their languages, in a science fiction program featuring space exploration. Thus Americans, Russians, Asians, Africans, Hispanics, and so on pursue common goals in a context of language and cultural plurality and maintenance.

In conclusion, bilingual education, and language education more generally, reveal fundamental concerns with the quality of American education. By pursuing the resolution of the pedagogical issues inherent in language education, we also pursue democracy in public education, the enhancement of the intellectual and social development of our populations, sensitivity to other peoples of the world, and competitiveness in an increasingly international arena of business, science, politics, and culture.

REFERENCES

Crandall, J., & Tucker, G. R. (1990). Content-based instruction in second and foreign languages. In A. M. Padilla, H. H. Fairchild, & C. M. Valadez (Eds.), *Foreign language education: Issues and strategies*. Newbury Park, CA: Sage.

Cummins, J. (1986). Empowering minority students: A framework for intervention. *Harvard Educational Review, 56*, 18–36.

Curtain, H. A., & Martínez, L. S. (1990). Elementary school content-based, foreign language instruction. In A. M. Padilla, H. H. Fairchild, & C. M. Valadez (Eds.), *Foreign language education: Issues and strategies*. Newbury Park, CA: Sage.

Fairchild, H. H. (1984). Creating, producing, and evaluating pro-social TV. *Journal of Educational Television, 10*(3), 161–183.

Fairchild, H. H. (1988). Creating positive television images. In S. Oskamp (Ed.), *Applied social psychology annual: Vol. 8. Television as a social issue* (pp. 270–279). Newbury Park, CA: Sage.

Fairchild, H. H., & Padilla, A. M. (1990). Innovations in foreign language education: Contributions from bilingual education. In A. M. Padilla, H. H. Fairchild, & C. M. Valadez (Eds.), *Foreign language education: Issues and strategies*. Newbury Park, CA: Sage.

Lindholm, K. J., & Padilla, A. M. (1990). A high school bilingual partial immersion program. In A. M. Padilla, H. H. Fairchild, & C. M. Valadez (Eds.), *Foreign language education: Issues and strategies*. Newbury Park, CA: Sage.

McGroarty, M., & Oxford, R. (1990). Language learning strategies: An introduction and related studies. In A. M. Padilla, H. H. Fairchild, & C. M. Valadez (Eds.), *Foreign language education: Issues and strategies*. Newbury Park, CA: Sage.

Padilla, A. M., Fairchild, H. H., & Valadez, C. M. (Eds.). (1990). *Foreign language education: Issues and strategies*. Newbury Park, CA: Sage.

Padilla, A. M., & Sung, H. (1990). Information processing and foreign language learning. In A. M. Padilla, H. H. Fairchild, & C. M. Valadez (Eds.), *Foreign language education: Issues and strategies*. Newbury Park, CA: Sage Publications.

Rhodes, N., Crandall, J., & Christian, D. (1990). "Key Amigos": A partial immersion program. In A. M. Padilla, H. H. Fairchild, & C. M. Valadez (Eds.), *Foreign language education: Issues and strategies*. Newbury Park, CA: Sage.

Rhodes, N., & Thompson, L. (1990). An oral assessment instrument for immersion students: COPE. In A. M. Padilla, H. H. Fairchild, & C. M. Valadez (Eds.), *Foreign language education: Issues and strategies*. Newbury Park, CA: Sage.

Shannon, S. M. (1990). Spanish for Spanish speakers: A translation skills curriculum. In A. M. Padilla, H. H. Fairchild, & C. M. Valadez (Eds.), *Foreign language education: Issues and strategies*. Newbury Park, CA: Sage.

Snow, M. A. (1990a). Language immersion: An overview and comparison. In A. M. Padilla, H. H. Fairchild, & C. M. Valadez (Eds.), *Foreign language education: Issues and strategies*. Newbury Park, CA: Sage.

Snow, M. A. (1990b). Instructional methodology in immersion foreign language education. In A. M. Padilla, H. H. Fairchild, & C. M. Valadez (Eds.), *Foreign language education: Issues and strategies*. Newbury Park, CA: Sage.

Snow, M. A. (1990c). Spanish language attrition of immersion graduates. In A. M. Padilla, H. H. Fairchild, & C. M. Valadez (Eds.), *Foreign language education: Issues and strategies.* Newbury Park, CA: Sage.

Stansfield, C. W., & Kenyon, D. M. (1990). Extension of ACTFL guidelines for less commonly taught languages. In A. M. Padilla, H. H. Fairchild, & C. M. Valadez (Eds.), *Foreign language education: Issues and strategies.* Newbury Park, CA: Sage.

Thompson, L., Christian, D., Stansfield, C. W., & Rhodes, N. (1990). Foreign language instruction in the United States. In A. M. Padilla, H. H. Fairchild, & C. M. Valadez (Eds.), *Foreign language education: Issues and strategies.* Newbury Park, CA: Sage.

Tucker, G. R. (1990). Second language education: Issues and perspectives. In A. M. Padilla, H. H. Fairchild, & C. M. Valadez (Eds.), *Foreign language education: Issues and strategies.* Newbury Park, CA: Sage.

Index

About the Editors

HALFORD H. FAIRCHILD received his Ph.D. in social psychology from the University of Michigan in 1977. He is a principal of Fairchild, Fairchild, and Associates, a Los Angeles-based planning, research, and development firm. His primary interests are in intergroup relations, educational opportunity, and mass media.

AMADO M. PADILLA received his Ph.D. in experimental psychology from the University of New Mexico in 1969. He is currently Professor of Education at Stanford University and has interests in language education, Hispanic issues in psychology, and interethnic relations.

CONCEPCIÓN M. VALADEZ received her Ph.D. in Education from Stanford University in 1976, where she also minored in linguistics. She is currently Associate Professor in the Graduate School of Education at the University of California, Los Angeles. Her interests include teacher education, language acquisition, and the academic achievement of minority students.

About the Contributors

DONNA M. BRINTON received her M.A. in Teaching English as a Second Language from the University of California, Los Angeles, in 1980. She is currently Lecturer and Audio-Visual Coordinator for the TESL/Applied Linguistics Department at UCLA. She has taught EFL and ESP courses in Germany and has been involved in ESL instruction and teacher training in the Los Angeles area for the past dozen years. Her primary interests are curriculum design, materials development, accent improvement, and instructional technology.

DONNA CHRISTIAN received her Ph.D. in sociolinguistics from Georgetown University in 1978. She is Director of the Research Division at the Center for Applied Linguistics in Washington, D.C. Her research concerns the role of language in education, including issues of second-language education and dialect diversity.

JOANN CRANDALL received her Ph.D. in sociolinguistics from Georgetown University in 1982. She is director of the International and Corporate Education Division at the Center for Applied Linguistics. Her primary interests are in teacher education and curriculum development, with a focus on the integration of academic content and culture into language education.

STEPHANIE EDWARDS-EVANS received her Ed.D. in 1977 in Higher Education from the University of California, Los Angeles, Graduate School of Education. An urban education specialist, she is currently Professor of Educational Foundations at

California State University, Los Angeles. Her research interests are in the education of African American children, dialect, and organizational and community development.

CLEMENTINA PATIÑO GREGOIRE received her Ed.D. from the University of California, Los Angeles, Graduate School of Education, in 1985. She is the Coordinator for the New Teachers' Program for the Los Angeles Unified School District and was a Research Associate with the Center for Language Education and Research at UCLA. Her research interests include teacher development, bilingualism, and foreign language education.

KENJI HAKUTA received his Ph.D. in Experimental Psychology from Harvard University in 1979. He is currently Professor of Education at Stanford University. Formerly he was on the faculty at Yale University and the University of California, Santa Cruz. His interests are in language and cognitive development, particularly as they relate to the education of language minority children.

EVELYN JACOB is a cultural anthropologist and Associate Professor of Education at George Mason University, Fairfax, Virginia. Much of her previous research has focused on literacy and "informal education." She currently is studying language minority students within cooperative learning classrooms.

KATHRYN LINDHOLM received her Ph.D. in developmental psychology from the University of California, Los Angeles, in 1981. She is now Assistant Professor of Education at San Jose State University. Her main areas of interest are bilingual and second-language development, cognitive development, factors associated with school achievement, and bilingual education.

MARGUERITE MALAKOFF is a Mellon Fellow at Yale University. Her doctoral dissertation in developmental psychology is on the study of translation abilities in bilingual children.

BEVERLY MATTSON has worked for 12 years as an educational diagnostician, consultant, and researcher. She is currently a doctoral student at George Mason University. Her dissertation applies the theory L. S. Vygotsky to the study of children's development of social communication skills.

JOY KREEFT PEYTON received her Ph.D. in sociolinguistics from Georgetown University. She is a member of the professional staff at the Center for Applied Linguistics in Washington, D.C., and is involved in research on the writing development of hearing-impaired students.

CARMEN SIMICH-DUDGEON received her Ph.D. from Georgetown University in 1984. She is currently Education Program Specialist in the Division of State and Local Programs, Office of Bilingual Education and Minority Languages Affairs, U.S. Department of Education. Her main interest is the study of academic language development through teacher-student verbal interactions in the elementary grades.

CATHERINE E. SNOW received her Ph.D. from McGill University in psychology. She is currently Professor of Human Development and Psychology at the Harvard Graduate School of Education. She conducts research on first-language acquisition, social interaction between parents and children, literacy acquisition, and second-language learning.

MARGUERITE ANN SNOW received her Ph.D. in applied linguistics from the University of California, Los Angeles, in 1985. She is currently Assistant Professor in the School of Education at California State University, Los Angeles. Her primary areas of interest are immersion language education, foreign language attrition, and TESL methodology.

GEORGE SPANOS received his Ph.D. in oriental studies from the University of Arizona in 1977. Currently he is Research Associate at the Center for Applied Linguistics in Washington, D.C. His interests include teacher training, curriculum development, math and science problem solving, and language-sensitive content instruction.

KAREN WILLETTS received her Maîtrise-es-lettres Spécialisee de Linguistique in 1982 from the Université Center for Applied Linguistics in Washington, D.C., where she is also Project Director for a Department of Education teacher training grant, "Improving Foreign Language Instruction Through the Use of Technology." Her interests include language planning and literacy in developing nations and foreign language education.